T0181173

Lecture Notes
in Business Information Processing 508

Series Editors

Wil van der Aalst(iD), *RWTH Aachen University, Aachen, Germany*

Sudha Ram(iD), *University of Arizona, Tucson, AZ, USA*

Michael Rosemann(iD), *Queensland University of Technology, Brisbane, QLD, Australia*

Clemens Szyperski, *Microsoft Research, Redmond, WA, USA*

Giancarlo Guizzardi(iD), *University of Twente, Enschede, The Netherlands*

LNBIP reports state-of-the-art results in areas related to business information systems and industrial application software development – timely, at a high level, and in both printed and electronic form.

The type of material published includes

- Proceedings (published in time for the respective event)
- Postproceedings (consisting of thoroughly revised and/or extended final papers)
- Other edited monographs (such as, for example, project reports or invited volumes)
- Tutorials (coherently integrated collections of lectures given at advanced courses, seminars, schools, etc.)
- Award-winning or exceptional theses

LNBIP is abstracted/indexed in DBLP, EI and Scopus. LNBIP volumes are also submitted for the inclusion in ISI Proceedings.

Abhishek Kathuria · Prasanna P. Karhade ·
Kexin Zhao · Devina Chaturvedi
Editors

Digital Transformation in the Viral Age

21st Workshop on e-Business, WeB 2022
Copenhagen, Denmark, December 10, 2022
Revised Selected Papers

 Springer

Editors
Abhishek Kathuria 🄳
#6104
Indian School of Business
Hyderabad, Telangana, India

Prasanna P. Karhade 🄳
Chinese University of Hong Kong
Sha Tin District, Hong Kong

Kexin Zhao 🄳
University of North Carolina at Charlotte
Charlotte, NC, USA

Devina Chaturvedi 🄳
Indian School of Business
Hyderabad, Telangana, India

ISSN 1865-1348   ISSN 1865-1356 (electronic)
Lecture Notes in Business Information Processing
ISBN 978-3-031-60002-9   ISBN 978-3-031-60003-6 (eBook)
https://doi.org/10.1007/978-3-031-60003-6

© The Editor(s) (if applicable) and The Author(s), under exclusive license
to Springer Nature Switzerland AG 2024

This work is subject to copyright. All rights are solely and exclusively licensed by the Publisher, whether the whole or part of the material is concerned, specifically the rights of translation, reprinting, reuse of illustrations, recitation, broadcasting, reproduction on microfilms or in any other physical way, and transmission or information storage and retrieval, electronic adaptation, computer software, or by similar or dissimilar methodology now known or hereafter developed.
The use of general descriptive names, registered names, trademarks, service marks, etc. in this publication does not imply, even in the absence of a specific statement, that such names are exempt from the relevant protective laws and regulations and therefore free for general use.
The publisher, the authors and the editors are safe to assume that the advice and information in this book are believed to be true and accurate at the date of publication. Neither the publisher nor the authors or the editors give a warranty, expressed or implied, with respect to the material contained herein or for any errors or omissions that may have been made. The publisher remains neutral with regard to jurisdictional claims in published maps and institutional affiliations.

This Springer imprint is published by the registered company Springer Nature Switzerland AG
The registered company address is: Gewerbestrasse 11, 6330 Cham, Switzerland

Paper in this product is recyclable.

Preface

The Workshop on e-Business (WeB) is a premier annual conference on electronic business. The purpose of WeB is to provide a forum for researchers and practitioners to discuss findings, novel ideas, and lessons learned, to address major challenges, and to map out the future directions for e-business. Since 2000, WeB has attracted valuable, novel research that addresses both the technical and organizational aspects of e-business. The 21st Annual Workshop on e-Business (WeB 2022) was held in a hybrid format, partially virtually and partially in presence, at the IT University of Copenhagen in Copenhagen, Denmark, on December 10, 2022. This book constitutes revised selected papers from this conference.

The WeB 2022 theme was "Digital Transformation in the Viral Age." The past decade has witnessed exponential growth in digital and e-business technologies that transform how we interact, live, and work – from communication to entertainment to employment. Adopting these technologies has never been more critical than it is currently. The coronavirus and the COVID-19 pandemic shut down the physical world, and many business industries, ranging from retail, restaurants, and finance to education, were compelled to migrate to remote/digital environments to survive. The virus is here to stay in some form or another, and we live in the viral age. As the world has slowly recovered from this unprecedented event, the sustainability and longevity of such rapid digital transformation is now a matter of debate. The recent war in Europe has also added to the ongoing crises and is creating massive global shifts. Consequently, global rebalancing of power is creating situations vital for leveraging digital transformation.

WeB 2022 allowed academic scholars and practitioners worldwide to exchange ideas and share research findings that explored the issues, opportunities, and solutions related to e-business, digital transformation, and IT-enabled recovery in the viral age. The articles presented at the workshop covered a broad range of issues from multiple perspectives. They employed various business research methods such as surveys, analytical modeling, experiments, computational models, data science, and design science.

The eight edited papers included in this LNBIP volume were carefully reviewed and selected from 31 submissions. We are grateful to the reviewers and editors for providing insightful feedback and to the authors for their contributions.

February 2024

Abhishek Kathuria
Prasanna Purushottam Karhade
Kexin Zhao
Devina Chaturvedi

Organization

Honorary Chairs

Hsinchun Chen   University of Arizona, USA
Michael J. Shaw   University of Illinois at Urbana-Champaign, USA
Andrew B. Whinston   University of Texas at Austin, USA
Benn R. Konsynski   Emory University, USA

Conference Co-chairs

Prasanna P. Karhade   Chinese University of Hong Kong, China
Abhishek Kathuria   Indian School of Business, India
Keong Tae Kim   Chinese University of Hong Kong, China
Weiquan Wang   Chinese University of Hong Kong, China
Kexin Zhao   University of North Carolina at Charlotte, USA

Advisory Committee

Kenny Cheng   University of Florida, USA
Ming Fan   University of Washington, USA
Karl Lang   City University of New York, USA
Jennifer Xu   Bentley University, USA
Han Zhang   Georgia Institute of Technology, USA
Bin Zhu   Oregon State University, USA

Program Committee

Arthur Goncalves De Carvalho   Miami University, USA
Hsin-Lu Chang   National Chengchi University, Taiwan
Xiaohui Chang   Oregon State University, USA
Michael Chau   University of Hong Kong, China
Cheng Chen   University of Illinois at Chicago, USA
Ching-Chin Chern   National Taiwan University, Taiwan
Su Dong   Elon University, USA
Aidan Duane   Waterford Institute of Technology, Ireland

Giang Hoang   National University of Singapore, Singapore
Yuheng Hu   University of Illinois at Chicago, USA
Seongmin Jeon   Gachon University, South Korea
Chunghan Kang   Georgia Institute of Technology, USA
Timothy Kaskela   Oregon State University, USA
Sarah Khan   North Carolina State University, USA
Kelvin King   Syracuse University, USA
Anthony Lee   National Taiwan University, Taiwan
Sam Lee   Texas State University, USA
Chenwei Li   University of Hong Kong, China
Hongxiu Li   Tampere University, Finland
Shengli Li   Peking University, China
Xitong Li   HEC Paris, France
Jifeng Luo   Shanghai Jiao Tong University, China
Xin Luo   University of New Mexico, USA
Selwyn Piramuthu   University of Florida, USA
Liangfei Qiu   University of Florida, USA
Yufei Shen   HEC Paris, France
Vijayan Sugumaran   Oakland University, USA
Kai Wang   National University of Kaohsiung, Taiwan
Jason Xiong   Appalachian State University, USA
Ling Xue   Georgia State University, USA
Dezhi Yin   University of South Florida, USA
Adeel Zaffar   Lahore University of Management Sciences,
                              Pakistan
Peiqin Zhang   Texas State University, USA
Wei Zhou   ESCP Europe, France
Wenqi Zhou   Duquesne University, USA

Contents

Contents

Profiting from High Frequency Market Psychology Data with Deep Learning

Jiancheng Shen[1] , Jia Wang[2], Hongwei Zhu[2](✉) , Yu Cao[2] , and Benyuan Liu[2]

[1] Soochow University, Suzhou, Jiangsu, China
jcshen@suda.edu.cn
[2] University of Massachusetts Lowell, Lowell, MA 01854, USA
{hongwei_zhu,yu_cao,benyuan_liu}@uml.edu

Abstract. It is challenging to predict financial markets, but there have been continued efforts to develop improved prediction methods. With availability of high frequency market psychology data, and guided by design science principles, this research iteratively develops and comprehensively evaluates *DeepPsych*, a deep learning system that leverages market psychology data to gain prediction advantage. Using two convolutional sequence-to-sequence channels to extract local and temporal features from psychology and trading data separately, the system outperforms other leading machine learning and deep learning models in both machine learning metrics and economic values realized through trading strategy based on the prediction. This research contributes to both information systems design science through innovation in deep learning and finance by providing empirical evidence about the predictive power of high frequency market psychology data. The research also benefits practice by producing a validated Fintech artifact.

Keywords: Deep Learning · Market Psychology · Financial Market Prediction

1 Introduction

It is difficult to predict the financial market. However, the potential huge profit from even a slight predictive advantage has led to continued effort in developing various prediction methods. Extensive research in finance and related fields has identified numerous factors that influence asset price and market movement. As a good start, trading data such as price and volume provide the basis for trend analysis. Numerous technical indicators (TIs) have been hand crafted from trading data to derive trading signals. Financial markets are also influenced by the psychology of investors [7]. Empirical studies have found evidence to support that news and social media psychology measurements are good predictors for current and short-term future returns in three financial markets: equity, and fixed income [2, 3, 17, 18]. We use the term *market psychology* to refer to market participants' overall sentiment associated with a tradable asset. Market psychology is typically derived from news and social media, and it has become increasingly available as computing technology continues to advance. For example, derived from more than two million news articles daily and contents of all major social media outlets, the Thompson

© The Author(s), under exclusive license to Springer Nature Switzerland AG 2024

A. Kathuria et al. (Eds.): WeB 2022, LNBIP 508, pp. 1–11, 2024.
https://doi.org/10.1007/978-3-031-60003-6_1

Reuters *MarketPsych* Indices (TMRIs) are updated every minute to provide a near-real-time measurement of market psychology for any tradable asset [15]. Although extant empirical research has confirmed the *explanatory* power of market psychology, there has been no *predictive* model that takes advantage of high frequency psychology data. This leads to the question that motivates this research: how can we use high frequency market psychology data to better predict price movement?

We focus on the development of deep learning models to address the main research question. Guided by design science principles [6, 14], we have iteratively developed and rigorously evaluated the building blocks and the integrated *DeepPsych* system to harness the power of high frequency TMRI psychology data for market prediction. There are several innovations in this research. First, by developing a novel 1D cross data type (CDT) convolutional neural network (CNN) model, we can extract informative features from basic trading data (volume and prices) to achieve higher performance than other machine learning models that rely on highly engineered and sophisticated inputs. Second, we integrate the 1D CDT CNN model into a regularized convolutional sequence-to-sequence (CS) model with attention mechanism that incorporates daily and intra-day temporal context to further improve model performance. Third, we develop a dual channel model to extract features from trading data and market psychology data separately; with this model, additional information embedded in high frequency psychology data helps to further improve the prediction. Fourth, by framing the prediction problem as classification of price directions, we develop a backtesting method based on prediction-directed paper trades to assess the *economic value* of the model when it is used to guide automated trading.

Through comprehensive evaluations using up to eight years of market data for four commodities and three equities, we find that DeepPsych can effectively extract and combine features from both trading data and market psychology data. The model outperforms state-of-the-art deep learning models that do not use market psychology data or simply combine the data with other types of input. We further find that for psychology data to improve model performance, there must of sufficient amount of it (i.e., it cannot be overly sparse).

This research contributes to both design science and finance. First, we develop and validate DeepPsych, a deep learning model that achieves prediction performance significantly higher than other machine learning and deep learning models. More importantly, our model is the first that successfully combines high frequency market psychology data with trading data to improve prediction performance. Our method of extracting features from different data types is applicable in other contexts, and the method of using multiple channels is extensible to accommodate any number of data types. Second, we contribute to the empirical literature on the relationship between investor psychology and financial markets. Our findings suggest that the market is not perfectly efficient, and the interaction between investors and the market may be bidirectional in that they influence one another in a complex manner. Using a sophisticated model like the one developed in this research, we demonstrate that useful information can be extracted from this complex interaction to identify profitable trades.

An immediate practical implication is that this research produces an artifact, the DeepPsych system, which can be used in practice with minimal adaptation. It can enable automated trading, provide advice to human traders, and produce useful input to other systems such as those for portfolio and risk management.

2 Literature Review and Research Questions

2.1 Market Psychology

Market psychology reflects the collective emotions of individual market participants. Investor emotions affect their perceptions of risk, and subsequently their risk-taking behaviors [10] and trading performance [12]. The Wall Street motto "buy on fear, sell on greed" also indicates that financial professionals understand the importance of market psychology in affecting trading behaviors. Investor emotions are often influenced by the emotions of others, the market psychology, and other factors. For example, investors often attempt to "sense" the emotions of executives during their conference calls through vocal cues [13, 16] and facial expressions [1]. Market psychology "sensed" from news and social media can also explain current and short-term returns of major asset classes [3, 17, 18]. Known as the "sunlight effect", even the weather can influence investor mood and subsequently the market [8].

These studies have developed inference models to establish empirical evidence for the interaction between market psychology and market movement. It remains a challenge to leverage high frequency market psychology to predict the market and identify profitable trades. In this research, we aim to develop a deep learning model that solves the prediction problem.

2.2 Machine Learning and Financial Market Prediction

Asset pricing research has adopted machine learning algorithms to predict stock returns [4, 5]. The conventional machine learning algorithms used in these studies rely on feature engineering, which tends to introduce human bias and produce inflexible models.

Deep learning research has developed methods for automatic feature extraction. For example, vocal cues can be extracted from conference calls, and such automatically extracted features are more informative than engineered features in predicting post-conference-call stock volatility [20]. However, convolutional neural network (CNN) is designed to process inputs with the same data type, whereas different data types are involved for market prediction; other variants fail to exploit joint distribution of the data. There is also the challenge of capturing temporal patterns of different time horizons without overfitting the model. In this research, we aim to address these challenges.

2.3 Research Questions

Based on the literature review and analysis of research gap, we formulate our research questions as the following hypotheses:

H1. High frequency market psychology contains useful information for market prediction; this information, when properly extracted and combined with other features extracted from the market, can improve model performance.

H2. Using trading data can produce better prediction than using other hand-crafted features.

H3. Temporal patterns can be exploited to further improve prediction performance.

3 Model Development

We developed the deep learning model using an iterative process. For presentation, we provide an overview of the integrated architecture first, followed by a description of the building blocks.

3.1 Model Input

We use high frequency trading data and TMRI market psychology indicators as the main input to the model. Trading data are at 5-min interval with five attributes: volume, open price, close prices, high price, low price. To test research questions, we also evaluate model performance with technical indicators as input. The TMRIs are at 1-min interval; in experiments with the single channel model, we aggregate the data to align it with the 5-min-granuality trading data. Additional details of the datasets are provided in the Model Evaluation section.

3.2 Target Variable

The target variable is the price movement direction. We adopt a dynamic labeling strategy [190 to take price (p) and its volatility (v) into concertation using Eq. (1):

$$y_{t+1} = \begin{cases} \text{up,} & \text{if } p_{t+1} \geq p_t(1 + \alpha v_t) \\ \text{down,} & \text{if } p \leq p_t(1 - \alpha v_t) \\ \text{flat,} & \text{otherwise} \end{cases} \qquad (1)$$

where α is a parameter to adjust sensitivity and class mix; we set it to 0.55 in early phase of the research and developed a weighted F score to evaluate prediction; later we adjusted the value to yield balanced classes and simply used the mean accuracy of the three classes for evaluation.

3.3 DeepPsych Architecture

The DeepPsych architecture is illustrated in Fig. 1. Market psychology indicators (labeled as Historical Sentiment Data) are fed through a network of sequence-to-sequence (seq2seq) with attention to extract both local and temporal features; trading data are fed through a separate channel of the same architecture. The extracted features from both channels are then concatenated and fed to the fully connected (FC) layers for target prediction. We use this architecture and other alternatives to test H1.

A main building blocks of the architecture is the 1D cross data type CNN, developed in this research to address the limitations of conventional CNN that requires same data type in the input layer or uses 1D convolution that fails to extract features from joint

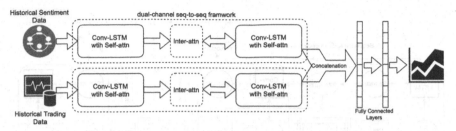

Fig. 1. Schematic of DeepPsych architecture: dual channel convolutional seq2seq (CS).

distribution. As illustrated in Fig. 2, input data is still organized into 2D frames, where the x-axis denotes time and the y-axis contains inputs of various data types. All kernels are one-dimensional and only scan along the x-axis. After each convolutional layer, a max-pooling layer is used to reduce the x-axis dimension of the feature maps.

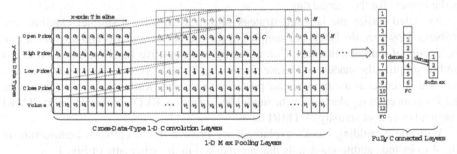

Fig. 2. 1-D cross data type (CDT) convolution architecture for extracting local features.

The kernel scan strategy is different from that of the regular 1D or 2D convolution: all the kernels scan along the x-axis; once a kernel finishes scanning a row, it moves to the next row until all positions of the 2D frames are scanned. As illustrated in Fig. 2, the 1×3 red and blue kernels scan the whole 2D input frame to produce their own respective convolution layers (C' and C"). In addition to overcoming the limitation of conventional CNN, the scan strategy can extract features from the joint distribution of different types of data through parameter sharing. Prior research has found that features based on joint distribution offer stronger prediction power than marginal distributions [11]. We use this architecture and other alternatives to test H2.

The 1D cross data type CNN is designed to extract local features (within a 30-min window), but it is unable to exploit intra- and inter-day temporal patterns that are useful for prediction. We develop a sequence-to-sequence architecture, as shown in Fig. 3, that includes convolutional long short-term memory (LSTM) units and other mechanisms to improve performance without overfitting. We limit to two consecutive days to avoid training convergence issues that often arise when longer spans are used.

The convolutional LSTM units are designed with the hidden layers (which are typically fully connected) replaced with 1D cross data type CNNs. The 2-layer encoder and decoder take prior day and current day data as input, respectively. A self-attention

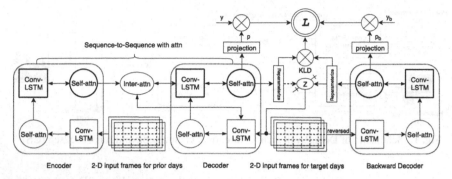

Fig. 3. Convolutional sequence-to-sequence (CS) architecture for temporal feature extraction.

module is used in both the encoder and the decoder to highlight parts of the sequence of daily data frames. An inter-attention module is used to highlight parts of the prior day as the context for the second day.

As stated earlier, the labeling strategy allows us to solve a simpler classification problem. However, the labels are samples of the market movements and do not capture the details of market dynamics. Consequently, the objective function based on labels tend to simplify the market and cause overfitting. To address this issue, we introduce a backward decoder as the approximate posterior to generate Kullback-Leibler divergence (KLD) as an extra regularizer for the model optimization. KLD is not used for the TMRI channel because of sparsity of TMRI data.

With these building blocks explained, we present the DeepPsych architecture in Fig. 4 to include additional details that are masked in the schematic of Fig. 1.

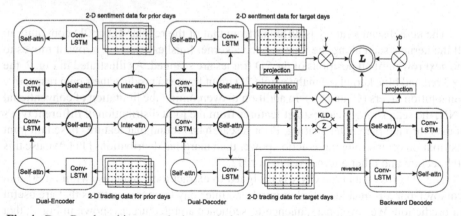

Fig. 4. DeepPsych architecture: dual convolutional seq2seq with attention and regularization.

The convolutional LSTM units have kernel size of 1×3 and output size of 32. Both the encoder and the decoder are a stack of two convolutional LSTM units, and the discriminator consists of a 200-unit and 50-unit FC layer and a softmax layer. The backward decoder for approximate posterior has the same structure as the decoder. For the reparametrization tricks [9], the multi-variant Gaussian distributions for the prior and the posterior distribution are formed by a 512-unit and 256-unit FC layer, respectively. Other specs are omitted for brevity.

4 Model Evaluation

We have conducted a range of experiments to train and comprehensively evaluate the DeepPsych model and its components. Data and evaluation methods are described in this section.

4.1 Datasets

Our evaluations involve trading data and market psychology data of different periods from 2001 to 2017. Various technical indicators derived from trading data are also used in experiments.

Trading data include 5-min interval volume and prices (open, close, high, low) of four commodity futures, two equity futures, and one equity index ETF: WTI crude oil (CL), natural gas (NG), soybeans (S), gold (GC), E-mini Nasdaq 100 (NQ), E-mini S&P 500 (ES), and SPDR S&P 500 Trust ETF (SPY).

We choose technical indicators according to their functionality and popularity. For lagging indicators, which are often used to identify and confirm the strength of a pattern or trend, we pick Exponential Moving Average (EMA), Moving Average Convergence Divergence (MACD) Histogram, and Bollinger Bands. For leading indicators, which usually change before a trend or pattern and are thus used during periods of sideways or non-trending ranges, we pick Relative Strength Index (RSI), Commodity Channel Index (CCI), Volume Weighted Average Price (VWAP), On-balance Volume (OBV), Average Directional Index (ADX), Accumulation Distribution Line (ADL), and Chaikin Money Flow (CMF). We also include technical indicators regarded as neither lagging nor leading such as Rate of Change (ROC), which is used to measure the change of prices over time. Different time spans are used to generate EMA, MACD Histogram, Bollinger Bands, ROC, RSI, CCI, CMF, and ADX - this produces 41 technical indicator attributes used in relevant experiments.

TMRIs consist of dozens of indexes based on more than 4,000 psychology variables derived every minute from news and social media content in the past 24 h. The index *buzz* indicates the overall media attention to a given asset. There are 14 other indexes that are available for all asset classes. Since the dataset is very sparse, we choose to use buzz and four other least sparse indexes: *sentiment, optimism, fear,* and *joy*. For architectures that have convolution, we align the TMRI with trading data using an operation analogous to right-join on timestamp (trading data on the right). For architectures that do not have convolution, we generate 30-min aggregate index values that are weighted using the buzz index.

4.2 Training and Tuning

We use sequential training sessions with moving windows to prevent data leakage. Each window has training, validation, and test datasets with typical sizes of 2-year, 4-week, and 2-week, respectively. We use the Adam optimizer with a learning rate of 0.001. Due to space limitation, we do not report other model-specific parameters, which are available upon request.

4.3 Evaluation Methods

We evaluate model performance using two methods: prediction accuracy and profitability of prediction-directed trading.

Prediction evaluation. We use weighted F-score (early stage of research) or mean accuracy of 3-class predictions (later stage, with balanced datasets). The two metrics produce qualitatively the same result, which is further validated with profitability evaluation.

Profitability evaluation. We evaluate the economic value of the model using backtesting, which is based on a strictly followed prediction-directed trading strategy. Starting with $100 K cash position, the first up or down prediction renders the test into a long or short trade, respectively; the position remains until the next opposite prediction, which leads to opposite trades. For example, if the current position is a long trade, up or flat predictions do not trigger any trading; upon the first down prediction, trades are triggered to exit the long position and enter a short position. We use higher than real-life transaction cost ($42.75 per initial trade and $85.50 per subsequent round-trip trade) to obtain a conservative profit estimate. The economic value is evaluated using portfolio performance metrics including cumulative or periodic returns, Sharpe ratio, and daily Jensen alpha.

A model with better prediction generally produces better profitability, but not always because profitability also depends on the number trades and the size of gain or loss of each trade.

5   Results

5.1   DeepPsych Performance and Power of High Frequency Market Psychology (H1)

We conduct experiments with seven different model specifications to test H1. The dataset is for SPY from 2001 and 2006. Conventional LSTM (without convolution) and the single channel convolutional seq2seq (CS) architecture developed in this research are benchmark cases; we vary the input (e.g., trading data, with or with technical indicators and TMRIs) for different specifications. The results are summarized in Table 1.

We make the following observations: (1) DeepPsych performs significantly better than all other benchmarks, providing support for H1. (2) the convolutional seq2seq model developed in the research performs remarkably well (third to last row), suggesting its ability to effectively extract features from trading data; but when TMRIs are used as just another data type, the performance drops (second to last row) - this suggests the importance of using separate channels. (3) the experiments for LSTM specifications show that LSTM cannot effectively extract features from trading data alone, but it can benefit from additional features such as technical indicators and TMRIs; performance also drops when using technical indicators and TMRIs together.

Table 1. Performance comparison between DeepPsych and other benchmark architectures

Architecture	Input data	Accuracy	Annual return	Sharpe ratio	Daily Jensen alpha	Annual Jensen alpha
LSTM	Trading	42.00%	−19.90%	−1.45	−0.12%	−21.30%
LSTM	Trading + TI	46.00%	34.20%	1.75	0.24%	43.60%
LSTM	Trading + TMRI	45.50%	32.80%	1.27	0.24%	41.90%
LSTM	Trading + TI + TMRI	45.70%	28.90%	1.08	0.22%	37.20%
CS	Trading	46.10%	48.00%	2.11	0.24%	57.90%
CS	Trading + TMRI	45.40%	29.50%	1.1	0.14	35.60%
DeepPsych	Trading + TMRI	**50.70%**	**57.30%**	**3.01**	**0.29%**	**65.00%**

Additional experiments are conducted to compare the top two models (DeepPshcy and CS with trading data) during bull market (5/2003 to 3/2004) and bear market (3/2002 to 7/2002). Results show the DeepPsych model outperforms the benchmark by a large margin in all measures, e.g., in terms of Sharpe ratio: 4.42 vs 1.58 during the bull market and 6.40 vs 4.78 during the bear market.

However, the results of the two models for crude oil futures (CL) (2012 to 2017) suggest that DeepPsych is slightly disadvantaged, yielding a Sharpe ratio of 3.01, smaller than 3.99 of the CS model using trading data alone. Further investigation finds that, since SPY has nearly 500 components, it persistently has a much higher media buzz (monthly median buzz greater than 50), whereas CL is extremely sparse with a median value 0 for most of the months. Thus, when TMRIs are extremely sparse, they are essentially white noise; using noise as input degrades model performance, as similarly shown elsewhere [20].

5.2 1D Cross Data Type CNN and Local Feature Extraction from Trading Data (H2)

We compare the performance of 1D cross data type CNN with benchmark models that include support vector machine (SVM) using radial basis kernel, multi-layer perceptron (MLP) with six hidden layers, and regular 1D CNN with no parameter sharing among data types. Experiments are conducted using trading data with or without the derived technical indicators of six tradable futures from 1/2010 to 10/2017. The results are summarized in Table 2 (only Sharpe ratios are reported here; same conclusions can be drawn from F-scores and annual returns).

The results show that the 1D cross data type CNN with only trading data as input achieves the best performance, providing support for H2. Further, the comparison with

Table 2. Sharpe ration comparison between 1D cross data type CNN and benchmarks

Architecture	Input data	CL	NG	S	GC	NQ	ES
SVM	Trading	0.18	−0.95	−0.43	−1.45	−0.49	−0.85
MLP	Trading + TI	0.29	0.12	0.18	1.08	−0.10	−0.54
1D CNN	Trading	1.44	−0.05	0.28	2.11	−0.22	0.76
1D CDT CNN	Trading + TI	0.75	0.00	0.07	1.1	0.06	0.43
1D CDT CNN	Trading	**2.74**	**1.55**	**1.63**	**3.01**	**0.89**	**0.90**

the regular 1D CNN confirms the benefit of feature extraction based on joint distribution. The results hold across tests of all six futures.

5.3 Convolutional Seq2Seq and Temporal Feature Extraction (H3)

We compare the convolutional seq2seq (CS) framework with attention and KLD regularization against benchmarks that are components of the CS architecture. With increasing complexity, the benchmarks include 1D cross data type CNN, convolutional LSTM, seq2seq with attention, and CS without KLD regularization. The results are summarized in Table 3. With confirmation of H2, we only need to use trading data as input for all evaluations; data are from 1/2010 to 12/2017.

Table 3. Sharpe ratio comparison convolutional seq2seq and benchmarks

Architecture	CL	NG	S	GC	NQ	ES
1D CDT CNN	1.55	1.05	1.20	0.67	1.54	0.75
Conv. LSTM	1.12	1.23	1.13	0.82	1.26	0.62
Seq2Seq	1.02	1.11	1.17	0.79	1.28	0.67
CS, no KLD	2.69	2.23	1.66	1.08	1.85	1.02
CS, with KLD	**3.99**	**3.01**	**1.81**	**1.58**	**1.87**	**1.22**

The results show that the convolutional seq2seq (CS) framework with attention and KLD regularization achieves the best performance, providing support for H3.

6 Conclusion

Through iterative design and comprehensive evaluations, we develop DeepPsych, a deep learning model to effectively extract and combine features from trading data and high frequency market psychology data. The model achieves better performance than other existing leading models in prediction and profitability from prediction-guided trading. This research contributes to both design science in the IS field through innovation in deep learning and finance by providing empirical evidence about the predictive power of high frequency market psychology. The research also benefits practice by producing a validated Fintech artifact.

References

1. Akansu, A., Cicon, J., Ferris, S.P., Sun, Y.: Firm performance in the face of fear: how CEO moods affect firm performance. J. Behav. Financ. **18**(4), 373–389 (2017)
2. Deng, S., Huang, Z., Sinha, A.P., Zhao, H.: The interaction between microblog sentiment and stock returns: an empirical examination. MISQ **42**(3), 895–918 (2018)
3. Griffith, J., Najand, M., Shen, J.: Emotions in the stock market. J. Behav. Financ. **21**(1), 42–56 (2020)
4. Gu, S., Kelly, B., Xiu, D.: Empirical asset pricing via machine learning. Rev. Financ. Stud. **33**(5), 2223–2273 (2020)
5. Gu, S., Kelly, B., Xiu, D.: Autoencoder asset pricing models. J. Econometrics **222**(1), 429–450 (2021)
6. Hevner, A.R., March, S.T., Park, J., Ram, S.: Design science in information systems research. MISQ **28**(1), 75–201 (2004)
7. Hirshleifer, D.: Investor psychology and asset pricing. J. Financ. **56**(4), 1533–1597 (2001)
8. Hirshleifer, D., Shumway, T.: Good day sunshine: stock returns and the weather. J. Financ. **58**(3), 1009–1032 (2003)
9. Klingma, D.P., Welling, M.: Auto-encoding variational Bayes. In: Second International Conference on Learning Representations, April 14–16. Banff, Canada (2014)
10. Kuhnen, C.M., Knutson, B.: The influence of affect on beliefs, preferences, and financial decisions. J. Financ. Quant. Anal. **46**(3), 605–626 (2011)
11. Lo, A., Mamaysky, H., Wang, J.: Foundations of technical analysis: computational algorithms, statistical inference, and empirical implementation. J. Financ. **55**(4), 1705–1765 (2000)
12. Lo, A.W., Repin, D.V., Steenbarger, B.N.: Fear and greed in financial markets: a clinical study of day-traders. Am. Econ. Rev. **95**(2), 352–359 (2005)
13. Mayew, W.J., Venkatachalam, M.: The power of voice: managerial affective states and future firm performance. J. Financ. **67**(1), 1–43 (2012)
14. Padmanabhan, P., Fang, X., Sahoo, N., Burton-Jones, A.: Machine learning in information systems research. MISQ **46**(1), iii–xix (2022)
15. Peterson, R. L.: Trading on Sentiment: The Power of Minds Over Markets. Wiley (2016)
16. Price, S.M.K., Seiler, M.J., Shen, J.: Do investors infer vocal cues from CEOs during quarterly REIT conference calls? J. Real Estate Financ. Econ. **54**(4), 515–557 (2017)
17. Shen, J., Griffith, J., Najand, M., Sun, L.: Predicting Stock and Bond Market Returns with Emotions: Evidence from Futures Markets. J. Behav. Financ. **24**(3), 333–344 (2023)
18. Shen, J., Najand, M., Dong, F., Wu, H.: News and social media emotions in the commodity market. Rev. Behav. Financ. **9**(2), 148–168 (2017)
19. Sun, T., Wang, J., Zhang, P., Cao, Y., Liu, B., Wang, D.: Predicting stock price returns using microblog sentiment for Chinese stock market. In: Third International Conference on Big Data Computing and Communications (BIGCOM), pp. 87–96 (2017)
20. Yang, Y., Qin, Y., Fang, Y., Zhang, Z.: Unlocking the power of voice for financial risk prediction: a theory-driven deep learning design science approach. MISQ **47**(1), 63–96 (2023)

Understanding the Corporate Use of IT Security Labels for IoT Products and Services: A Literature Review

Lucas Pfannenberg$^{(\boxtimes)}$, Florian Schütz⑩, Sarah Gronemann, Eylert Spils ad Wilken, Kristin Masuch⑩, and Simon Trang⑩

University of Goettingen, Platz der Göttinger Sieben 5, 37073 Göttingen, Germany
`lucas-pf@freenet.de`

Abstract. The Internet of Things (IoT) has become part of everyday life and recorded an increasing number of users. However, security concerns have been raised regardless of the many benefits of the technology. Especially for consumers in online shopping, it is difficult to distinguish between more and less safe products. One proposal is to carry a security label to help consumers know which digital products to trust. Prior research only analyzes the impact of such labels from a consumer's perspective (i.e., the impact of security labeling on online consumer behavior). We currently lack an understanding of a manufacturer's perspective. Therefore, we conduct a literature review to identify factors influencing the decision to adopt security labels.

Keywords: Digital Consumer Protection · IT Security Label · IoT Device

1 Introduction

The Internet of Things (IoT) allows internet-enabled electronic devices to communicate and perform tasks fully automatically [1–3]. Typical applications are lighting control or voice control of smart TVs [4–7]. Thereby, many connected devices and services offer advantages over conventional products or even completely new solutions to consumers [8]. Thus, they have already become part of everyday life and still record increasing users [9]. Especially in the field of media and gaming, only 16% of consumers do not use IoT devices such as smart TVs or smart speakers [10]. Therefore, trends such as IoT and smart homes will continue to grow in the future [9, 11]. A study by Strategy Analytics confirms this assumption and estimates that the market for IoT smart home products will reach a spending volume of $173 billion worldwide by 2025 [12].

However, regardless of the many benefits of the technology, the high use of these vulnerable, interconnected products, combined with the risk of security incidents, poses a threat to consumers [8, 13]. This is because it is impossible to identify whether and how these devices and services offer potential attackers the opportunity to spy on data and exploit devices for criminal purposes [11]. Unfortunately, there is currently no general IT security standard for IoT products that minimizes these types of threats [14–16]. For

© The Author(s), under exclusive license to Springer Nature Switzerland AG 2024
A. Kathuria et al. (Eds.): WeB 2022, LNBIP 508, pp. 12–27, 2024.
https://doi.org/10.1007/978-3-031-60003-6_2

example, Myeonggeon et al. [17] revealed that attackers could use hardware or protocol flaws to eavesdrop on communications from wearable devices and steal personal data. Such security threats compromise consumers' privacy and expose them to the risk of identity theft [16]. Due to the lack of accessible information, it is difficult for consumers to assess the security of products [13, 18]. As a result, only 34% of consumers trust the manufacturer's security features [10]. Consumers thus value measures to protect themselves from security threats [13]. They also believe the government should help ensure such measures are in place [13]. These security concerns must be addressed to effectively build consumer trust in the IoT [3, 19]. Security labels are mechanisms to address these concerns, encouraging manufacturers to improve products' security features and increase consumer trust in IoT [20, 21].

The United Nations Guidelines for Consumer Protection (UNGCP) have highlighted that both governments and businesses should contribute to an effective consumer policy framework [22]. Many governments consider labels a potential IoT security solution [23]. Germany provides a legal basis to ensure IT security for digital products and introduced the IT security label with the IT Security Act 2.0 [24]. According to the German Federal Office for Information Security [24], the label creates transparency by making the security features of digital products visible so that consumers can assess a product's potential risk. The participating companies must comply with the security criteria required by the German Federal Office for Information Security [24].

Current studies focus on the impact of security labels on consumer behavior. In a discrete choice experiment by Johnson et al. [20], it was shown that security labels positively affected online consumers' purchasing decisions. Neither gender, age, nor self-reported security behavior appeared to influence whether the security label affected participants [20]. In another study by Emami-Naeini et al. [21], consumers were shown a privacy and security label prototype. They demonstrate that almost all consumers found the label accessible and valuable, additionally encouraging them to include privacy and security considerations in their IoT purchasing decisions [21]. There are currently few incentives for manufacturers to offer secure products and reduce information asymmetries between manufacturers and consumers [20, 25, 26].

Despite the increasing relevance of the topic, especially in practice, there has been a lack of a holistic view of factors that the adoption of security labels, in particular the IT security label, can entail from a company's perspective. We follow the research appeal by Jentzsch [27] to fill this research gap and focus our study on providing an overview of which conditions companies would invest in labels and under which they would stop using them. This leads us to our two key research questions:

- **RQ1**: What are the motivators for suppliers of IoT products and services for the corporate use of IT security labels?
- **RQ2**: What are the demotivators for suppliers of IoT products and services for the corporate use of IT security labels?

This research project aims to identify the motivators and demotivators influencing companies' decision-making to adopt security labels. These factors should be determined to incentivize participation in or improve the adoption of IT security labels. An IT security label enables a "security by design" approach, i.e., important security requirements should already be met during the development of IoT devices and services, which then protect the consumer [24]. While there are many areas of applications, in this article, we focus on consumer IoT. These are IoT products found at home and can be bought and owned by consumers [28]. Therefore, our research objective is to provide an overview of factors influencing the decision to adopt security labels, such as the IT security label, based on a structured literature review. These are IoT products found at home and can be bought and owned by consumers [28]. Therefore, our research objective is to provide an overview of factors influencing the decision to adopt security labels, such as the IT security label, based on a structured literature review.

2 Research Background

The following section examines the theoretical background for this research. First, we discuss companies' importance in signaling their product attributes and how they contribute to digital consumer protection. Second, we present security labels as one possible trust-building signal instrument in online shopping environments.

2.1 Digital Consumer Protection

Through the impact of digitalization and irrational behavior, approaches such as behavioral economics and security nudges are becoming increasingly relevant for consumer protection in the digital consumer market [29–31]. The starting point is a classification of consumer types. In consumer research, Kenning and Wobker [32], Micklitz et al. [33] and Reisch et al. [34] differentiate between three categories:

- **Trusting consumers** trust politics and market players and do not spend much time on consumption decisions [32]. For example, they accept privacy policies without thoroughly reading them [34].
- **Responsible consumers** feel responsible for themselves and the environment and collect information even if this involves resources [32]. For example, they encrypt their emails and switch to paid but data-secure alternatives [34].
- **Vulnerable consumers** have low problem-solving skills and limited knowledge about products and rights [32]. For example, they lack information security awareness, making them cybercrime targets [34].

The neoclassical economic theory assumes that people are entirely rational [35]. As homo oeconomicus, they can collect and process all relevant information autonomously [36]. Consequently, there is no need to protect consumers [30]. However, there is an important limitation: the fact that humans can rationally collect and process information does not mean that they are fully informed [30]. According to Simon [37, 38] from behavioral economics, the theory of bounded rationality reveals that although people seek to process all information, they do not have the necessary cognitive capacities and lack relevant information. In addition, time constraints limit the ability to cognitively process a situation, analyze it, and make an optimal decision [38].

This leads to us being quickly overloaded when confronted with too much or too complex information and, therefore, making suboptimal decisions [39]. Especially in the IoT context, there is an increasing lack of transparency for consumers due to the rising complexity and rapid changes of products and the associated difficulty in comparing functionality and quality [8]. The neoclassical approach of simply providing more information to reduce information asymmetries is no longer sufficient when behavioral economic insights, such as bounded rationality, are considered [30].

Consumers' purchase and service decisions involve information [39, 40]. Uncertainties arise for consumers when knowledge about certain characteristics of devices and services is not observable [41]. For example, security is often intangible, and thus products are not rewarded in the market for their higher security [18]. The lack of information can lead to information asymmetry between suppliers and consumers [42]. Thereby, Akerlof [42] refers to adverse selection when a seller has pre-contractual hidden information about the product quality. As a result, the consumer is unaware of the actual quality of the product or service and is, therefore, less willing to pay [30]. Thus, suppliers with higher-quality devices and services cannot gain an advantage over companies with lower-quality features [30]. This leads to market failure, and companies with high quality have to leave the market because they cannot achieve sales advantages over suppliers with lower quality and have to accept cost disadvantages [30, 43].

In summary, consumers risk making wrong decisions or even having their lack of knowledge exploited by companies [30]. Governments attempt to address these risks in market-based processes by providing consumer protection [30]. This paper uses the UNGCP as a starting point for consumer protection [22]. This approach is also recommended by the OECD [44] in its report on Key issues for digital transformation in the G20. These principles aim to create, maintain and continuously improve conditions for consumers so that markets are seen as trustworthy and functioning in the best interest of consumers [45]. The measures taken on the consumer and supplier sides by consumer policy are numerous, and the OECD [46] has categorized them for ease of reference. Thus, consumer protection is faced with the challenge of digitalization and has to design measures so that they are applicable in real life [45].

On the one hand, consumer protection aims to influence the behavior of companies positively and, on the other hand, to provide aid to the consumer [45, 46]. The focus on supply-side consumer protection is on regulations, e.g., through standards or prohibitions, which serve to affect firm behavior [46]. The focus of demand-side consumer protection is on consumer empowerment, which involves, in particular, improving the quality of available information as well as reducing unfair conditions of consumer contracts [46].

2.2 Security Labels

Behavioral economics has explored ways to reduce those existing information asymmetries in the consumer sector, which is intended to influence consumer risk evaluation and, thus, decision-making [31]. For this reason, suppliers and demanders apply mechanisms to reduce information asymmetry: signaling and screening [30]. In contrast to signaling, with screening, the consumer becomes active and collects information themselves to reduce information asymmetry [47, 48]. Since in screening, especially the less well-informed market side wants to reduce information asymmetry [30], this does not apply to the better-informed manufacturers concerning security features in our study.

One method to reduce information asymmetry is signaling, e.g., by using labels issued by trustworthy institutions that can "signal" to the consumer that certain security requirements have been fulfilled so that the consumer himself can assess the hazard potential of a product [23, 31]. Such signals ensure that a given quality limit is not missed and thus minimize the risk of making the wrong decision for the consumer [30]. In addition to mandatory signals (e.g., best before date), companies have the opportunity to use voluntary signals, such as certificates and quality seals [30].

However, there is no uniform scientific definition of the term "label" [49]. In the literature are several terms used synonymously, some of which are also understood as subcategories of labels, such as a seal of approval, quality seal, or certificate [49, 50]. Sander et al. [49] define labels as information for consumers presented in a compressed form to assist consumers in selecting and evaluating products or services for environmental, social, or quality-relevant characteristics. Thus, the consumer can distinguish between products since the labels are intended to signal that the respective product contains different or additional features compared to similar products [49].

A study by Blythe and Johnson [51] examined the effectiveness of existing labels in the food and energy sectors. While consumers prefer labels because of their simplicity, they have unintended consequences such as dichotomous thinking, e.g., mistakenly assuming that a product with a label is better than one without, and halo effects, e.g., a false perception of security [20]. The adoption of product labels for security and privacy information was examined in user studies. Kelley et al. [52] investigated whether food nutrition labels can be adapted to make the privacy policies of websites more understandable. The investigations by Emami-Naeini et al. [21] and Morgner et al. [53] show that security and privacy labels represent a possible approach to regulating the IoT market with regard to security. Lastly, effective labeling helps consumers distinguish between a secure and a less secure product, providing a feeling of confidence [20].

Studies of the design and deployment of security labels have highlighted that labels help manufacturers differentiate their devices and services from competitors and strategically position them in the market [20, 23, 54]. It is also known that several different labels can reduce the impact of the signal [27, 31]. Willingness to pay (WTP) is the amount a consumer is willing to pay for a product [55–57]. WTP is useful for marketers to understand consumer demand and can be used for tactical pricing [58].

Current research by Blythe et al. [20] shows that participants are willing to pay more for a secure product. Furthermore, they found that the presence of security information may prime consumers and consequently influence their purchasing behavior. Spindler [31] shares a similar assessment as Johnson et al. [20], but the findings from behavioral economics raise doubts about the suitability of labels for improving product security. The influence of labels on consumers' purchasing decisions depends on whether the label is perceived as the only relevant criterion and if the consumer is aware of the meaning of the label at all [31]. According to Enste et al. [30], signaling and screening thus have a particular effect on responsible consumers because they are the ones most willing to seek information about the quality of a product. However, in this context, the question arises as to what extent consumers inform themselves or perceive risks in the course of information processing [33]. On the other hand, trusting and vulnerable consumers spend less time searching for information [32]. If many consumers do not fully use the possibilities of signaling and screening due to limited cognitive resources or bounded rationality, consumer policies that rely on empowered consumers may not be effective [30]. Based on these findings, we expect that there are both motivators and demotivators that influence the adoption of security labels from the company's perspective. Hereafter, we have analyzed the literature on security labels and consumer protection to provide an overview of these factors.

3 Methodology

We follow a literature-based research approach to address this gap and to answer our research questions. We conduct a structured literature review to identify factors influencing the decision to use security labels, such as the IT security label. The proposed concept considers both motivating and demotivating factors for using such labels. Our literature review is based on Fettke [59], vom Brocke et al. [60], and Webster and Watson [61] in order to systematically analyze the existing state-of-the-art factors influencing the use of security labels. Figure 1 illustrates our literature selection process.

We searched nine scientific databases, such as AIS Electronic Library, ACM Digital Library, and IEEE Xplore Digital Library, to identify articles addressing the key motivators and demotivators influencing the use of security labels. The relevant articles had to include search strings (like "IT security label" OR "product label" OR "digital consumer protection" OR "IoT") in the title, keywords, or abstract to cover a wide range of articles. An overview of all our search strings is shown in Fig. 1.

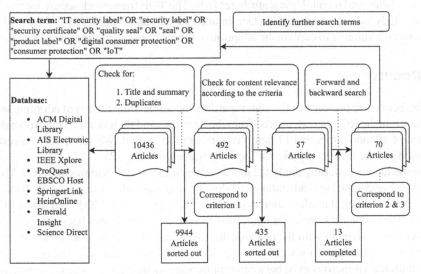

Fig. 1. Illustration of the Literature Selection Process

To ensure the high quality of the articles, we restricted the literature according to three content criteria (Table 1) and removed duplicates.

Table 1. Content Criteria

Criterion	Description
1	Refers only to irrelevant articles that address consumer protection without reference to security labels in the IoT context
2	Considers relevant articles that describe the two research areas of consumer protection and security labels in the IoT context
3	Deals with relevant articles from the topic area of security labels in the IoT context, but not directly in the area of consumer protection

The publications found are limited until the last criterion is reached. In addition, a forward and backward search was performed to increase the number of publications found. 10,436 articles were identified in the databases by using the procedure described above. Of these publications, 9944 articles were removed based on the title, abstract, and duplicate check. The remaining 492 articles were checked for content criteria, so a further 435 articles were removed. A subsequent forward and backward search added 13 articles. A total of 70 articles were identified that met the criteria. The review resulted in a list of 10 motivators and 11 demotivators that were referenced across 15 articles and thus collected. Based on that, we assign these motivators and demotivators from the literature to the three dimensions of the Technology-Organization-Environment Framework [62]. The TOE framework aids in explaining which influencing factors affect the adoption of new technologies by classifying them in environmental conditions, organizational characteristics, and technological attributes [63]. The TOE framework seems appropriate for our study as prior research like Doolin and Ali [63] and Angeles [64] show that the framework is suitable to explain the adoption of innovations in enterprises in IS research.

4   Results

In this section, we present our findings regarding the influencing factors of adopting security labels in the IoT context derived from the literature and their definitions (Appendix). A total of 10 motivators and 11 demotivators were identified. We subdivide our results according to the three categories of the TOE framework (Fig. 2).

Some factors generally apply to labels, such as increasing consumer trust (O1-MOT) or achieving competitive advantage (E1-MOT), whereas other factors result from the specifics of the digital market, such as increasing IT security (T3-MOT) and privacy (T5-MOT). The smaller database for demotivators is quite conspicuous because only a few authors have also dealt with the possible disadvantages of security labels. Nevertheless, more demotivators than motivators could be identified. Our literature review revealed that information asymmetries exist between suppliers and demanders. There is an increasing lack of transparency (T1-MOT) for consumers due to the rising complexity and rapid changes of IoT products and the associated difficulty in comparing secure and less secure products. Security labels offer manufacturers the opportunity to credibly and transparently signal compliance with security standards and legal requirements for IoT products (E3-MOT).

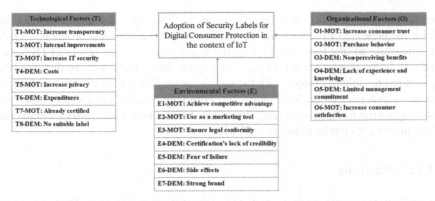

Fig. 2. Influencing Factors of the Adoption of Security Labels

During the audit process, a manufacturer may learn from the practices specified in a label, which could trigger internal improvements (T2-MOT). For example, creating documentation can shorten the training times for new employees. In addition, the acquired knowledge is no longer lost when employees leave. Through detailed documentation, internal risk controls and security optimizations take place. Depending on the label's focus, data protection can also be improved through compliance with applicable data protection laws, such as the General Data Protection Regulation. These are all opportunities to build consumer trust in the IoT. Moreover, studies have shown that consumers are willing to pay for more secure products (see Sect. 2.2); thus, security is a criterion for the purchase decision (O2-MOT). If a manufacturer cannot signal its information credibly, this can result in the adverse selection described in the research background (see Sect. 2.2). For manufacturers, the use of a label not only enhances their public image (E2-MOT) but also differentiates them from the competition. It is also known that several different labels may neutralise the impact of the signal (E6-DEM). Since such diversity can reduce comparability, consumers need to know the different criteria for awarding labels to be able to compare them (O6-MOT). Consequently, trust is mainly derived from the reputation of the independent institution. Manufacturers may reject such labels due to the lack of credibility caused by the poor reputation or low level of awareness of these institutions among consumers (E4-DEM).

Instead, they use their limited resources, e.g., financial and human resources, for other opportunities that are more appropriate to increase sales (O3-DEM). Another reason manufacturers use other opportunities is that they are already certified (T7-DEM) and therefore see no benefit in additional labels or found no suitable label. Similarly, the adoption of labels can be a legitimate concern of the company's top management to contribute to the company's strategy because there is a lack of experience and knowledge to obtain labels for devices and services (O4-DEM). Employees could also hinder the adoption because they are not sufficiently trained and supported or are unwilling to change their work processes (O5-DEM), especially when managers decide to focus on other opportunities better suited to increase sales because labels are unlikely to be adopted due to an almost exhausted budget. The economic disadvantages are related to the one-time and ongoing costs of the label for the manufacturers. These can be, for example, the costs for the labels themselves as well as expenses, e.g., personnel and time for the creation of the documentation and costs to maintain the products over the entire life cycle so that they comply with the requirements of the label (T4-DEM and T6-DEM). Some companies do not even try to introduce labels because they fear that they will not be able to comply with the requirements (E5-DEM) or only confirm the minimum standards (T8-DEM). Finally, if a company already has a strong brand and a good reputation in the market (e.g., Amazon), labels are not necessary as marketing tools to improve its public image (E7-DEM).

5 Contributions

The results of this study have both practical and theoretical implications. First, we expand the existing knowledge by contributing to the understanding of using security labels on IoT products. In this way, we can contribute to security research and consumer protection in general, which is supported by the recent call of UNGCP for further developments in this area [22]. Second, the results may help improve the adoption of security labels in companies as they explain and predict challenges. The overview could also incentivize other companies to implement conscious IT security management already in the development phase of new devices and services. Thus, our results are relevant for all well-known manufacturers of security-relevant end-consumer devices because they usually have their own online stores as well. Third, this research contains implications for improvements of such labels with regard to a European label [24] that can be derived from the results. Our results serve as a starting point for further studies, e.g., regarding overcoming challenges or investigating individual factors such as online purchase intention or trust toward online suppliers.

6 Conclusion and Further Outlook

This paper is the first part of a broader study. In this current phase, we provide an overview of factors that could influence the adoption of security labels for IoT products and services derived from the literature. The literature review resulted in a list of 10 motivators (RQ1) and 11 demotivators (RQ2) from the companies' perspective. Based on our findings, we classified the factors into three context categories according to the TOE framework (i.e., technological, organizational, and environmental). We plan to empirically evaluate and validate our findings through semi-structured interviews in the second phase. We will conduct the interviews with three focus groups, one with (1) suppliers who plan to implement a security label, especially the IT security label, another one with (2) suppliers who already use a security label, and (3) suppliers who do not currently have, nor plan to implement a security label for their products. In follow-up studies, the adoption of security labels for IoT products could be compared across specific organizational types and sizes, e.g., with a focus on cyber security start-ups as described by Schütz et al. [65]. In addition to the IT security labels examined, it may also be interesting for suppliers to evaluate offering add-on personal cyber insurance (e.g., as introduced by McGregor et al. [66] or Schütz et al. [67]) as a signal in the online purchasing process.

Appendix

Factors	Definition	References
Increase consumer trust	Allows for a reconsideration of belief formation related to the trustworthiness of a manufacturer and its products	[20, 27, 49, 54, 68–73]
Increase transparency	Enable the seeking of hidden information about the manufacturer's quality and its devices or services to their customers	
Purchase behaviour	Persuades consumers to buy from them because the label shows that they are audited by a third party and are therefore trustworthy	
Ensure legal conformity	Comply with the legal and regulatory requirements of its devices or services	[27, 68, 69, 71, 72, 74, 75]
Increase IT security	IT security standards can be assessed and improved	[27, 68, 69, 71–75]
Use as a marketing tool	Exploit the popularity and credibility of the labels to improve their public image	[23, 27, 49, 69, 70, 73, 75]
Achieve competitive advantage	Allow them to differentiate themselves from their competitors to create strategic value or necessary to retain their reputation in the market	
Internal Improvements	During the audit process, a manufacturer may learn from the practices specified in a label, which could trigger internal improvements	[23, 27, 69, 70, 73, 75]
Increase privacy	The manufacturer complies with applicable data protection laws	[27, 68, 69, 72, 74]
Increase consumer satisfaction	The purchasing behaviour of consumers is based on their personal needs and desires	[69]
Already certified	Some companies do not seek additional labels because they are already "certified" and therefore see no benefit in adding additional labels to their devices or services	

(continued)

(*continued*)

Factors	Definition	References
Lack of experience and knowledge	Lack of experience and knowledge to obtain labels for devices and services	
Strong brand	If a company already has a "strong brand" and a good reputation in the market (e.g., Amazon), labels are not necessary as marketing tools	
No suitable label	No suitable label, only confirmation of the minimum standards	
Limited management commitment	Due to insufficient training and support or the lack of willingness of staff and management to implement labels	
Fear of failure	Some companies do not even try to introduce labels because they fear that they will not be able to comply with the requirements	
Side effects	For some labels, consumer ratings are linked to the label (e.g., Trusted Shop), so the companies fear negative consumer reactions could neutralise the effect of the label	
Costs	Direct costs are specifically related to the actual process and the costs it causes. The direct costs are related to the expenditures incurred	[27, 30, 69, 70, 75]
Expenditures	Indirect costs arise due to necessary changes in the product or the development process	[69, 75]
Non-perceiving benefits	Usage of limited resources (e.g., financial, human resources) for other opportunities that are more capable ways to increase sales	[27, 69]
Certification's lack of credibility	Lack of credibility resulting from poor reputation of the independent institution or the low level of awareness of these institutions among consumers	[31, 75]

References

1. Kim, Y., Oh, H., Kang, S.: Proof of concept of home IoT connected vehicles. Sensors **17**(6), 1289 (2017). https://doi.org/10.3390/s17061289
2. Bello, O., Zeadally, S., Badra, M.: Network layer inter-operation of Device-to-Device communication technologies in Internet of Things (IoT). Ad Hoc Netw. **57**, 52–62 (2017). https://doi.org/10.1016/j.adhoc.2016.06.010
3. AlHogail, A.: Improving IoT technology adoption through improving consumer trust. Technologies **6**(3), 64 (2018). https://doi.org/10.3390/technologies6030064
4. Alaa, M., Zaidan, A.A., Zaidan, B.B., Talal, M., Kiah, M.: A review of smart home applications based on Internet of Things. J. Netw. Comput. Appl. **97**, 48–65 (2017). https://doi.org/10.1016/j.jnca.2017.08.017
5. Feng, S., Setoodeh, P., Haykin, S.: Smart home: cognitive interactive people-centric Internet of Things. IEEE Commun. Mag. **55**, 34–39 (2017). https://doi.org/10.1109/MCOM.2017.160 0682CM
6. Isyanto, H., Arifin, A.S., Suryanegara, M.: Design and implementation of IoT-based smart home voice commands for disabled people using Google assistant. In: 2020 International Conference on Smart Technology and Applications (ICoSTA), Surabaya, Indonesia, pp. 1–6. https://doi.org/10.1109/ICoSTA48221.2020.1570613925
7. Park, J.-S., Jang, G.-J., Kim, J.-H., Kim, S.-H.: Acoustic interference cancellation for a voice-driven interface in smart TVs. IEEE Trans. Consum. Electron. **59**(1), 244–249 (2013). https://doi.org/10.1109/TCE.2013.6490266
8. Knips, J., Gries, C.-I. and Wernick, C.: Consumer-IoT in Deutschland. Anwendungsbereiche und möglicher Regelungsbedarf. WIK Diskussionsbeitrag, No. 471 (2020). http://hdl.handle.net/10419/228684
9. Statista: Digital Market Outlook. Prognose zur Anzahl der Smart Home Haushalte nach Segmenten in Europa für die Jahre 2017 bis 2025 (in Millionen), p. 4 (2021). https://de.statista.com/statistik/studie/id/6638/dokument/smart-home/
10. Stenkamp, D.: TÜV Consumer IoT Zertifizierung – mehr Sicherheit für smarte Produkte. Pressekonferenz (2021). https://www.tuev-verband.de/?tx_epxelo_file%5Bid%5D=831592&cHash=1d5eb42a2fe855c4182fe148983f8185
11. Raffman, M.S., Russo, A.H.: Mitigating transactional risk in the Internet of Things. J. Private Equity **21**, 65–73 (2018). https://doi.org/10.3905/jpe.2018.21.2.065
12. businesswire: Strategy Analytics: Global Smart Home Market Roaring Back in 2021 (2022). https://www.businesswire.com/news/home/20210706005692/en/Strategy-Analytics-Global-Smart-Home-Market-Roaring-Back-in-2021
13. Badran, H.: IoT Security and Consumer Trust. In: Proceedings of the 20th Annual International Conference on Digital Government Research (dg.o 2019), pp. 133–140. Association for Computing Machinery, New York, NY, USA (2019). https://doi.org/10.1145/3325112.3325234
14. Kolias, C., Kambourakis, G., Stavrou, A., Voas, J.: DDoS in the IoT: Mirai and other botnets. Computer **50**(7), 80–84 (2017). https://doi.org/10.1109/mc.2017.201
15. Khan, W.Z., Aalsalem, M.Y., Khan, M.K.: Communal acts of IoT consumers: a potential threat to security and privacy. IEEE Trans. Consum. Electron. **65**(1), 64–72 (2019). https://doi.org/10.1109/TCE.2018.2880338
16. Maras, M.-H.: Internet of Things: security and privacy implications. Int. Data Privacy Law **5**(2), 99–104 (2015). https://doi.org/10.1093/idpl/ipv004
17. Myeonggeon, L., Kyungmook, L., Jaewoo, S., Seong-je, C., Jongmoo, C.: Security threat on wearable services: empirical study using a commercial smartband. In: 2016 IEEE International Conference on Consumer Electronics-Asia (ICCE-Asia), Seoul, Korea (South), pp. 1–5. https://doi.org/10.1109/ICCE-Asia.2016.7804766

18. Woods, D.W., Moore, T.: Cyber warranties: market fix or marketing trick? Commun. ACM **63**(4), 104–107 (2020). https://doi.org/10.1145/3360310
19. Yildirim, H., Ali-Eldin, A.M.: A model for predicting user intention to use wearable IoT devices at the workplace. J. King Saud Univ. Comput. Inform. Sci. **31**(4), 497–505 (2019). https://doi.org/10.1016/j.jksuci.2018.03.001
20. Johnson, S.D., Blythe, J.M., Manning, M., Wong, G.T.W.: The impact of IoT security labelling on consumer product choice and willingness to pay. PLoS ONE **15**, e0227800 (2020). https://doi.org/10.1371/journal.pone.0227800
21. Emami-Naeini, P., Dixon, H., Agarwal, Y., Cranor, L.F.: Exploring how privacy and security factor into IoT device purchase behavior. In: Proceedings of the 2019 CHI Conference on Human Factors in Computing Systems (CHI 2019). Association for Computing Machinery, New York, NY, USA, vol. 534, pp. 1–12. https://doi.org/10.1145/3290605.3300764
22. United Nations Conference on Trade and Development (UNCTAD): United Nations Guidelines for Consumer Protection (2016). https://unctad.org/system/files/official-document/dit ccplpmisc2016d1_en.pdf
23. Garg, V.: A lemon by any other label. In: Proceedings of the 7th International Conference on Information Systems Security and Privacy (ICISSP 2021), pp. 558–565 (2021). https://doi.org/10.5220/0010295205580565
24. Bundesamt für Sicherheit in der Informationstechnik (BSI): Bericht zum Digitalen Verbraucherschutz 2021 (2022). https://www.bsi.bund.de/SharedDocs/Downloads/DE/BSI/Pub likationen/DVS-Berichte/dvs-bericht_2021.pdf?__blob=publicationFile&v=4
25. Halderman, J.A.: To strengthen security, change developers' incentives. IEEE Secur. Priv. **8**(2), 79–82 (2010). https://doi.org/10.1109/MSP.2010.85
26. Serabian, D.: Consumer Protection and Cybersecurity: The Consumer Education Gap (2015). https://digitalscholarship.unlv.edu/brookings_pubs/33/
27. Jentzsch, N.: Was können Datenschutz-Gütesiegel leisten? Wirtschaftsdienst **92**, 413–419 (2012). https://doi.org/10.1007/s10273-012-1397-9
28. Blythe, J.M., Johnson, S.D.: A systematic review of crime facilitated by the consumer Internet of Things. Secur. J. **34**, 97–125 (2021). https://doi.org/10.1057/s41284-019-00211-8
29. Dold, M., Krieger, T.: Cyber-security aus ordnungspolitischer Sicht: Verfügungsrechte. Wettbewerb und Nudges. Wirtschaftsdienst **97**, 559–565 (2017). https://doi.org/10.1007/s10273-017-2176-4
30. Enste, D., Ewers, M., Heldman, C. and Schneider, R.: Verbraucherschutz und Verhaltensökonomik. Zur Psychologie von Vertrauen und Kontrolle. IW-Analysen, No. 106 (2016). http://hdl.handle.net/10419/157153
31. Spindler, G.: Behavioral economics und Verbraucherschutz sowie Sicherheitsrecht in der IT-Welt. Wirtschaftsdienst **100**, 97–99 (2020). https://doi.org/10.1007/s10273-020-2576-8
32. Kenning, P., Wobker, I.: Ist der "mündige Verbraucher" eine Fiktion? Zeitschrift für Wirtschafts- und Unternehmensethik **14**(2), 282–300 (2013). https://doi.org/10.5771/1439-880X-2013-2-282
33. Micklitz, H.-W., Oehler, A., Piorkowsky, M.-B., Reisch, L., Strünck, C.: Der vertrauende, der verletzliche oder der verantwortungsvolle Verbraucher? Stellungnahme des Wissenschaftlichen Beirats Verbraucher- und Ernährungspolitik beim BMELV (2010). https://www.vzbv.de/sites/default/files/downloads/Strategie_verbraucherp olitik_Wiss_BeiratBMELV_2010.pdf
34. Reisch, L., Büchel, D., Joost, G., Zander-Hayrat, H.: Sachverständigenrat für Verbraucherfragen: Digitale Welt und Handel. Verbraucher im personalisierten Online-Handel, Berlin (2016)
35. Simon, H.A.: Rationality in psychology and economics. J. Bus. **59**(2), 209–224 (1986)

36. Levine, J., Chan, K.M., Satterfield, T.: From rational actor to efficient complexity manager: exorcising the ghost of Homo economicus with a unified synthesis of cognition research. Ecol. Econ. **114**, 22–32 (2015). https://doi.org/10.1016/j.ecolecon.2015.03.010

37. Simon, H.A.: A behavioral model of rational choice. Q. J. Econ. **69**(1), 99 (1955). https://doi.org/10.2307/1884852

38. Simon, H.A.: Bounded Rationality. In: Eatwell, J., Milgate, M., Newman, P. (eds.) Utility and Probability, pp. 15–18. Palgrave Macmillan UK, London (1990). https://doi.org/10.1007/978-1-349-20568-4_5

39. Gao, J., Zhang, C., Wang, K., Ba, S.: Understanding online purchase decision making: the effects of unconscious thought, information quality, and information quantity. Decis. Support. Syst. **53**(4), 772–781 (2012). https://doi.org/10.1016/j.dss.2012.05.011

40. Murray, K.B.: A test of services marketing theory: consumer information acquisition activities. J. Mark. **55**(1), 10–25 (1991). https://doi.org/10.1177/002224299105500102

41. Rubik, F., Weskamp, C.: Verbraucherschutz durch Produktkennzeichnung. Gutachten im Auftrag des Bundesministeriums für Wirtschaft (Forschungsauftrag Nr. 24/94) (1996). https://www.ioew.de/fileadmin/_migrated/tx_ukioewdb/IOEW_SR_098_Verbrauch erschutz_durch_ProduktkennzeichnungTeil1.pdf

42. Akerlof, G.A.: The Market for "Lemons". quality uncertainty and the market mechanism. Q. J. Econ. **84**(3), 488–500 (1970). https://doi.org/10.2307/1879431

43. Jahn, G., Schramm, M., Spiller, A.: The reliability of certification: quality labels as a consumer policy tool. J. Consum. Policy **28**, 53–73 (2005). https://doi.org/10.1007/s10603-004-7298-6

44. OECD: Key Issues for Digital Transformation in the G20. Report prepared for a joint G20 German Presidency/OECD conference. OECD Publishing, Paris (2017). https://www.oecd.org/G20/key-issues-for-digital-transformation-in-the-G20.pdf

45. Thorun, C., Diels, J.: Consumer protection technologies: an investigation into the potentials of new digital technologies for consumer policy. J. Consum. Policy **43**, 177–191 (2020). https://doi.org/10.1007/s10603-019-09411-6

46. Organisation for Economic Co-operation and Development (OECD): Consumer Policy Toolkit, vol. (2010). https://doi.org/10.1787/9789264079663-en

47. Spence, M.: Job market signaling. Q. J. Econ. **87**(3), 355–374 (1973). https://doi.org/10.2307/1882010

48. Stiglitz, J.E.: The theory of "screening," education, and the distribution of income. Am. Econ. Rev. **65**(3), 283–300 (1975)

49. Sander, M., Heim, N., Kohnle, Y.: Label-Awareness. Wie genau schaut der Konsument hin? Eine Analyse des Label-Bewusstseins von Verbrauchern unter besonderer Berücksichtigung des Lebensmittelbereichs. Berichte über Landwirtschaft - Zeitschrift für Agrarpolitik und Landwirtschaft **94**(2), 1–20 (2016). https://doi.org/10.12767/buel.v94i2.120

50. Pollrich, M., Wagner, L.: Gütesiegel. Zu detaillierte Angaben können die Funktionsfähigkeit der Zertifikate schmälern. DIW Wochenbericht **80**, 15–18 (2013)

51. Blythe, J., Johnson, S.D.: Rapid evidence assessment on labelling schemes and implications for consumer IoT security. PETRAS IoT Hub, pp. 1–19 (2018). https://www.gov.uk/govern ment/publications/rapid-evidence-assessment-on-labelling-schemes-for-iot-security

52. Kelley, P.G., Bresee, J., Cranor, L.F., Reeder, R.W.: A 'nutrition label' for privacy. In: Proceedings of the 5th Symposium on Usable Privacy and Security (SOUPS 2009), vol. 4, pp. 1–12. Association for Computing Machinery, New York, NY, USA (2009). https://doi.org/10.1145/1572532.1572538

53. Morgner, P., Mai, C., Koschate-Fischer, N., Freiling, F., Benenson, Z.: Security update labels: establishing economic incentives for security patching of IoT consumer products. In: 2020 IEEE Symposium on Security and Privacy (SP), San Francisco, CA, USA, pp. 429–446 (2020). https://doi.org/10.1109/sp40000.2020.00021

54. Emami-Naeini, P., Agarwal, Y., Cranor, L., Hibshi, H.: Ask the experts. What should be on an IoT privacy and security label?. In: IEEE Symposium on Security and Privacy (SP), San Francisco, CA, USA,, pp. 447–464 (2020). https://doi.org/10.1109/sp40000.2020.00043
55. Wertenbroch, K., Skiera, B.: Measuring consumers' willingness to pay at the point of purchase. J. Mark. Res. **39**(2), 228–241 (2002). https://doi.org/10.1509/jmkr.39.2.228.19086
56. Kalish, S., Nelson, P.: A comparison of ranking, rating and reservation price measurement in conjoint analysis. Mark. Lett. **2**, 327–335 (1991). https://doi.org/10.1007/BF00664219
57. Simonson, I., Drolet, A.: Anchoring effects on consumers' willingness-to-pay and willingness-to-accept. SSRN Electron. J (2003). Stanford GSB Working Paper No. 1787. https://doi.org/10.2139/ssrn.383341
58. Miller, K.M., Hofstetter, R., Krohmer, H., Zhang, Z.J.: How should consumers' willingness to pay be measured? An empirical comparison of state-of-the-art approaches. J. Mark. Res. **58**(1), 172–184 (2011). https://doi.org/10.1509/jmkr.48.1.172
59. Fettke, P.: State-of-the-Art des State-of-the-Art. Eine Untersuchung der Forschungsmethode „Review" innerhalb der Wirtschaftsinformatik. WIRTSCHAFTSINFORMATIK **48**, 257–266 (2006). https://doi.org/10.1007/s11576-006-0057-3
60. vom Brocke, J., Simons, A., Riemer, K., Niehaves, B., Plattfaut, R., Cleven, A.: Standing on the shoulders of giants: challenges and recommendations of literature search in information systems research. Commun. Assoc. Inform. Syst. **37**, 206–220 (2015). https://doi.org/10.17705/1CAIS.03709
61. Webster, J., Watson, R.T.: Analyzing the past to prepare for the future. Writing a literature review. MIS Q. **26**(2), xiii–xxiii (2002)
62. Tornatzky, L.G., Fleischer, M.: The Processes of Technological Innovation. Lexington Books, Lexington (1990)
63. Doolin, B., Ali, E.A.H.: Adoption of mobile technology in the supply chain: an exploratory cross-case analysis. In: Electronic Business: Concepts, Methodologies, Tools, and Applications. IGI Global, pp. 1121–1136 (2008). https://doi.org/10.4018/9781605660561.ch070
64. Angeles, R.: Using the technology-organization-environment framework and Zuboff'S concepts for understanding environmental sustainability and RFID: two case studies. Int. J. Econ. Manage. Eng. **7**, 2878–2887 (2013). https://doi.org/10.5281/zenodo.1088850
65. Schütz, F., Spierau, B., Rampold, F., Nickerson, R., Trang, S.: Chasing cyber security unicorns: a taxonomy-based analysis of cyber security start-ups' business models. In: ECIS 2023 Research Papers, Kristiansand, Norway, vol. 262, pp. 1–19 (2023)
66. McGregor, R., Reaiche, C., Boyle, S., Corral de Zubielqui, G.: Cyberspace and personal cyber insurance: a systematic review. J. Comput. Inform. Syst. **64**(1), 157–171 (2023). https://doi.org/10.1080/08874417.2023.2185551
67. Schütz, F., Rampold, F., Kalisch, A., Masuch, K.: Consumer cyber insurance as risk transfer: a coverage analysis. Procedia Comput. Sci. **219**, 521–528 (2023). https://doi.org/10.1016/j.procs.2023.01.320
68. Lansing, J., Benlian, A., Sunyaev, A.: Unblackboxing' decision makers' interpretations of IS certifications in the context of cloud service certifications. J. Assoc. Inf. Syst. **19**(11), 1064–1096 (2018). https://doi.org/10.17705/1jais.00520
69. Lins, S., Kromat, T., Löbbers, J., Benlian, A., Sunyaev, A.: Why don't you join in? A typology of information system certification adopters. Decis. Sci. **53**, 452–485 (2020). https://doi.org/10.1111/deci.12488
70. Volkamer, M., Hauff, H.: Zum Nutzen hoher Zertifizierungsstufen nach den Common Criteria (II). Datenschutz und Datensicherheit **31**, 766–768 (2007). https://doi.org/10.1007/s11623-007-0250-6
71. Lins, S., Sunyaev, A.: Unblackboxing IT certifications: a theoretical model explaining IT certification effectiveness. In: ICIS 2017 Proceedings, Seoul, Korea (South), vol. 26, pp. 1–13 (2017)

72. Gadatsch, A., Klein, H., Münchhausen, M.: Zertifizierte IT-Sicherheit für Cloud Services. Wirtschaftsinformatik Management **6**, 88–97 (2014). https://doi.org/10.1365/s35764-014-0388-6
73. Konrad, W. , Scheer, D.: Grenzen und Möglichkeiten der Verbraucherinformation durch Produktkennzeichnung. In: BfR-Wissenschaft, 05/2020, pp. 1–220 (2010). http://www.bfr.bund.de/cm/238/grenzen_und_moeglichkeiten_der_verbraucherinformation_durch_produkt kennzeichnung.pdf
74. Schumacher, A.: Akkreditierung und Zertifizierung von De-Mail-Diensteanbietern. Datenschutz und Datensicherheit **34**, 302–307 (2010). https://doi.org/10.1007/s11623-010-0092-5
75. Blomer, J., et al.: Software Zertifizierung. In: Interner Bericht 2008-4, pp. 1–221. https://doi.org/10.5445/IR/1000008070

Software as a Service – A Key Enabler for Digital Transformation in Organization - A Multi-disciplinary Information Systems Research Agenda

Himanshu Warudkar(✉)

Indian School of Business, Hyderabad, India
himanshu_warudkar2024@efpm.isb.edu

Abstract. Software as a Service (SaaS) is a segment within the technology services industry that has shown continued resilience and strong growth. SaaS is software owned, delivered, and managed remotely by one or more providers. It offers value to businesses by reducing the total cost of ownership through complete outsourcing, leveraging data and analytics to understand customers better, and making data-driven solutions that enhance performance. SaaS is highly scalable and generates reliably recurring revenue, making it an attractive acquisition target for B2B SaaS players. SaaS is seen as a key enabler of business value and transformation. One of the key factors that enables organizations to extract value is the maturity of architectures and better integration of new technologies. Enterprises are looking at SaaS as an alternative to purchasing, installing, and maintaining modifiable off-the-shelf software packages, offering flexibility in pricing and modular usage of features. Although SaaS offerings have been around for more than a decade, firms are still learning to realize value from their co-existence. However, implementing SaaS solutions comes with challenges and risks. In this chapter, we look at these factors and put forward several propositions laying down the foundation for empirical and qualitative research to be conducted for validation of the hypothesis.

Keywords: Software as a Service (SaaS) · data-driven solutions · business value and transformation

1 Introduction – SaaS as an Enabler for Digital Transformation

Organisations all around are undergoing massive digital transformation. According to a recent consulting report, Software as a Service (SaaS) is one of the segments within the technology services industry that has shown continued resilience and strong growth[1]. Software as a service (SaaS) is defined as "software owned, delivered and managed remotely by one or more providers"[2]. Some of the key features of SaaS are a common

---

[1] https://www.bcg.com/publications/2023/winning-strategies-of-hypergrowth-saas-champions.

[2] https://www.gartner.com/en/information-technology/glossary/software-as-A-service-saas.

© The Author(s), under exclusive license to Springer Nature Switzerland AG 2024
A. Kathuria et al. (Eds.): WeB 2022, LNBIP 508, pp. 28–37, 2024.
https://doi.org/10.1007/978-3-031-60003-6_3

set of code and data definitions that is consumed in a one-to-many model by all contracted customers at any time on a pay-for-use basis or as a subscription based on use metrics.

For businesses, SaaS solutions offer value on multiple levels a) by reducing the total cost of ownership (TCO) through complete outsourcing i.e., hosting and maintenance of infrastructure, b) by having a common code and data definitions that enable analytics to understand customers better, improve products and services, and make data-driven solutions—all of which will enhance performance. Moreover, because they are highly scalable and generate reliably recurring revenue, B2B SaaS players have become attractive acquisition targets.

There are various types of software services, each designed to address specific needs and provide different functionalities. These software services cater to various needs, from infrastructure management and application development to collaboration, security, and data analytics. Therefore, organizations can choose the services that best align with their goals, budgets, and technical requirements. They are often delivered through cloud computing models, including Software as a Service (SaaS), Platform as a Service (PaaS), and Infrastructure as a Service (IaaS).

SaaS is seen as a critical enabler of business value and transformational potential [21]. Further, organizational assets complement the business value of SaaS in value creation. One of the key factors that enables organizations to extract value is through mature architectures and better integration of new technologies into the organization. Many firms are learning how to combine them to put them to strategic use. Even though SaaS offerings have been around for more than a decade, firms are still learning to realize value from their co-existence.

Given, that Software as a Service (SaaS) delivers a bundle of applications and services over the Internet, its on-demand feature allows users to enjoy full scalability and to handle possible demand fluctuations (also called as infrastructure elasticity) at no risk. As such, enterprises are looking at SaaS as an alternative to purchasing, installing, and maintaining modifiable off-the-shelf (MOTS) software packages [20]. This offers flexibility in pricing, modular usage of features more.

However, there are several factors, including challenges and risks associated with the implementation of SaaS solutions within an organization. In this chapter, we look at these factors from a practitioner's perspective and put forward several propositions laying down the foundation for empirical and qualitative research to be conducted for validation of the hypothesis.

2   Choice of SaaS vs. On-Premises Implementation

Every SaaS implementation has a lifecycle of its own, and factors within this lifecycle affect the choice of whether an organization should go for a SaaS implementation. For example, research has been conducted on a) the factors that determine the magnitudes of operational and innovational benefits and. b) the contribution of these benefits to firm performance [19, 30]. However, several critical decisions must be made in implementing SaaS software, starting from whether firms should adopt SaaS and, if so, how they can gain more benefits and positively impact firm performance. Figure 1 provides a simple decision tree to navigate this decision process.

The choice between SaaS (Software as a Service) and on-premises software depends on various factors and is primarily driven by the needs of an organization, its resources, and its long-term goals. Each approach has its advantages and disadvantages. Table 1 gives us a comparison of the SaaS versus the on-premise model.

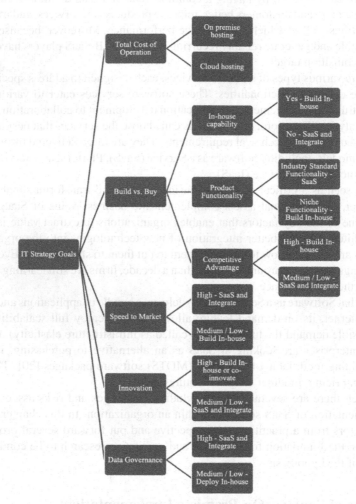

Fig. 1. Choice of SaaS Implementation

Ultimately, the choice between SaaS and on-premises software should align with an organization's specific needs, budget, and long-term strategy. Many businesses opt for a hybrid approach, using both SaaS and on-premises solutions to meet different requirements.

Table 1. – Comparison of SaaS vs. On-Premise Deployment

Factors	SaaS Model	On-Premise Model
Deployment and Maintenance	SaaS applications are hosted on the cloud thereby eliminating the need for organisations to install and maintain software devices on their own infrastructure. The SaaS provider is responsible for the end-2-end service i.e., techno-functional updates, cybersecurity, maintenance and production services	On-premise software deployment requires organizations to set up and manage their own infrastructure. This approach offers more control but comes with the need for ongoing maintenance of infrastructure including regular version upgrades and greater management oversight
Cost	SaaS services are subscription-based models thereby allowing users to pay on a recurring basis. This can be more cost-effective for many organizations, as it eliminates the upfront costs of hardware, software licenses, and ongoing maintenance. From an accounting perspective this cost becomes an operational expenditure as opposed to capital expenditure	On-premise software often requires significant upfront capital expenditure for hardware, software licenses, and infrastructure. This may result in a greater total cost of ownership due to continuous maintenance and upgrade requirements
Accessibility	Given SaaS applications are hosted on the cloud are accessible from anywhere over the internet promoting remote work and collaboration. This provides greater flexibility to organizations to have a distributed workforce	Access to on-premise software is strictly governed by the organizational network and needs to be accessed over VPN as such restricting flexibility in remote work capabilities
Scalability	SaaS applications are designed for scalability. Users can horizontally and vertically scale their subscriptions as well as infrastructure to accommodate peaks and troughs in usage	Scalability for on-premise software requires investing in and maintaining additional infrastructure making it less flexible in accommodating peak usage. Further during troughs spare infrastructure is unused thereby locking the organization in greater capital and operational expenditure

(*continued*)

Table 1. (*continued*)

Factors	SaaS Model	On-Premise Model
Customization	SaaS providers allow users to configure and customize software. Instead of "eat all you can" the approach is "buy what you need". However, customization may be limited to maintain the multi-tenant architecture	On-premise software offers greater customization as users can modify it according to their needs. However, the risk is also in having multiple instances of the same software, particularly in the case of a globally distributed organization
Security and Compliance	SaaS providers are responsible for cybersecurity and data protection regulations. Organizations must carefully assess the provider's compliance with cybersecurity and regulatory laws	Cybersecurity in on-premise software is the responsibility of the organization and provides control but requires substantial efforts to ensure compliance with cybersecurity and regulatory laws
Integration	SaaS applications typically offer APIs for easy integration with other software systems particularly start-ups and other externally hosted applications	On-premise software allows for more extensive custom integrations and can be better suited for organizations with complex integration requirements

3 Factors Affecting Success of SaaS Implementation

Organizations must select the right Software as a Service (SaaS) provider. The right choice can significantly enhance the organizational ability to serve its customers effectively, and the wrong one can lead to costly errors such as data losses, cyber-attacks, and a long time to market due to integration issues. To ensure organizations make an informed choice, the key steps to be followed in selecting a SaaS provider and the success of its implementation are described in Fig. 2.

A few more factors that must be considered in the selection of a SaaS provider and during implementation:

1. *Cybersecurity Controls and Compliance*: Cybersecurity is a top priority as such organizations need to ensure that the SaaS provider has robust cybersecurity measures and complies with all the regulations applicable to the industry domain.
2. *Scalability and Performance*: Organizations must assess the scalability of SaaS solutions and the ability to accommodate changes in user numbers and data volumes.
3. *User-Friendly Interfaces*: Organizations should evaluate the user interface to ensure it is user-friendly and intuitive. Conducting usability tests across a wide range of users is highly advisable.

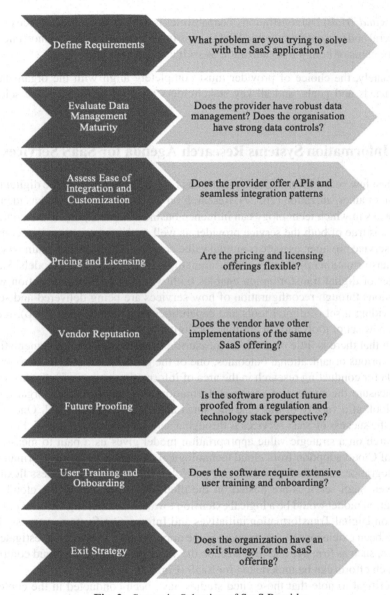

Fig. 2. Stages in Selection of SaaS Provider

4. Support and Service Level Agreements (SLAs): Organizations must review the Service Level Agreements (SLAs) that guarantee service levels and response times and ensure they are fit for purpose in line with organizational expectations from a service criticality and geographical spread.

5. *Legal and Contractual Aspects*: Organizations must carefully review the terms and conditions of the legal and contractual agreement, including liabilities, openness to audit, and access to code in escrow as a safety measure.

6. *Demos and Trials*: Demonstration of capabilities is a must, and mere reliance on sales collateral and presentations could lead to gaps in understanding the techno-functional requirements of both the organization as well as SaaS provider.

Ultimately, the choice of provider must completely align with the organization's specific needs and goals, and all key stakeholders must be involved in the selection process.

4 An Information Systems Research Agenda for SaaS Services

For the past few years, Information Systems has been a key enabler for the digital transformation of an organization [26, 27]. Research on digital transformation has identified various ways in which technology can influence business models [18]. In the context of SaaS, this is true of both the service provider as well as the organization that contracts with the service provider, as there is mutual value creation. There are two main ways that digital transformation might influence different organizations' business models. SaaS as an enabler of digital transformation enables both ways – i.e., experimentation within organizations through reconfiguration of how services are being delivered and second is in providing a set of digital tools and capabilities (e.g., Salesforce, Zoho), thereby adding a new set of tools and capabilities for digital knowledge workers.

Given that there is little research on measuring the effects of the implementation of SaaS on various organizational outcomes, one of the goals of this chapter is to provide an agenda for conducting research in the area of information systems for SaaS services.

To measure the success of various Information Systems initiatives, organizations need to look at a variety of outcome measures and success factors [23]. One way to research the success of SaaS services is through a value appropriation model. For example, research on a strategic value appropriation model gives us a path to measure the success of Cloud adoption from cloud technological capability to firm performance via cloud integration capability, cloud service portfolio capability, and business flexibility. [14]. Given SaaS services are hosted on the cloud, an extension of the cloud value appropriation model would be a logical extension towards researching the effect of SaaS services on Digital Transformation initiatives and Information Systems success. There have also been extensions to the strategic value appropriation model to investigate contingencies, such as firm age and firm size, on the value generated from cloud computing [6, 7]. Such efforts can be undertaken for SaaS (Fig. 3).

It is critical to note that these cited studies have been conducted in the context of GREAT domains [2, 9, 10]. There have been calls to conduct research in such domains [9] because research shows that findings from Western countries do not necessarily hold in other contexts (e.g., [11, 12]). As a result, there is an increasing number of studies in GREAT domains such as India (e.g., [9, 12, 13, 22, 25, 28, 29]) and other developing countries (e.g., [1, 4, 5, 8]). Research has found many reasons for these differences, including managerial priorities [15] and differences in the ability of foreign and domestic firms to leverage IT in these contexts [5, 16, 17]. Research on the success of SaaS initiatives should therefore be conducted in GREAT and Western domains and also consider differences across foreign and domestic firms.

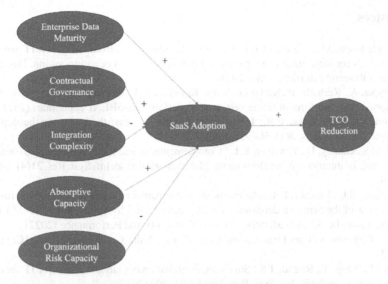

Fig. 3. Conceptual Model for SaaS Effectiveness

Another model for measuring IS success is that of DeLone and McLean (D&M) [3, 24]. The D&M model has been found to be a useful framework for organizing measurements of the success of Information Systems. The model has been widely used by IS researchers for understanding and measuring the dimensions of IS success. Furthermore, each of the variables describing the success of an information system was consistent with one or more of the six major success dimensions of the updated D&M model [23]. The dimensions of success included in the D&M model: a) System quality b) Information quality c) Service quality d) System use e) User satisfaction f) Net benefits.

5 Conclusion

Software as a Service (SaaS) has emerged as a key enabler for digital transformation. The ability to accelerate time to market also directly impacts a company's ability to respond to market demands, outpace competitors, and capture new opportunities. While it's important to expedite product development, ensuring product quality and cybersecurity standards is crucial. Many SaaS companies focus on achieving a minimum viable product quickly and then iteratively improving it based on user feedback and evolving market needs. Research needs to be conducted both from a SaaS provider as well as recipient perspective on both the technical and design aspects of SaaS products[3].

SaaS is a dynamic industry and several emerging technologies would play a key role in the continuous innovation. To stay competitive, organizations would need to continually assess their strategies and leverage opportunities in the SaaS landscape.

---

[3] https://hbsp.harvard.edu/product/ISB290-PDF-ENG.

References

1. Andrade-Rojas, M. G., Saldanha, T., Kathuria, A., Khuntia, J., Boh, W.F.: How IT overcomes deficiencies for innovation in SMEs: closed innovation versus open innovation. Information Systems Research, (forthcoming) (2024)
2. Dasgupta, A., Karhade, P., Kathuria, A. and Konsynski, B.: Holding space for voices that do not speak: design reform of rating systems for platforms in GREAT economies (2021)
3. DeLone, W.H., McLean, E.R.: Information systems success: the quest for the dependent variable. Inf. Syst. Res. 3(1), 60–95 (1992)
4. Dewan, S., Ganley, D., Kraemer, K.L.: Complementarities in the diffusion of personal computers and the internet: implications for the global digital divide. Inf. Syst. Res. 21(4), 925–940 (2010)
5. Jarvenpaa, S.L., Leidner, D.E.: An information company in mexico: extending the resource-based view of the firm to a developing country context. Inf. Syst. Res. 9(4), 342–361 (1998)
6. Jha, S., Kathuria, A.: Size Matters for Cloud Capability and Performance (2022)
7. Jha, S., Kathuria, A.: How Firm Age and Size Influence Value Creation from Cloud Computing (2023)
8. Kanat, I., Hong, Y., Raghu, T.S.: Surviving in global online labor markets for IT services: a geo-economic analysis. Inf. Syst. Res. 29(4), 893–909 (2018)
9. Karhade, P., Kathuria, A.: Missing impact of ratings on platform participation in India: a call for research in GREAT domains. Commun. Assoc. Inf. Syst. 47(1), 19 (2020)
10. Karhade, P., Kathuria, A., Dasgupta, A., Malik, O. and Konsynski, B. R. 2020. "Decolonization of digital platforms: a research agenda for GREAT domains. In: Garimella, A., Karhade, P., Kathuria, A., Liu, X., Xu, J., Zhao, K. (eds.) Proceedings of Workshop on E-Business, pp. 51–58. Springer, Cham. https://doi.org/10.1007/978-3-030-79454-5_5
11. Kathuria, A., Karhade, P.P.: You are not you when you are hungry: machine learning investigation of impact of ratings on ratee decision making. In: Xu, J.J., Zhu, B., Liu, X., Shaw, M.J., Zhang, H., Fan, M. (eds.) WEB 2018. LNBIP, vol. 357, pp. 151–161. Springer, Cham (2019). https://doi.org/10.1007/978-3-030-22784-5_15
12. Kathuria, A., Karhade, P.P., Konsynski, B.R.: In the realm of hungry ghosts: multi-level theory for supplier participation on digital platforms. J. Manag. Inf. Syst. 37(2), 396–430 (2020)
13. Kathuria, A., Karhade, P.P., Ning, X., Konsynski, B.R.: Blood and water: information technology investment and control in family-owned businesses. J. Manag. Inf. Syst. 40(1), 208–238 (2023)
14. Kathuria, A., Mann, A., Khuntia, J., Saldanha, T.J., Kauffman, R.J.: A strategic value appropriation path for cloud computing. J. Manag. Inf. Syst. 35(3), 740–775 (2018)
15. Kathuria, R., Kathuria, N.N., Kathuria, A.: Mutually supportive or trade-offs: an analysis of competitive priorities in the emerging economy of India. J. High Technol. Managem. Res. 29(2), 227–236 (2018)
16. Khuntia, J., Kathuria, A., Andrade-Rojas, M.G., Saldanha, T., Celly, N.: How foreign and domestic firms differ in leveraging IT-enabled supply chain information integration in BOP markets: the role of supplier and client business collaboration. J. Assoc. Inf. Syst. 22(3), 6 (2021)
17. Khuntia, J., Kathuria, A., Saldanha, T.J., Konsynski, B.R.: Benefits of IT-enabled flexibilities for foreign versus local firms in emerging economies. J. Manage. Inf. Syst. 36(3), 855–892 (2019)
18. Lanzolla, G., Lorenz, A., Miron-Spektor, E., Schilling, M., Solinas, G., Tucci, C.L.: Digital transformation: what is new if anything? Emerging patterns and management research. Academy of Management Briarcliff Manor, NY, City (2020)

19. Loukis, E., Janssen, M., Mintchev, I.: Determinants of software-as-a-service benefits and impact on firm performance. Decis. Support. Syst. **117**, 38–47 (2019)
20. Ma, D., Seidmann, A.: Analyzing software as a service with per-transaction charges. Inform. Syst. Res. **26**(2), 360–378 (2015)
21. Malladi, S., Krishnan, M.: Does Software-as-a-Service (SaaS) has a role in IT-enabled Innovation?–An Empirical Analysis (2012)
22. Mani, D., Srikanth, K., Bharadwaj, A.: Efficacy of R&D work in offshore captive centers: an empirical study of task characteristics, coordination mechanisms, and performance. Inf. Syst. Res. **25**(4), 846–864 (2014)
23. Petter, S., DeLone, W., McLean, E.: Measuring information systems success: models, dimensions, measures, and interrelationships. Eur. J. Inf. Syst. **17**, 236–263 (2008)
24. Petter, S., DeLone, W., McLean, E.R.: Information systems success: the quest for the independent variables. J. Manag. Inf. Syst. **29**(4), 7–62 (2013)
25. Ramakrishnan, T., Kathuria, A., Khuntia, J. and Konsynski, B. IoT Value Creation Through Supply Chain Analytics Capability (2022)
26. Saldanha, T.J.V., Kathuria, A., Khuntia, J., Konsynski, B.R.: Ghosts in the machine: how marketing and human capital investments enhance customer growth when innovative services leverage self-service technologies. Inf. Syst. Res. **33**(1), 76–109 (2022)
27. Saldanha, T.J.V., Lee, D., Mithas, S.: Aligning information technology and business: the differential effects of alignment during investment planning, delivery, and change. Inf. Syst. Res. **31**(4), 1260–1281 (2020)
28. Venkatesh, V., Bala, H., Sambamurthy, V.: Implementation of an information and communication technology in a developing country: a multimethod longitudinal study in a bank in India. Inf. Syst. Res. **27**(3), 558–579 (2016)
29. Venkatesh, V., Sykes, T.A.: Digital divide initiative success in developing countries: a longitudinal field study in a village in India. Inf. Syst. Res. **24**(2), 239–260 (2013)
30. Xiao, X., Sarker, S., Wright, R.T., Sarker, S., Mariadoss, B.J.: Commitment and replacement of existing SaaS-delivered applications: a mixed-methods investigation. MIS Q. **44**, 4 (2020)

Earnings Call Transcripts as a Source and Resource for Information Systems Research

Ria Sonpatki[1]([envelope]) [iD], Abhishek Kathuria[1] [iD], and Shakti Sethi[2]

[1] Indian School of Business, Hyderabad, India
{ria_sonpatki,abhishek_Kathuria}@isb.edu
[2] UBC Saunder School of Business, Vancouver, Canada
shakti.sethi@saunder.ubc.ca

Abstract. Quarterly earnings conference calls are used by publicly traded firms to share detailed information about their financial performance with external stakeholders. Earnings calls consist of two parts: a prepared remarks section by the company's leadership and a section for questions and answers with analysts. *Earnings Call Transcripts* are textual narratives of these calls and serve as a crucial source of information for analysts, investors, and researchers. These transcripts have historically played a pivotal role in offering insights into the financial performance, strategic direction, and overall dynamics of publicly traded firms. Despite their significance, *Earnings Call Transcripts* have been the subject of study predominantly within finance and accounting literature. It is noteworthy that these studies have neglected the vast potential that *Earnings Call Transcripts* hold for the field of information systems, such as the ability to infer digital endowments and strategies. The objective of this chapter is to present an extensive review of the literature on *Earnings Call Transcripts*, clarifying their structural intricacies and historical development and highlighting their untapped potential for the information systems field. We explain how the data expressed in *Earnings Call Transcripts* can provide a rich resource to analyze organizational strategies and outcomes related to digital and information technologies. To illustrate this assertion, we provide an analysis of *Earnings Call Transcripts* from the S&P1500 firms for a period of 15 years, starting from 2006 and ending in 2021, which consists of nearly 44 million unique questions and answers statements. Overall, the primary motivation of this chapter is to encourage scholars within the IS domain to recognize and utilize *Earnings Call Transcripts* as a valuable resource for their research.

Keywords: Information System · Earnings Call Transcripts · Business Value of IT

1 Introduction

Quarterly earnings conference calls serve as vital assets that provide a financial narrative of publicly listed corporations through open communication with the investor community. These calls are conducted via teleconference or webcast. Earnings calls consist of

© The Author(s), under exclusive license to Springer Nature Switzerland AG 2024
A. Kathuria et al. (Eds.): WeB 2022, LNBIP 508, pp. 38–63, 2024.
https://doi.org/10.1007/978-3-031-60003-6_4

two parts: a prepared remarks section by the company's leadership and a section for questions and answers with analysts. They constitute a significant communication event that thoroughly examines a company's financial performance for a certain reporting period. During these conversations, metrics such as net income and profits per share are the focus of the conversation as they enable analysts and investors to assess the company's financial health thoroughly.

While earnings calls are not mandated by law, publicly traded corporations use these occasions to share detailed information about their financial performance. The voluntary disclosure literature, with a traditional emphasis on disclosure activities related to predictable accounting releases, such as management forecasts before earnings announcements [1], expanded press releases, and clarifying conference calls during earnings announcements [2, 3] has surmised that voluntary disclosure through earnings calls is a calculated and strategic choice of firms [4]. This option provides for a variety of communication tactics, emphasizing the flexibility of these disclosures. Not every company engages in this journey, with some completely bypassing it. Unexpected occurrences, like mergers or acquisitions, might result in the unexpected cancellation of scheduled calls. This interruption causes a momentary pause in frequent interaction with investors, allowing researchers to analyze and consider the benefits and drawbacks of such approaches. Under certain conditions, companies may choose to proceed with the planned call even if unexpected events occur in order to ensure the timely dissemination of critical information to relevant parties and thus provide scholars with a valuable framework to better understand the dynamics of corporate communication in unforeseen circumstances.

Despite the lack of a legal mandate, the strategic importance of earnings calls in determining market sentiment cannot be underestimated. These calls have a direct impact on new and existing investors' perceptions of the firm, which in turn influence their investment decisions and, in fact, stock prices. Earnings calls are more than just a formality; they are a tool that allows firms to actively manage what they share with the financial community, establishing transparency as well as confidence. This, in turn, can have a huge influence on market performance and the value of the organization.

The transcripts of quarterly earnings conference calls are formally termed *Earnings Call Transcripts*. These transcripts, which function as textual narratives, provide analysts, investors, and researchers with a complete description of earnings calls, revealing insights into the financial status, strategic decision-making, and communication methods of the organization [5]. As a result, there have been an increasing number of academic studies, across various management disciplines, that utilize *Earnings Call Transcripts* as a valuable source of data and context.

Scholars have utilized linguistic analysis, sentiment analysis, and natural language processing (NLP) approaches to extract valuable insights from *Earnings Call Transcripts*, identifying hidden signals such as management sentiment, risk disclosures, and forward-looking comments. Research has highlighted that investors and stakeholders not only react to the information that managers communicate but also to the manner in which it is expressed, emphasizing substantial differences in word choice [6]. Consequently, *Earnings Call Transcripts* have been used extensively across multiple management fields, with Finance and Accounting leading the way. However, the full potential of leveraging *Earnings Call Transcripts* in Information Systems research remains untapped. The objective of this chapter is to present an extensive review of the literature on *Earnings Call Transcripts*, clarifying their structural intricacies and historical development and highlighting their mostly untapped potential for the Information Systems field.

The rest of this chapter is organized as follows. We first understand the historical growth of *Earnings Call Transcripts*. We then explain the structure of *Earnings Call Transcripts*. We then explicate a thematic analysis of prior research that utilizes *Earnings Call Transcripts* and categorize the expansive evolution of these studies into two distinct types. One examines and evaluates the content within and topics covered in these conference calls, whereas the other focuses on collecting and analyzing data from these conference calls. We then present two ways by which information systems scholars can use *Earnings Call Transcripts* in their research. We explicate how IS researchers can develop natural language processing (NLP) and machine learning techniques to better extract, analyze, and display textual data. We also explain how the data expressed in *Earnings Call Transcripts* can provide a rich resource for analyzing information, gender dynamics, tone, and other factors that may greatly improve our collective understanding of strategy, tactics, and decision-making processes related to digital and information technologies. To illustrate this assertion, we provide an analysis of *Earnings Call Transcripts* from the S&P1500 firms for a period of 15 years, starting from 2006 and ending in 2021, which consists of nearly 44 million unique questions and answers statements. Finally, we make a call for information systems researchers to use *Earnings Call Transcripts* by elaborating upon three broad themes of research that could benefit from *Earnings Call Transcripts* as a source of data.

Overall, the primary motivation of this chapter is to encourage scholars within the information systems domain to recognize the immense potential offered by *Earnings Call Transcripts*. These possibilities lie in not only the development of techniques to better extract information from *Earnings Call Transcripts* but also several thematic areas of future research that are proffered by *Earnings Call Transcripts* as a source of firm-level data on digital and information technologies.

2   A Historical Perspective of Earnings Call Transcripts

The history of *Earnings Call Transcripts* began during the 1929 stock market crisis, which caused a fundamental disruption in the financial domain. This transformation resulted in the establishment of regulatory bodies, particularly the *Securities and Exchange Commission* (SEC). The SEC proposed several regulations. A goal of this regulatory framework for the securities industry was to increase transparency and secure investor interests.

As guidelines developed, publicly traded corporations were mandated to provide financial information regularly, leading to an era of routine quarterly financial reporting for enterprises listed on stock exchanges. Technology emerged as a game changer during these shifts, enabling companies to conduct, record, and transcribe earnings conference calls to the public. These conversations introduced a new era of open communication in the financial sector, serving as a conduit for direct engagement between business executives and stakeholders. The *Wall Street Journal* recognized their growing importance and specified that "During the peak earnings reporting season after each quarter ends, the whole Wall Street community is glued to the telephone of the conference call."

Recognizing the essential significance of these calls, organizations such as the *National Investor Relations Institute* and the *Association of Investment Management and Research* emphasized the importance of quarterly earnings calls as the primary means of communication with analysts and portfolio managers. This recognition inspired scholars to consider quarterly earnings conference calls as an important tool for researching the dissemination of financial information. The popularity of *Earnings Call Transcripts* surged as research demonstrating their beneficial effects began to emerge. Early studies examined various aspects, such as whether or not these calls offered useful information to stock market participants. They additionally examined the readily available information provided to all investors and why certain companies held conference calls despite these being voluntary [7]. This research demonstrated that firms conducting conference calls tended to be larger, more profitable, and more closely followed by analysts [8]. Furthermore, although most early studies on smaller and medium-sized enterprises relied heavily on analyst rankings, earnings conference calls became an important channel for examining disclosures among these firms.

The SEC approved *Regulation Fair Disclosure* (Reg FD) in 2000, thus contributing to the growing popularity of earnings conference calls [9]. Regulation FD attempted to address the issue of selective disclosure of pertinent information to financial professionals by encouraging corporations to provide such information in a press release or conference call that was available to all investors. The implementation of Reg FD resulted in more studies on its usefulness, with academics seeking to uncover if this law successfully limited selective information disclosure to individual analysts while not reducing the overall quantity of information given. Evidence revealed that, following the adoption of Reg FD, information exchanged with analysts' clients did not decrease dramatically [10], illustrating that *Earnings Call Transcripts* already contained sufficient information to derive inferences.

As rules and regulations continued to influence the financial system, scholars sought to answer novel questions while ensuring that the specialization of the Accounting and Finance fields advanced. The dynamic character of the financial industry, along with technical improvements, motivated researchers to perform more research on the influence of *Earnings Call Transcripts* on market dynamics, corporate governance, and investor relations [11, 12].

From a corporate governance viewpoint, academics assessed how CEOs or CFOs determined when to issue earnings statements, typically in cooperation with the audit committee (which included the investor relations manager and legal counsel). These studies demonstrated that most corporations conducted quarterly earnings conference calls (mostly with sell-side analysts) shortly after the earnings release, usually within a few hours or the next morning. The time between the announcement of financial results and the quarterly earnings conference call enabled analysts and investors to process the material before asking further questions of management [13]. With this knowledge, scholars analyzed the data to show that internal corporate governance has an important role in deciding the timing of announcements.

Subsequent research analyzed the complicated nature of conference call content by examining call frequency and tone [14], as well as the language and sentiment expressed by company executives and analysts. This research attempted to determine if the linguistic characteristics of quarterly earnings conference calls could predict corporate performance [15], managerial credibility, and probable future issues. Furthermore, the development of Machine Learning and Natural Language Processing methods created new opportunities for researchers to examine *Earnings Call Transcripts* [16]. Thereby, automated analysis of large volumes of *Earnings Call Transcripts* became possible, allowing for a more detailed comprehension of the material spoken during those conversations.

3   The Structure of Earnings Call Transcripts

To analyze the attributes of quarterly earnings conference calls, researchers should familiarize themselves with the structure of the transcripts they receive. Recognizing the significance of the earnings call structure is essential as it helps to extract and present information from transcripts effectively. Prior to an earnings call, companies often announce the event through an earnings call calendar. This serves as a practice to draw the attention of interested parties such as investors, equity analysts, and business journalists. These calls, especially for large companies, receive significant coverage in business media.

The transcript of an earnings call typically follows a structured format. It begins by prominently displaying the company's name and details regarding the specific quarter and date of the conference call. Immediately thereafter, it offers a summarized view in a tabular format, with the company's revenue for the current quarter, including the expected values. Additionally, this table provides consensus figures for the next quarter, the current financial year, and the subsequent financial year. Furthermore, the introductory pages feature a graphical representation of the stock price versus volume, with further information regarding earnings surprises. This graphic representation generally spans the preceding four quarters, visually depicting the performance trends of the organization. Before proceeding into the communication transcripts from the earnings call, the document provides a list of participants, including executives and analysts, along with their affiliations. The transcript then contains the conversations that took place throughout the call (Fig. 1).

Quarterly earnings conference calls usually commence with a 'safe harbor' statement conducted by the company's management. This statement serves as a cautionary note to participants, forewarning them that the discussion of financial results may include forward-looking statements. This disclaimer intends to alert participants that estimates based on these forward-looking statements might significantly deviate from actual results, aiming to limit the company's liability in case of such discrepancies. Following the safe harbor statement, the reins of the call are taken up by the managers of the company, typically represented by C-level executives, with the CEO and CFO being consistent fixtures. This portion of the quarterly earnings conference call is termed the prepared remarks section. In this portion, as executives discuss the financial results for the specified reporting period, they concurrently provide valuable insights into upcoming company goals, milestones, and the anticipated impact on future financial performance (Fig. 2).

ABC Holdings FQ1 2019 EARNINGS CALL | MAY 04, 2016

Fig. 1. Prototypical Earnings Call Transcript (Presentation Section)

The latter part of the earnings call is dedicated to the Q&A session. This segment holds immense importance, as it often serves as a platform where substantial information is disclosed to researchers and analysts keen on understanding the performance and prospects of the organization. Here, participants, including investors and analysts, pose questions regarding the financial results presented to the firm's senior management. Each analyst usually gets an opportunity to ask 2–3 questions, though the management retains the right to decline or defer specific inquiries. The conclusion of the call entails closing remarks from the management, summarizing the discussions held throughout the call. The entire process is facilitated by an Operator, who manages the sequence of questions posed by analysts to the team.

While a quarterly earnings conference call typically spans 45 to 60 minutes, no statutory guidelines dictate its duration. The length of the call largely hinges on the duration of the Q&A session, the extent of information shared by the management, and the company's performance during the specified period. This structured format allows

ABC Holdings FQ1 2019 EARNINGS CALL | MAY 04, 2016
$7.2 billion, funded with $4 billion in debt, $1.1 billion in preferred stock and $2.1 billion in equity. Cannae's $500 million equity
investment represents an approximate 24.5% equity interest in EL&NM.

As President of ABC's Board of Directors, I am working very closely with EL&NM's management team to unlock the substantial potential that
we see in this company. As we discussed on our fourth quarter earnings call, I am working with Snape and Hagrid on the execution of 3
near-term initiatives, which include: first, EL&NM's organizational structure and leadership; two, our cost reduction plan; and three,
enhancing revenue growth. Each of these initiatives is designed to reinvigorate EL&NM and position the company to drive long-term value
to its customers, employees and its new shareholders.

Question and Answer

Operator

[Operator Instructions] Our first question comes from Harry Potter with Hogwarts.

Harry Potter
Hogwarts, Research Division

On EL&NM, I mean it seems like a great start on the cost side. You guys kind of came out of the gates pretty hot. On the rev side, can you just
maybe talk to the shift in the go-to market strategy? That's something you guys can outline, maybe what you're doing there and whether you
guys are seeing a pretty clear path to modest organic growth in time.

Albus Dumbledore
President

Yes. Well, thanks for the question. On the cost-cutting side, we're really ahead of schedule. We're doing --- the guys are doing a great job. We've got
our new management team in place and all of our business unit leaders in place. And D&B was organized not by product, and everything really kind of
rolled up to the CEO for final approval. And so no one was accountable in the entire system for their revenue or their profitability. And so we have
basically matrixed the -- each business unit and then each supporting unit. And we really feel like we're going to start seeing the benefits of this new
matrix that we have established for our business units fairly quickly, but maybe a quarter or 2. And the growth will start slowly, but we have really
significant opportunities in international, which they've largely ignored, and they're also not very -- not as strong as we want them to be in analytics.
On -- if you're marketing or selling analytics attached to the data that you're providing, usually you get 2.5 or 3x of revenue out of that kind of sale.

Harry Potter
Hogwarts, Research Division

Great. That's great color. I appreciate all the detail. And I might have misheard you, but did you say that Snape is now the sole CEO? So there's no
longer a co-CEO structure?

Albus Dumbledore
President

No, he is the sole CEO. Snape splits his time between Sirius Black and EL & NM. But Snape is really -- he's the day-to-day on-site.

Operator

Ladies and gentlemen, we've reached the end of the question-and-answer session. At this time, I'd like to turn the call back to Mr. Albus for
closing comments.

Albus Dumbledore
President

To conclude, we're very pleased with the success we've already achieved reducing EL & NM's cost structure, and are well on our way to
achieving our goal of reducing EL & NM's expense base by $200
million by year-end 2016. Additionally, we have taken meaningful steps to reinvigorate the go-to-market strategy and are optimistic that it'll
result in improved sales over the balance of the year.
To be truly successful in this turnaround and unlock the value that we see in this investment for our shareholders, we need to not only
reduce cost but also drive improved sales growth. We look forward to updating you further on our second quarter call in August. Thanks
again for your time today.

Operator

This concludes today's conference. You may disconnect your lines at this time, and we thank you for your participation.

2

Fig. 2. Prototypical Earnings Call Transcript (Question and Answer Section)

for a comprehensive understanding of the financial performance, future outlook, and strategic direction of the firm, making earnings calls a valuable source of information for stakeholders and researchers alike.

4 Thematic Analysis of Research Using Earnings Call Transcripts

The initial research that used *Earnings Call Transcripts* was driven by scholars from the finance area who sought to understand how the reactions of analysts to quarterly earnings conference calls influenced stock prices. However, the purpose of such research has expanded to encompass the content of conference calls themselves and their influence on financial markets. This research has evaluated the internal workings and communication practices of firms, as revealed within *Earnings Call Transcripts*, and their immediate implications for market dynamics.

We categorize this expansive evolution of studies into two distinct types. The first type is more comprehensive and examines and evaluates the content within and topics covered in these conference calls. Scholars monitored the themes, topics, tonality, sentiment, and inconsistencies in these encounters in an attempt to get useful insights.

The second type, however, focuses on collecting and analyzing data from these conference calls. In these types of studies, the emphasis is on the analytical extraction, processing, and interpretation of data retrieved from these calls, with the goal of using them as a source of usable data points for future analysis. This comprehensive progression has broadened the purview of *Earnings Call Transcripts* research beyond its financial origins and enabled a more profound understanding of corporate communications and operational strategies, separating the field into two distinct but related streams of study with different techniques and scopes.

4.1 Content Within Earnings Call Transcripts

Information asymmetry is an important subject in the financial world, inspiring a significant quantity of research on how businesses may efficiently manage and eradicate it. Voluntary disclosures became an important tool for rectifying information asymmetry, particularly via conference calls. Scholars have been studying how information asymmetry impacts firms, focusing on the voluntary nature of these conference calls. Analyses reveal that these calls are critical to the long-term reduction in information asymmetry among stock investors.

Examining the association between quarterly earnings conference calls and information asymmetry has revealed intriguing results. While some scholars claim that the disclosure environment in the United States is too diverse and homogeneous to evaluate information asymmetry, other research provides an alternate perspective [17]. For example, Brown's [11] study indicated a substantial negative association between the frequency of quarterly earnings conference calls and the resulting knowledge gap inside firms. Another insight is that more quarterly earnings conference calls tend to be related to less trading by informed investors than their less knowledgeable counterparts, which is also significant. This pattern suggests firms may unintentionally increase trade volumes undertaken without the necessary comprehension if they supply more information [18, 19].

The underlying causes of information asymmetry extend beyond trading patterns and impact management conduct during conference calls. Scholars have tried to discern between genuine and deceitful managers based on their communication styles. Particularly, the concept of 'big bath' events, in which managers purposefully incorporate unpleasant news into current profits to lower future performance expectations or obtain incentives, has gained traction. The fundamental concern is how the untruthfulness or vague communication by management during these episodes impacts the subsequent information asymmetry. According to research findings, when CEOs are found to be deceitful during discussions about their firm's financial achievements, they enhance information asymmetry following 'big bath' events compared to their less deceptive counterparts [20].

Empirical studies point out the importance of conference calls in improving information asymmetry among stock investors. In another study, Brown [21] emphasized that quarterly earnings conference call frequency significantly contributes to eliminating information asymmetry. However, this decrease is not the only predictor; it also influences management credibility. For example, if a manager involved with a "big bath" event appears genuine, investors may view the event as credible, thereby reducing information asymmetry. In contrast, a deceitful manager's participation in a "big bath" event may exacerbate information asymmetry in part to reduced credibility.

In sum, voluntary disclosures, particularly via quarterly earnings conference calls, play an important role in reducing information asymmetry among stock investors. However, the influence depends on a variety of circumstances, including management communication and trustworthiness during critical moments. Understanding these details is critical for both investors and businesses to successfully negotiate the complexities of information distribution and imbalance in financial markets. Scholars have ventured further in their research to include gender dynamics in financial talks and quarterly earnings conference calls. This has enabled academics to explore the unique interactions between analysts and CEOs influenced by gender dynamics. Relevant studies of these calls analyze both questioners (analysts) and those being questioned (managers).

Research has observed that female analysts tend to adopt a more positive tone, praising management [15]. Building on this work, further research has found that female analysts were more positive and accurate in their speech, utilizing fewer number references and expressing fewer hesitations than their male colleagues [22]. When female analysts used more upbeat tones, their verbal aggression (measured by questioning style) was much lower than that of male analysts [23]. This difference in verbal aggression was particularly noticeable when the CEO in question was female, suggesting a potential gender-based out-of-group bias influencing communication dynamics.

Researchers examining communication dynamics with females detected a significant gender ratio discrepancy. Although they observed a gradual increase in the percentage of female journalists participating in these conferences—from around 10 percent in the 1950s to approximately 40 percent by the late 1990s—it served as a spur for further research for studying differences in verbal aggressiveness between male and female journalists. As a result, researchers have attempted to uncover changes in communication philosophies and how they have evolved over time in these conversations. As scholars advanced their studies into the gender-based disparities in analysts' questioning approaches, they ascertained consequential insights into the potential career implications stemming from these differences.

Researchers gained more insight into gender dynamics in financial communications when they learned that male analysts asked more verbally aggressive questions compared to their female counterparts [24]. This study revealed that female analysts who used verbal aggression in their questioning were more likely to be recognized and ranked among the top three analysts in the *Institutional Investor's Annual List of Best Analysts*. This result identified a complicated relationship between verbal communication styles and job success in a gender-specific environment. It addressed previous beliefs about the possible backlash female professionals may experience for forceful communication, demonstrating that in certain cases, such boldness may be favorably correlated with professional recognition and success.

As researchers attempted to extract complete insights from *Earnings Call Transcripts* based on gender preferences, they faced an obstacle: the proverbial fourth wall, which precluded direct study around these recordings. The visible transcripts and audio recordings accessible to investors held limitations, concealing minute details perceptible only to analysts during these conference calls. Peng [25] delved into this uncharted territory, searching into the world of first impressions and their critical role in shaping analyst outcomes. They conducted unconventional research, looking into aspects including beauty, dominance, trustworthiness, and face width-to-height ratio. Using face recognition software on LinkedIn profile images of US sell-side analysts, they discovered surprising connections between facial impressions and later analyst performance. Their analysis proved gender differences in such associations, with highly dominant female analysts projecting lower accuracy in their forecasts compared to their male counterparts, despite female analysts, on average, providing more accurate forecasts.

Furthermore, studies into gender and racial diversity among executives participating in quarterly earnings conference calls uncovered noteworthy disparities. While the number of female and racial minority executives attending these calls has gradually increased, their participation—especially in speaking roles—has not significantly improved. Miller [26] noted that female and racial minority C-suite executives, despite their increased presence within these organizations, were much less likely to speak during these conversations, indicating ongoing differences in participation and representation. These thorough assessments carried out during quarterly earnings conference calls, illustrated the links between gender dynamics, communication preferences, career repercussions, and other factors that impact perceptions and outcomes.

With technological advancement over time, researchers have incorporated tonality models, which have aided in evaluating models that comprise a body of meanings, a language used to communicate meanings and a process. Moreover, this technological progress has enabled a deeper examination of linguistic details, allowing for a more comprehensive understanding of communication dynamics during various contexts, including financial discussions and corporate communications. As a result, researchers have used these models to understand better how managerial language affects information transmission and market perception through *Earnings Call Transcripts*. Consequently, studies have determined that management language choices have a significant influence on the quantity and quality of released information [15, 27]. These studies have also demonstrated how such choices shape market reactions.

However, exploring earnings-announcement-related conference calls introduced a new perspective. Contrary to conventional wisdom, the tone within these calls did not directly correlate with current or future performance indicators. Instead, it reflects managerial traits, such as early career experiences and charitable involvement. This indicated that the linguistic tone might reflect intrinsic tendencies toward optimism or pessimism among managers rather than just reflecting the company's performance or prospects [28].

Expanding on this notion, a closer examination of gender dynamics in managerial communication during such calls surfaced intriguing distinctions. A study revealed that female executives tended to adopt a more positive and less vague tone than their male counterparts. This discovery might suggest differences in communication methods or preferences between genders [29]. Nevertheless, it is important to note that financial analysts responded throughout during these calls. They appeared to have a gender bias, portraying less positivity and more vagueness while interacting with female executives. This gap in how analysts respond to different genders raises questions regarding the biases within the financial industry, thus influencing the reception and interpretation of managerial communication.

Aside from management gender, scholars have studied the impact of a manager's ethnic-cultural background on investor communication [30]. Managers from ethnic groups characterized by more individualistic cultures tended to employ an optimistic tone and emphasized self-reference in their disclosures. This choice of language and communication style resonated positively with financial analysts. Those analysts only responded more positively when the management shared the same ethnic background. In doing so, the research highlighted the relevance of a manager's ethnicity in communication dynamics with analysts and the following consequences on the capital market.

Each of these findings contributes to nuances in our understanding of the complexity of management speech in business communication. Language choices reflect human attributes, gender dynamics, and cultural influences, in addition to delivering information. Understanding these notions from *Earnings Call Transcripts* is essential to understanding the association between content and market response. Summatively, this research emphasizes the significance of more inclusive and complete analyses in *Earnings Call Transcripts* research and the need to be aware of biases and various perspectives of language choices.

4.2 Information Derived from Earnings Call Transcripts

Researchers increasingly recognize *Earnings Call Transcripts* as helpful instruments for collecting information about firms. Beyond providing insights into the financial condition of a company, *Earnings Call Transcripts* provide insight into strategic decision-making processes and the complex opinions of executives representing the organization. Analysts are able to decode the exact views of these leaders, thereby providing an understanding of the culture of the organization. Furthermore, *Earnings Call Transcripts* can be used to evaluate possible biases, such as disparities in treatment between male and female analysts. Researchers assess how gender discrimination is addressed within organizations by examining the involvement of female executives in the call as well as the general distribution of speaking positions of power. Likewise, the inclusion of diversity, not just on paper but also in active participation during calls, is an important component in determining the commitment of a firm to encouraging inclusivity. These are only a few of the many insights academics can derive from the information contained in *Earnings Call Transcripts*, thereby helping them better understand organizational dynamics and practices.

Building on information derived from *Earnings Call Transcripts*, research has examined information asymmetry by focusing on buy-side analysts' dynamics [31]. This study found that bid-ask spreads increased significantly when buy-side analysts asked aggressive questions during essential disclosure events. This rise in spreads indicated greater information asymmetry among market participants [12]. The aggressive engagement of buy-side analysts in conference calls serves as a signal, but selective disclosure creates a gap between public knowledge and analysts' insights, highlighting the interplay between informed investor engagement and market asymmetry. The use of *Earnings Call Transcripts* in these studies reinforces the quarterly earnings conference calls as a key source from which nuanced information about firms can be extracted.

Besides analysts, journalists also cover quarterly earnings conference calls. Another study found that 64% of journalists who were surveyed said they were very likely to actively listen to quarterly earnings conference calls. This desire for audio involvement was supported by journalists admitting that, when time allowed, they would consult transcripts. The rationale for this dual method was based on the benefits of auditory involvement in capturing the tone of voice and spotting minor signs such as stuttering or nervous ticks. This technique of concurrently using information contained within the audio and transcript of quarterly earnings conference calls stresses the significance of identifying minor linguistic signals during conference calls [15].

The researchers also learned of a variation in journalistic conduct during public quarterly earnings conference calls. Archival research often reveals that journalists prefer not to ask questions during these calls [32]. The reluctance of journalists to engage in direct questions stems from a strategic inclination to infer knowledge during the conversation so that they may express their views logically in their reporting. This strategic method helps to eliminate any knowledge gaps between the quarterly earnings conference calls and subsequent reporting, underlining the commitment of journalists to giving accurate and well-informed narratives to their audience.

Scholars have utilized several approaches to extract entire data from a quarterly earnings conference call, outlining the value of *Earnings Call Transcripts* as a dataset. One study focuses on the acquisitive tendencies demonstrated by extroverted CEOs. The study applies language analysis algorithms to unscripted *Earnings Call Transcripts* material, concentrating on CEOs who expressed their thoughts in length, over 500 words. The research team evaluated linguistic patterns to examine assertiveness, positive impacts, decision-making approaches, and social involvement. Their findings shed insight into how these qualities influenced the strategic decisions of CEOs and overall behavioral dynamics within their respective firms [33].

A distinctive component of the above research is the addition of control variables, namely the gender of CEOs and the number of female directors inside the organization, which were both derived from the *Earnings Call Transcripts*. This not only maintained a complete analytical approach but also permitted researchers to account for potential gender-related variables and the impact of board diversity in their regression models. The research methodology emphasizes the versatility of *Earnings Call Transcripts* as a reliable data source, providing insight into the various elements impacting CEO behavior and strategic decision-making processes.

Along with examinations of gender diversity on the board of directors, researchers have used *Earnings Call Transcripts* to explore diversity, equality, and inclusion (DEI) related issues at the senior management level of organizations. Capital markets potentially incentivize firms to achieve diversity that maximizes shareholder profits. One particular study involved assessing the valuation impact of a firm's exposure to diversity and its responses to societal pressures, specifically in the aftermath of George Floyd's tragic murder – an event widely regarded as a catalyst prompting firms to address issues related to race-related diversity. The analysis in this study commences by establishing the socially significant nature of George Floyd's murder, which became an issue of corporate importance. Analysis indicated that approximately 29% of all firms engaged in discussions related to diversity in at least one quarterly earnings conference call following the event. This prompted the examination of follow-up questions concerning the valuation effects of a firm's exposure to race-related diversity issues [34]. *Earnings Call Transcripts* are useful since they allow researchers to derive information on how businesses would approach these issues [34].

In another detailed examination of diversity dynamics, researchers widen their emphasis beyond the higher echelons of management to include the diversity of analysts participating in earnings conference calls. A crucial component of their inquiry is determining whether ethnic minority and non-minority sell-side analysts are underrepresented in conference Q&A sessions. Furthermore, the study investigates the prioritizing levels experienced by minority analysts actively participating in these conversations and compares them to their non-minority counterparts. The study found that extroverted minority analysts have greater involvement rates, as predicted. However, a more surprising finding is that the negative correlation between minority status and conference call involvement is amplified under certain conditions. This link is particularly strong when there are more time limits during calls, less diversity among executive teams, and analysts hail from less reputable brokerage companies [35].

This research highlights significant mediating factors, stating that fixed effects related to quarterly earnings conference calls and firms help mitigate around half of the reduced minority participation rates. This emphasizes the complicated interaction of numerous factors impacting the representation of minority analysts on quarterly earnings conference calls. The wider implications of this study lie in the detailed picture provided by it, wherein it shows that managers' and analysts' decisions are crucial in determining how many minority analysts participate in the field. This research provides strong proof of the interwoven effect of decisions made by managers and analysts in this environment, in addition to documenting the underrepresentation of minority analysts [35].

In the rapidly changing realm of corporate communication in the digital age, executives have at their disposal a wider range of tools than merely quarterly earnings conference calls to express their opinions and insights about their organizations. This change has led academics to explore novel methods for evaluating executive activity. Notably, research by Lee [36] investigates overconfidence, which is measured by combining modern media, such as Twitter, with conventional data, such as *Earnings Call Transcripts*. This analysis provides subtle patterns in CEO behavior through several channels of communication.

This study adopts a unique approach by focusing specifically on the differences between founding CEOs and "professional CEOs" in the context of large S&P 1500 businesses. The purpose of this comparison lens is to identify any differences in overconfidence levels according to the leadership style and background of the CEO. This research stands out as it measures overconfidence holistically. The study does not rely on a single source; instead, it integrates a variety of data sources, such as public remarks, tweets from CEOs, and, most importantly, the demeanor displayed on quarterly earnings conference calls. This extensive approach enables a detailed examination of the language clues and general emotions conveyed by CEOs. Through close examination of communication patterns across a range of platforms, the researchers seek to identify minute differences in the words CEOs use to talk about their firms. The study's conclusions make for an intriguing discovery: founder CEOs speak with a far higher level of optimism on Twitter and in quarterly earnings conference calls than their professional peers [36]. This language discrepancy is a significant indicator that provides insightful information about possible variations in the degree of overconfidence that founder CEOs and professional CEOs may possess. In order to obtain a comprehensive knowledge of executive behavior in the modern corporate environment, it emphasizes the significance of taking into account a variety of communication channels in addition to *Earnings Call Transcripts*.

5 Earnings Call Transcripts in Information Systems Research

The practical application of *Earnings Call Transcripts* provides several insights that extend beyond finance and corporate communication to a wide range of fields, including, potentially, the field of Information Systems. Information systems researchers can use *Earnings Call Transcripts* in at least two ways.

First, IS researchers can develop natural language processing (NLP) and machine learning techniques to better extract, analyze, and display textual data. By identifying language signals that indicate variable levels of asymmetry, IS systems may be constructed to combine sentiment analysis algorithms while allowing for real-time monitoring of market attitudes and asymmetrical information distribution. Second, the data expressed in *Earnings Call Transcripts* can provide a rich resource for analyzing information, gender dynamics, tone, and other factors that may greatly improve our collective understanding of strategy, tactics, and decision-making processes related to digital and information technologies.

6 IS Research to Extract Information from Earnings Call Transcripts

While prior studies in finance and accounting have extensively examined the relationship between executives' verbal language during earnings conference calls and various aspects such as firm performance, market reactions, and financial inaccuracy reporting [37–40], there is a significant gap in understanding the significance of nonverbal vocal cues in an identical setting. Nonverbal vocal cues, such as the tone of voice used to convey a verbal message, are important in nonverbal communication [41]. Human voices and speech patterns rely on a range of vocal signals, including pitch and volume. A similar relationship between managers' voice tones and stock prices has been studied [42].

Researchers in the field of IS have achieved significant advances in this arena. They have analyzed unstructured multimedia data (text and audio), which could offer previously unnoticed opportunities to make actionable decisions in the financial sector, notably in areas such as risk and portfolio management. Design Science offers an intriguing possibility of developing advanced techniques to analyze *Earnings Call Transcripts.*

We illustrate this possibility with a detailed example. In a design science paper, researchers created *DeepVoice*, a revolutionary nonverbal predictive analytic system optimized for financial risk prediction, for which they used data from quarterly earnings conference calls. Their research sought to create a design artifact that surpasses past efforts in predicting a company's financial risk by utilizing management speech signals. They used the design paradigm [43, 44] to steer forward the development of the IT component. In doing so, they used Mehrabian's communication model (MCM) [41] as the kernel theory [45].

Using the MCM theory as a framework, the research determined meta-requirements for a specific design and proposed meta-designs to address three major problems. The first challenge was the temporal changes in managers' voice characteristics during conference calls. For example, during sections of the presentation where managers read forward-looking statements, the voice pitch could stay consistent, or it may shift during the question-and-answer time due to fear or enthusiasm [46]. However, research suggests that voice pitch is lower in conversations with analysts than in presentation sessions [42]. This component of managers' vocal signals that varies over time might be a valuable source of information.

The subsequent issue was Vocal-Verbal Integration, addressed utilizing Mehrabian's theory of nonverbal communication [33]. Vocal signals are crucial because they can affirm or deny a message. When a manager speaks with optimism but utilizes a dismal tone, listeners may interpret the message differently. To effectively interpret managerial communication, researchers had to combine spoken language with accompanying voice cues. Finally, there was a lack of agreement on models for assessing emotional state, sentiments, and trust, making it difficult to identify specific acoustic patterns in the speech [15].

Ongoing controversy exists about the optimum approach to integrating voice inputs to detect emotional states, which may result in considerable measurement errors [47]. To solve these challenges, the meta-designs employed a two-stage LSTM neural network to understand the links between consecutive vocal and verbal cues, where meta-learnings have been incorporated into a financial risk prediction model and basic vocal cues are used as features in voice data. Introducing a novel framework demonstrates the Deep-Voice framework's extraordinary effectiveness, as indicated by a significant increase in out-of-sample R^2 compared to benchmark predictions. This framework is versatile and applicable to a wide range of actual commercial applications. For example, in the customer service sector, where significant audio data is created through client phone conversations, audio analysis can deliver succinct summaries of customer interactions, increasing overall customer satisfaction [48].

The use of revolutionary frameworks based on the DeepVoice offers new possibilities for IS researchers. As digital and information technologies continue to evolve, IS researchers would be empowered to develop better and more frameworks that would help decipher information from *Earnings Call Transcripts*. This would enable the extraction of information, allowing researchers to conduct studies on innovative topics regarding organizational behavior, strategy, and firm performance from *Earnings Call Transcripts*.

Most importantly, as digital and information technologies become ubiquitous and necessary for firm performance, their incidence in *Earnings Call Transcripts* will increase, thereby enhancing data availability for IS research. As we navigate the era of data abundance, IS scholars are empowered to attain better insight and promote novelty in the field of IS.

7 IS Research to Utilize Information from Earnings Call Transcripts

There are few publicly available sources of firm-level data pertaining to digital and information technologies. Current research has used either proprietary sources of such data or constructed novel datasets from proprietary or publicly available information. Proprietary datasets that have been used as a source of digital and information technology include the InformationWeek dataset for firm-level data from the United States [49], Prowess for data from Indian firms [50], and the Harte Hanks dataset for data for firms from the United States or elsewhere [51]. A commonly used approach used by researchers to construct datasets is using news announcements, press releases, and 10K filings [52–54].

Earnings Call Transcripts can fill this critical gap by serving as a source of such data for the discipline of Information Systems. *Earnings Call Transcripts* can facilitate researchers to derive information pertaining to a firm's intended and executed strategies related to digital and information technologies. This pathway can enable the exploration of several research ideas at the firm level, providing significant perspectives on strategic decision-making and strengthening the understanding of organizational dynamics in the digital age. *Earnings Call Transcripts* can also provide insights into the use and leverage of digital and information technologies within firms, lending opportunities to the examination of a multitude of research questions.

We illustrate these possibilities through an examination of *Earnings Call Transcripts*. We collect *Earnings Call Transcripts* from the S&P1500 firms for a period of 15 years, starting from 2006 and ending in 2021. Thus, our sample contains *Earnings Call Transcripts* from 2202 unique firms over 60 quarters. This provides us with 44,05,136 usable observations or unique *Earnings Call Transcripts* for analysis. Our sample is representative of the US economy as the S&P1500 is a composite index made up of 500 large, 500 medium, and 500 small firms, hailing from diverse industries.

Our analysis model consists of the following steps: (i) pre-processing of raw text, (ii) section separation, (iii) keyword detection, and (iv) construct extraction, in that order. Specifically, first, we pre-process the raw text of *Earnings Call Transcripts* by text analytics. Then, we separated each section of each Earnings Call Transcript and discarded the text from the prepared remarks section. We then built a seed keyword list consisting of terms that are relevant to digital and information technology at the firm level. This keyword list is based on a combination of Google's online glossary of digital and information technology terms and keywords from prior literature that has used such an approach to parse news announcements for a similar purpose [55–63]. We then manually refined this list for fit and relevance to the context of *Earnings Call Transcripts*. We further validated each term's inclusion by asking three academic experts to assess each term independently and found high inter-rater concordance scores. We then searched through the *Earnings Call Transcripts* corpora for dictionary keyword matches and calculated the incidence corresponding to each term. Finally, we created a summative construct for each *Earnings Call Transcript*, which measures the number of Digital and Information Technology related terms occurring within the *Earnings Call Transcript*.

Based on the keyword list, we measure Digital and Information Technology (DIT) Incidence as a variable that represents the proportion of digital words spoken within a given context, expressed as the ratio of digital words spoken to the total words spoken. For a preparatory understanding of data from *Earnings Call Transcripts* to be utilized in IS research we conducted a pairwise correlation of DIT Incidence on firm attributes such as Tobins's q and the six dimensions of strategy – advertising intensity, inventory level, plant and equipment newness, research and development intensity, nonproduction overhead and financial leverage.

Table 1. Pairwise Correlation of Tobins Q and DIT Incidence

DIT Incidence	Tobins Q		
	Low	Medium	High
Low	0.005*	−0.001	−0.004*
Medium	−0.004*	0.001*	0.002*
High	−0.003*	0.000	0.003*

Notes: 1) Low DIT Incidence indicates $= 0$. 2)*** $p < 0.01$, ** $p < 0.05$, * $p < 0.1$

Our key observations from this exercise are as follows. There is a significant correlation between the frequency of digital and information technology-related terms mentioned in firms' *Earnings Call Transcripts* and Tobin's q (Table 1). This aligns with the literature suggesting a correlation between a firm's emphasis on digital and information technologies and its market value [64]. Therefore, it implies that *Earnings Call Transcripts* serve as a preferable source for proxying digital and information technology in further research within the field of Information Systems. Similarly, we observe a significant positive correlation between high DIT Incidence and high Advertising intensity (Table 2). In line with previous literature, there is a positive association between Research and Development (R&D) investment and a focal firm's market value [65] we find similar correlation between DIT incidence and Research and development (Table 3). Understanding this relationship can help us infer the impact of DIT incidence on firms that innovate and influence on their advertising intensities.

For researchers studying the capabilities of core interorganizational processes, leveraging the *Earnings Call Transcripts* database could prove invaluable. Our analysis reveals a negative correlation between firms discussing DIT incidence and their inventory levels (Table 4). While previous studies have explored supply chain strategies aimed at improving and innovating end-to-end processes between firms and their suppliers [66, 67], as well as how companies utilize their IT infrastructure to optimize their supply

Table 2. Pairwise Correlation of Advertising Intensity and DIT Incidence

	Advertising Intensity		
Incidence	Low	Medium	High
Low	0.005*	0.001	−0.002*
Medium	−0.003*	0.000	0.001
High	−0.004*	−0.001	0.001*

Notes: 1) Low Incidence indicates = 0. 2) Low Advertising Intensity indicates = 0. 3)*** p < 0.01, ** p < 0.05, * p < 0.1

Table 3. Pairwise Correlation of Research and Development Intensity and Incidence

	Research and Development Intensity		
Incidence	Low	Medium	High
Low	0.009*	−0.001	−0.006*
Medium	−0.008*	−0.001	0.007*
High	−0.004*	0.002*	0.001

Notes: 1) Low Incidence indicates = 0. 2) Low Research and Development Intensity indicates = 0. 3)*** p < 0.01, ** p < 0.05, * p < 0.1

chain operations [68], this database can provide insights into similar inquiries. Our premiliminary analysis represents when firms mention DIT Incidence at a moderate level there might be positive correlation with firms plant and equipment newness (Table 5).

Table 4. Pairwise Correlation of Inventory Level and Incidence

	Inventory Level		
Incidence	Low	Medium	High
Low	−0.005*	0.006*	−0.002*
Medium	0.005*	−0.007*	0.003*
High	0.002*	−0.001*	−0.001

Notes: 1) Low Incidence indicates = 0. 2)*** p < 0.01, ** p < 0.05, * p < 0.1

Unlike other strategic dimensions, we find no significant correlation between DIT Incidence and non-production overheads of firms and firms financial leverage (Tables 6 and 7).

Table 5. Pairwise Correlation of Plant and Equipment Newness and Incidence

Incidence	Plant and Equipment Newness		
	Low	Medium	High
Low	0.003*	−0.003*	0.001
Medium	−0.003*	0.003*	−0.001
High	−0.001	0.001*	0.000

Notes: 1) Low Incidence indicates = 0. 2)*** p < 0.01, ** p < 0.05, * p < 0.1

Table 6. Pairwise Correlation of Non-Production Overhead and Incidence

Incidence	Non-Production Overhead		
	Low	Medium	High
Low	−0.003*	−0.001	0.001*
Medium	0.002*	0.001	−0.001
High	0.002*	0.000	−0.001

Notes: 1) Low Incidence indicates = 0. 2) Low Non Prodcution Overhead indicates = 0. 3)*** p < 0.01, ** p < 0.05, * p < 0.1

Table 7. Pairwise Correlation of Financial Leverage and Incidence

Incidence	Financial Leverage		
	Low	Medium	High
Low	−0.003*	−0.001	0.001*
Medium	0.002*	0.001	−0.001
High	0.002*	0.000	−0.001

Notes: 1) Low Incidence indicates = 0. 2) Low Financial Leverage indicates = 0. 3)*** p < 0.01, ** p < 0.05, * p < 0.1

8 Future IS Research Using Earnings Call Transcripts

As illustrated in the prior section, *Earnings Call Transcripts* offer immense potential to researchers in the field of information systems. Beyond the development of techniques to better extract information from *Earnings Call Transcripts*, several thematic areas of future research are proffered by *Earnings Call Transcripts* as a source of firm-level data on digital and information technologies. We elaborate upon three broad themes of research that could benefit from *Earnings Call Transcripts* as a source of data.

First, *Earnings Call Transcripts* could offer intriguing possibilities for research in the broad domain of the business value of IT [50, 60–62, 69–73]. These possibilities include examining the operating, financial, or market performance implications of digital and information technologies that are present in *Earnings Call Transcripts* [74–76]. Research utilizing *Earnings Call Transcripts* could also uncover different variables, such as resources [61], capabilities [77], intermediate outcomes like innovation [78–90], firm characteristics such as ownership [91], and environmental contingencies such as uncertainty [92], that may mediate or moderate this relationship.

Second, *Earnings Call Transcripts* can allow future research in the area of digital globalization and internationalization in the digital age [50, 93]. The worldwide prevalence of Quarterly Earnings Conference Calls presents a unique and promising avenue for researchers to look into and evaluate varied global settings. For example, comparing and contrasting *Earnings Call Transcripts* across countries can enlighten cross-national disparities in the context of digital and information technologies, an intriguing research avenue. This can also provide insights into how analysts inquiries and investor responses to the queries differ across various regions and reveals the environmental and cultural factors influencing executive behavior during these conversations and their financial implications. Digging into linguistic distinctions in textual disclosures can enrich such investigations, enabling researchers to evaluate how regional variances in language may influence interpretation and decision-making related to digital and information technologies.

In the context of this global perspective, there is increasing awareness among researchers about the predominant focus of scientific studies within Western, Educated, Industrialized, Rich and Democratic (WEIRD) domains [94]. While research efforts have expanded into broader settings, particularly within information systems field [cite our papers and three others], the majority of research is still centered around WEIRD contexts. Recognizing this trend is vital, especially considering the transformative potential that research in alternative settings, such as Growing, Rural, Eastern, Aspirational, and Transitional (GREAT) regions, holds for theory development [95, 96]. Connecting these two perspectives emphasizes the need for a comprehensive exploration of *Earnings Call Transcripts* not only as a global phenomenon but also as an avenue to bridge the gap in understanding diverse economic and cultural contexts, ultimately enriching the broader research landscape in the field.

Furthermore, *Earnings Call Transcripts* can also enable an exploration of specific contexts, such as GREAT domains. As an illustrative case, significant research has been undertaken in areas like strategic management and operations management within the Indian context [97–99]. Though there are notable exceptions [99–106], there remains a noticeable gap in exploring India as a context for theory or data in the information systems area. Considering India's status as one of the fastest-growing major economies in Asia and the world, it becomes imperative to examine such questions. By exploring *Earnings Conference Calls* as a source of data, researchers can uncover unique insights into the intersection of corporate communication strategies, financial performance, and the rapidly evolving technological landscape of India.

Expanding the scope of research beyond individual countries, a comparative analysis between Indian firms and their counterparts in the United States could offer a novel and insightful avenue for investigation. A cross-country examination of *Earnings Conference Calls* could shed light on the nuanced differences in corporate communication strategies, investor responses, and financial implications related to digital and information technologies. The comparison between Indian and US firms provides an opportunity to discern how cultural, regulatory, and economic variations influence the dynamics of these communication events in the technology context. Investigating such cross-country disparities could contribute not only to the understanding of global financial markets but also offer practical insights for multinational corporations navigating diverse business environments.

Third, information within *Earnings Call Transcripts* could enable researchers to discern organizational strategies and responses to digital and information technology-related events and contexts. For instance, analyses of *Earnings Call Transcripts* could offer information regarding how firms interact and handle cybersecurity incidents. Researchers can assess a firm's readiness and flexibility in the face of security threats by examining executive statements on incident response plans, communication procedures, and resilience methods discussed on quarterly earnings conference calls. Scholars can additionally learn more about the cybersecurity commitment of organizations by analyzing discussions regarding investments in security technology and infrastructure upgrades. Examining these financial allocations can enable a more in-depth investigation of the link between a firm's financial responsibilities and its overall cybersecurity capability. This approach will not only reveal the tactical steps firms take to counter cyber threats but will also illuminate the strategic and financial factors that support these actions. The results of these studies would greatly advance firm-level research on cybersecurity by improving our understanding of the relationships between monetary investments, operational resilience, and cybersecurity outcomes.

To conclude, *Earnings Call Transcripts* offer myriad untapped opportunities for information systems researchers. Thus, through this book chapter, we make a call for information systems research that leverages *Earnings Call Transcripts*.

References

1. Baginski, S.P., Hassell, J.M.: Determinants of management forecast precision. Account. Rev. **72**, 303–312 (1997)
2. Francis, J., Schipper, K., Vincent, L.: Expanded disclosures and the increased usefulness of earnings announcements. Account. Rev. **77**(3), 515–546 (2002)
3. Bowen, R.M., Davis, A.K., Matsumoto, D.A.: Do conference calls affect analysts' forecasts? Account. Rev. **77**(2), 285–316 (2002)
4. Allee, K.D., DeAngelis, M.D.: The structure of voluntary disclosure narratives: evidence from tone dispersion. J. Account. Res. **53**(2), 241–274 (2015)
5. Allee, K.D., Do, C., Sterin, M.: Product market competition, disclosure framing, and casting in earnings conference calls. J. Account. Econ. **72**(1), 101405 (2021)
6. Price, S.M., et al.: Earnings conference calls and stock returns: the incremental informativeness of textual tone. J. Bank. Finance **36**(4), 992–1011 (2012)
7. Frankel, R., Johnson, M., Skinner, D.J.: An empirical examination of conference calls as a voluntary disclosure medium. J. Account. Res. **37**(1), 133–150 (1999)
8. Tasker, S.C.: Voluntary disclosure as a response to low accounting quality: evidence from quarterly conference calls. Massachusetts Institute of Technology (1997)
9. Ke, B., Petroni, K.R., Yu, Y.: The effect of regulation FD on transient institutional investors' trading behavior. J. Account. Res. **46**(4), 853–883 (2008)

10. Zitzewitz, E.: Regulation Fair Disclosure and the private information of analysts. SSRN 305219 (2002)
11. Frankel, R., Mayew, W.J., Sun, Y.: Do pennies matter? Investor relations consequences of small negative earnings surprises. Rev. Acc. Stud. **15**, 220–242 (2010)
12. Brown, L.D., Call, A.C., Clement, M.B., Sharp, N.Y.: Managing the narrative: investor relations officers and corporate disclosure☆. J. Account. Econ. **67**(1), 58–79 (2019)
13. Michaely, R., Rubin, A., Vedrashko, A.: Corporate governance and the timing of earnings announcements. Rev. Financ. **18**(6), 2003–2044 (2014)
14. Blau, B.M., DeLisle, J.R., Price, S.M.: Do sophisticated investors interpret earnings conference call tone differently than investors at large? Evidence from short sales. J. Corp. Finan. **31**, 203–219 (2015)
15. Mayew, W.J., Venkatachalam, M.: The power of voice: managerial affective states and future firm performance. J. Financ. **67**(1), 1–43 (2012)
16. Frankel, R., Jennings, J., Lee, J.: Disclosure sentiment: machine learning vs. dictionary methods. Manage. Sci. **68**(7), 5514–5532 (2022)
17. Leuz, C., Verrecchia, R.E.: The economic consequences of increased disclosure. J. Account. Res. **38**, 91 (2000). https://doi.org/10.2307/2672910
18. Fishman, M.J., Hagerty, K.M.: Disclosure decisions by firms and the competition for price efficiency. J. Financ. **44**(3), 633–646 (1989)
19. Merton, R.C.: A simple model of capital market equilibrium with incomplete information. J. Financ. **42**(3), 483 (1987). https://doi.org/10.2307/2328367
20. Hope, O.-K., Wang, J.: Management deception, big-bath accounting, and information asymmetry: evidence from linguistic analysis. Acc. Organ. Soc. **70**, 33–51 (2018)
21. Brown, S., Hillegeist, S.A., Lo, K.: Conference calls and information asymmetry. J. Account. Econ. **37**(3), 343–366 (2004)
22. Francis, B.B., Shohfi, T.D., Xin, D.: Gender and earnings conference calls. SSRN Electron. J. **25**, 2020 (2020)
23. Kumar, A.: Self-selection and the forecasting abilities of female equity analysts. J. Account. Res. **48**(2), 393–435 (2010)
24. Gao, M., Ji, Y., Rozenbaum, O.: When do associate analysts matter? Manage. Sci. **68**(5), 3925–3948 (2022)
25. Peng, L., Teoh, S.H., Wang, Y., Yan, J.: Face value: trait impressions, performance characteristics, and market outcomes for financial analysts. J. Account. Res. **60**(2), 653–705 (2022)
26. Miller, G.S., Naranjo, P.L., Yu, G.: Gender and Racial Diversity: Evidence from Earnings Conference Calls. SSRN (2022)
27. Tetlock, P.C.: Giving content to investor sentiment: the role of media in the stock market. J. Financ. **62**(3), 1139–1168 (2007)
28. Davis, A.K., Ge, W., Matsumoto, D., Zhang, J.L.: The effect of manager-specific optimism on the tone of earnings conference calls. Rev. Acc. Stud. **20**, 639–673 (2015)
29. De Amicis, C., Falconieri, S., Tastan, M.: Sentiment analysis and gender differences in earnings conference calls. J. Corp. Finan. **71**, 101809 (2021)
30. Brochet, F., Miller, G.S., Naranjo, P., Yu, G.: Managers' cultural background and disclosure attributes. Account. Rev. **94**(3), 57–86 (2019)
31. Call, A.C., Sharp, N.Y., Shohfi, T.D.: Which buy-side institutions participate in public earnings conference calls? Implications for capital markets and sell-side coverage. J. Corp. Finan. **68**, 101964 (2021)
32. Jung, M.J., Wong, M.F., Zhang, X.F.: Buy-side analysts and earnings conference calls. J. Account. Res. **56**(3), 913–952 (2018)
33. Malhotra, S., Reus, T.H., Zhu, P., Roelofsen, E.M.: The acquisitive nature of extraverted CEOs. Adm. Sci. Q. **63**(2), 370–408 (2018)

34. Balakrishnan, K., Copat, R., De la Parra, D., Ramesh, K.: Racial diversity exposure and firm responses following the murder of George Floyd. J. Account. Res. **61**(3), 737–804 (2023)
35. Flam, R.W., et al.: Ethnic minority analysts' participation in public earnings conference calls. J. Account. Res. **61**(5), 1591–1631 (2023)
36. Lee, J.M., Hwang, B.H., Chen, H.: Are founder CEOs more overconfident than professional CEOs? Evidence from S&P 1500 companies. Strateg. Manag. J. **38**(3), 751–769 (2017)
37. Larcker, D.F., Zakolyukina, A.A.: Detecting deceptive discussions in conference calls. J. Account. Res. **50**(2), 495–540 (2012)
38. Li, F.: Textual analysis of corporate disclosures: a survey of the literature. J. Account. Lit. **29**(1), 143–165 (2010)
39. Loughran, T., McDonald, B.: Textual analysis in accounting and finance: a survey. J. Account. Res. **54**(4), 1187–1230 (2016)
40. Yan, X., Zheng, L.: Fundamental analysis and the cross-section of stock returns: a data-mining approach. Rev. Financ. Stud. **30**(4), 1382–1423 (2017)
41. Mehrabian, A.: Nonverbal Communication. Routledge (2017)
42. Mayew, W.J., Sethuraman, M., Venkatachalam, M.: Individual analysts' stock recommendations, earnings forecasts, and the informativeness of conference call question and answer sessions. Account. Rev. **95**(6), 311–337 (2020)
43. Gregor, S., Hevner, A.R.: Positioning and presenting design science research for maximum impact. MIS Q. **37**(2), 337–355 (2013). https://doi.org/10.25300/MISQ/2013/37.2.01
44. Iivari, J.: Twelve theses on design science research in information systems. In: Design Research in Information Systems: Theory and Practice, pp. 43–62. Springer, Boston, MA (2010). https://doi.org/10.1007/978-1-4419-5653-8_5
45. Walls, J.G., Widmeyer, G.R., El Sawy, O.A.: Building an information system design theory for vigilant EIS. Inf. Syst. Res. **3**(1), 36–59 (1992)
46. Scherer, K.R.: Affect bursts. In: Emotions, pp. 175–208. Psychology Press (2014)
47. Schuller, B.: Voice and speech analysis in search of states and traits. In: Computer Analysis of Human Behavior, pp. 227–253. Springer (2011). https://doi.org/10.1007/978-0-85729-994-9_9
48. Guo, Y., Li, Y., Wei, Q., Xu, S.X.: IT-enabled role playing in service encounter: design a customer emotion management system in call centers (2017)
49. Saldanha, T.J., Andrade-Rojas, M.G., Kathuria, A., Khuntia, J., Krishnan, M.: How the locus of uncertainty shapes the influence of CEO long-term compensation on IT capital investments. MIS Q. (2023, forthcoming)
50. Kathuria, A., Karhade, P.P., Ning, X., Konsynski, B.R.: Blood and water: information technology investment and control in family-owned businesses. J. Manag. Inf. Syst. **40**(1), 208–238 (2023)
51. Kathuria, A., Karhade, P., Jaiswal, A., Mani, D.: Stock market reactions to IT endowment at the onset of COVID-19. In: ICIS 2023 Proceedings. 5 (2023)
52. Haislip, J.Z., Karim, K.E., Lin, K.J., Pinsker, R.E.: The influences of CEO IT expertise and board-level technology committees on form 8-K disclosure timeliness. J. Inf. Syst. **34**(2), 167–185 (2020)
53. Jing, J.: Information acquisition from sec filings and earnings management. Ph. D. thesis (2019)
54. Li, C., Peters, G.F., Richardson, V.J., Watson, M.W.: The consequences of information technology control weaknesses on management information systems: the case of Sarbanes-Oxley internal control reports. MIS Q. **36**(1), 179–203 (2012). https://doi.org/10.2307/41410413
55. Chatterjee, D., Richardson, V.J., Zmud, R.W.: Examining the shareholder wealth effects of announcements of newly created CIO positions. MIS Q. **25**(1), 43 (2001). https://doi.org/10.2307/3250958

56. Haislip, J.Z., Richardson, V.J.: The effect of CEO IT expertise on the information environment: evidence from earnings forecasts and announcements. J. Inf. Syst. **32**(2), 71–94 (2018)

57. Benaroch, M., Chernobai, A.: Operational IT failures, IT value destruction, and board-level IT governance changes. MIS Q. **41**(3), 729-A6 (2017)

58. Bose, I., Leung, A.C.M.: Adoption of identity theft countermeasures and its short- and long-term impact on firm value. MIS Q. **43**(1), 313–327 (2019). https://doi.org/10.25300/MISQ/2019/14192

59. Havakhor, T., Sabherwal, S., Sabherwal, R., Steelman, Z.R.: Evaluating information technology investments: insights from executives' trades. MIS Q. **46**(2), 1165–1194 (2022). https://doi.org/10.25300/MISQ/2022/16355

60. Andrade, M., Saldanha, T., Khuntia, J., Kathuria, A., Boh, W.: Overcoming deficiencies for innovation in SMEs: IT for closed innovation versus IT for open innovation. In: ICIS 2020 Proceedings, p. 9 (2020)

61. Khuntia, J., Saldanha, T., Kathuria, A., Tanniru, M.R.: Digital service flexibility: a conceptual framework and roadmap for digital business transformation. Eur. J. Inf. Syst. 1–19 (2022)

62. Chaturvedi, D., Kathuria, A., Andrade, M., Saldanha, T.: Navigating the paradox of IT novelty and strategic conformity: the moderating role of industry dynamism (2023)

63. Andrade-Rojas, M.G., Kathuria, A., Konsynski, B.R.: Competitive brokerage: how information management capability and collaboration networks act as substitutes. J. Manag. Inf. Syst. **38**(3), 667–703 (2021)

64. Bharadwaj, A.S., Bharadwaj, S.G., Konsynski, B.R.: Information technology effects on firm performance as measured by Tobin's q. Manage. Sci. **45**(7), 1008–1024 (1999)

65. McGahan, A.M., Silverman, B.S.: Profiting from technological innovation by others: the effect of competitor patenting on firm value. Res. Policy **35**(8), 1222–1242 (2006)

66. Lee, H.L., So, K.C., Tang, C.S.: The value of information sharing in a two-level supply chain. Manage. Sci. **46**(5), 626–643 (2000)

67. Tyndall, G., Gopal, C., Partsch, W., Kamauff, J.: Supercharging Supply Chains. New Ways to Increase Value Through Global Operational Excellence (1998)

68. Rai, A., Patnayakuni, R., Seth, N.: Firm performance impacts of digitally enabled supply chain integration capabilities. MIS Q. **30**(2), 225 (2006). https://doi.org/10.2307/25148729

69. Karhade, P., Kathuria, A., Malik, O., Konsynski, B.: Digital platforms and infobesity: a research agenda. In: Garimella, A., Karhade, P., Kathuria, A., Liu, X., Xu, J., Zhao, K. (eds.) WeB 2020. LNBIP, vol. 418, pp. 67–74. Springer, Cham (2021). https://doi.org/10.1007/978-3-030-79454-5_7

70. Ning, X., Khuntia, J., Kathuria, A., Konsynski, B.R.: Artificial Intelligence (AI) and cognitive apportionment for service flexibility. In: Xu, J.J., Zhu, B., Liu, X., Shaw, M.J., Zhang, H., Fan, M. (eds.) WEB 2018. LNBIP, vol. 357, pp. 182–189. Springer, Cham (2019). https://doi.org/10.1007/978-3-030-22784-5_18

71. Barua, A., Konana, P., Whinston, A.B., Yin, F.: Assessing internet enabled business value: an exploratory investigation. MIS Q. **28**(4), 585–620 (2004)

72. Kumar, R.L.: A framework for assessing the business value of information technology infrastructures. J. Manag. Inf. Syst. **21**(2), 11–32 (2004)

73. Kohli, R., Grover, V.: Business value of IT: an essay on expanding research directions to keep up with the times. J. Assoc. Inf. Syst. **9**(1), 1 (2008)

74. Chatjuthamard, P., Jiraporn, P.: Corporate culture, innovation and board size: recent evidence from machine learning and earnings conference calls. Corp. Governance Int. J. Bus. Soc. **23**(2), 1361–1378 (2023)

75. Chava, S., Du, W., Paradkar, N.: More than Buzzwords? Firms' discussions of emerging technologies in earnings conference calls. SSRN (2020)

76. Likitapiwat, T., Treepongkaruna, S., Jiraporn, P., Uyar, A.: Corporate culture, innovation, and female board representation: evidence from earnings conference calls. Q. J. Financ. **12**(04), 2250012 (2022)
77. Kathuria, A., Mann, A., Khuntia, J., Saldanha, T.J., Kauffman, R.J.: A strategic value appropriation path for cloud computing. J. Manag. Inf. Syst. **35**(3), 740–775 (2018)
78. Svahn, F., Mathiassen, L., Lindgren, R.: Embracing digital innovation in incumbent firms. MIS Q. **41**(1), 239–254 (2017)
79. Nambisan, S., Lyytinen, K., Majchrzak, A., Song, M.: Digital innovation management. MIS Q. **41**(1), 223–238 (2017)
80. Fichman, R.G., Dos Santos, B.L., Zheng, Z.: Digital innovation as a fundamental and powerful concept in the information systems curriculum. MIS Q. **38**(2), 329-A15 (2014)
81. Karhade, P.P., Dong, J.Q.: Innovation outcomes of digitally enabled collaborative problemistic search capability. MIS Q. **45**(2), 693–717 (2021)
82. Ye, H., Kankanhalli, A.: User service innovation on mobile phone platforms. MIS Q. **42**(1), 165-A9 (2018)
83. Nambisan, S., Agarwal, R., Tanniru, M.: Organizational mechanisms for enhancing user innovation in information technology. MIS Q. **23**(3), 365 (1999). https://doi.org/10.2307/249468
84. Saldanha, T.J., Mithas, S., Krishnan, M.S.: Leveraging customer involvement for fueling innovation. MIS Q. **41**(1), 267–286 (2017)
85. Fichman, R.G.: The role of aggregation in the measurement of IT-related organizational innovation. MIS Q. **25**(4), 427 (2001). https://doi.org/10.2307/3250990
86. Xue, L., Ray, G., Sambamurthy, V.: Efficiency or innovation: how do industry environments moderate the effects of firms' IT asset portfolios? MIS Q. **36**, 509–528 (2012)
87. Lucas, H.C., Swanson, E.B., Zmud, R.: Implementation, innovation, and related themes over the years in information systems research. J. Assoc. Inf. Syst. **8**(4), 8 (2008)
88. Guo, F., Li, Y., Maruping, L.M., Masli, A.: Complementarity between investment in information technology (IT) and IT human resources: implications for different types of firm innovation. Inf. Syst. Res. **34**(3), 1259–1275 (2023)
89. Melville, N.P.: Information systems innovation for environmental sustainability. MIS Q. **34**, 1–21 (2010)
90. Roberts, N., Campbell, D.E., Vijayasarathy, L.R.: Using information systems to sense opportunities for innovation: integrating postadoptive use behaviors with the dynamic managerial capability perspective. J. Manag. Inf. Syst. **33**(1), 45–69 (2016)
91. Chen, Y., Bharadwaj, A., Goh, K.-Y.: An empirical analysis of intellectual property rights sharing in software development outsourcing. MIS Q. **41**(1), 131–162 (2017)
92. Dwirandra, A.A.N.B., Astika, I.B.P.: Impact of environmental uncertainty, trust and information technology on user behavior of accounting information systems. J. Asian Financ. Econ. Bus. **7**(12), 1215–1224 (2020). https://doi.org/10.13106/jafeb.2020.vol7.no12.1215
93. Khuntia, J., Kathuria, A., Andrade-Rojas, M.G., Saldanha, T., Celly, N.: How foreign and domestic firms differ in leveraging IT-enabled supply chain information integration in BOP markets: the role of supplier and client business collaboration. J. Assoc. Inf. Syst. **22**(3), 6 (2021)
94. Henrich, J., Heine, S.J., Norenzayan, A.: The weirdest people in the world? Behav. Brain Sci. **33**(2–3), 61–83 (2010)
95. Dasgupta, A., Karhade, P., Kathuria, A., Konsynski, B.: Holding space for voices that do not speak: design reform of rating systems for platforms in GREAT economies. In: Proceedings of the 54th Hawaii International Conference on System Sciences (2021)
96. Karhade, P., Kathuria, A.: Missing impact of ratings on platform participation in India: a call for research in GREAT domains. Commun. Assoc. Inf. Syst. **47**(1), 19 (2020)

97. Celly, N., Kathuria, A., Subramanian, V.: Overview of Indian multinationals. In: Thite, M., Wilkinson, A., Budhwar, P. (eds.) Emerging Indian multinationals: Strategic players in a multipolar world. Oxford University Press, London, UK (2016)

98. Khuntia, J., Kathuria, A., Saldanha, T.J., Konsynski, B.R.: Benefits of IT-enabled flexibilities for foreign versus local firms in emerging economies. J. Manag. Inf. Syst. **36**(3), 855–892 (2019)

99. Kathuria, R., Kathuria, N.N., Kathuria, A.: Mutually supportive or trade-offs: an analysis of competitive priorities in the emerging economy of India. J. High Technol. Managem. Res.igh Technol. Managem. Res. **29**(2), 227–236 (2018)

100. Capelli, P.: The India way: how India's top business leaders are revolutionizing management. NHRD Network J. **3**(3), 74–74 (2010). https://doi.org/10.1177/0974173920100315

101. Ning, X., Khuntia, J., Kathuria, A., Karhade, P.: Ownership and management control effects on IT investments: a study of Indian family firms (2020)

102. Gupta, A.: Emergence of Indian multinationals. Technol. Exports **8**(3), 1–6 (2006)

103. Pradhan, J.P., Sauvant, K.P.: Introduction: the rise of Indian multinational enterprises: revisiting key issues. In: The Rise of Indian Multinationals: Perspectives on Indian Outward Foreign Direct Investment, pp. 1–23. Springer (2010). https://doi.org/10.1057/9780230011 4753_1

104. Kapur, D., Ramamurti, R.: India's emerging competitive advantage in services. Acad. Manag. Perspect. **15**(2), 20–32 (2001)

105. Kumar, N.: India's Global Powerhouses: How they are taking on the World. Sage, New Delhi (2010)

106. Nayak, A.K.J.R.: Growth of Indian multinationals. In: Nayak, A.K.J.R. (ed.) Indian Multinationals, pp. 49–91. Palgrave Macmillan UK, London (2011). https://doi.org/10.1057/978 0230308718_4

Systematic Literature Review of Cloud Computing Research Between 2010 and 2023

Shailaja Jha[1] and Devina Chaturvedi[2(⊠)]

[1] SP Jain Institute of Management and Research, Mumbai, India
shailaja.jha@spjimr.org
[2] Indian School of Business, Hyderabad, India
devina_chaturvedi@isb.edu

Abstract. We present a meta-analysis of cloud computing research in information systems. The study includes 152 referenced journal articles published between January 2010 to June 2023. We take stock of the literature and the associated research themes, research frameworks, the employed research methodology, and the geographical distribution of the articles. This review provides holistic insights into trends in cloud computing research based on themes, frameworks, methodology, geographical focus, and future research directions. The results indicate that the extant literature tends to skew toward themes related to business issues, which is an indicator of the maturing and widespread use of cloud computing. This trend is evidenced in the more recent articles published between 2016 to 2023.

Keywords: Cloud Computing · Meta-analysis · Literature Review · Review · Classification

1 Introduction

The widely accepted definition of cloud computing provided by the National Institute of Standards and Technologies (NIST) recognizes it as "a model for enabling ubiquitous, convenient, on-demand network access to a shared pool of configurable computing resources (e.g., networks, servers, storage, applications, and services) that can be rapidly provisioned and released with minimal management effort or service provider interaction" [64]. Cloud computing combines several IT technologies including hardware, virtualization, distributed computing, etc., whose development spans over multiple decades. Delivery of "IT as a service" over the Internet Cloud computing represents a groundbreaking technology that lowers initial infrastructure expenses, extends accessibility to computing and storage capabilities, and empowers businesses to drive innovation and maintain competitiveness in the digital age.

As Cloud computing enters the seventeenth year of its existence post the launch of the first public cloud (AWS), cloud computing has been the focus of several scholarly endeavours. Given the socio-technical nature of the subject [83], cloud computing has been the subject of research for both technical journals as well as management journals. Such research has been periodically reviewed, most notably by Yang & Tate, 2012

© The Author(s), under exclusive license to Springer Nature Switzerland AG 2024
A. Kathuria et al. (Eds.): WeB 2022, LNBIP 508, pp. 64–88, 2024.
https://doi.org/10.1007/978-3-031-60003-6_5

[108]; Schneider and Sunyaev, 2016 [85]; Wang et al., 2016 [101]; Muller et al., 2015 [70]; Wulf et al., 2021 [106] and Venters & Whitley, 2012 [100]. While these reviews provide useful information on the status of research on cloud computing, an updated review of the research landscape on cloud computing is warranted considering these earlier attempts only cover research published up to 2016. Post-2016, cloud adoption has become mainstream, and consequently, research on post-adoption issues has started to become a part of the discourse during this time. Accordingly, we conduct a systematic literature review [8, 95] using the period between January 2010 and June 2023 to synthesize cloud computing research relevant to the prevailing context.

The rest of this paper is organized as follows. We start with an overview of cloud computing including discussions on service and deployment models. The second section presents the classification framework employed for this literature review. The third section covers the methodology of this study, and the fourth section covers the findings from the study. The next section provides a more detailed narrative of the literature categorized into themes and the last section summarizes the paper with the contributions and directions for future research.

2 Overview of Cloud Characteristics and Categorizations

2.1 Fundamental Characteristics of Cloud Computing

The foundation of the cloud computing paradigm rests upon five fundamental characteristics that collectively define its operational framework.

First and foremost is the on-demand self-service feature, enabling users to provision and manage computing resources autonomously without direct human intervention. This empowers organizations with flexibility and agility, allowing them to scale resources according to their dynamic requirements. Broad network access is another pivotal characteristic, ensuring ubiquitous access to cloud services through a variety of devices, fostering accessibility and inclusivity across diverse platforms. Resource pooling is a central tenet, consolidating computing resources to serve multiple consumers, thus optimizing efficiency and utilization. Rapid elasticity is a hallmark of the cloud, facilitating the swift and automatic scaling of resources in response to demand fluctuations. This elasticity ensures that organizations can seamlessly adapt to varying workloads without compromising performance or incurring unnecessary costs. Finally, measured service introduces transparency and accountability by monitoring and controlling resource usage. This pay-as-you-go model allows users to pay for only the resources consumed, promoting cost-effectiveness.

Collectively, these characteristics not only distinguish cloud computing from traditional models but also lay the foundation for its transformative impact on modern IT infrastructures, offering unprecedented flexibility, scalability, and efficiency.

2.2 Categorization of Cloud Models

The classification of cloud computing extends beyond its essential characteristics to encompass three distinct service models and four deployment models. Broadly categorized, cloud computing services are characterized as information as a service (IaaS), platform as a service (PaaS), and software as a service (SaaS), each catering to specific user needs and demands. Moreover, the relationship between service providers and users further delineates cloud computing into four deployment models: public cloud computing, private cloud computing, community cloud computing, and hybrid cloud computing.

SaaS, which replaced the Application Service Providers (ASPs) model, is characterized by NIST as the model that provides consumers with the capability to "use the provider's applications running on a cloud infrastructure" [64]. This means that the end user does not oversee or govern the foundational cloud infrastructure, encompassing aspects such as network, servers, operating systems, storage, and even specific application functionalities. However, the user may be provided with the ability to make limited configurations to application settings tailored to their specific needs. SaaS today contributes to a wide range of software categories such as database management systems, office suites, enterprise resource planning, customer relationship management, supply chain management, business intelligence applications, marketing and advertising applications, and workplace collaboration management tools.

PaaS provides a platform and environment for developers to build, deploy, and manage applications without worrying about the underlying infrastructure and its complexities. In the PaaS model, the cloud provider offers a set of tools, services, and development frameworks to streamline the application development process. The client organization using the PaaS platform typically provides the application layer as well as the database schemas and objects that run on the database chosen in the PaaS configuration. PaaS enables organizations to concentrate on their application layer and leverage modern features provided including containers, Kubernetes services, and serverless components, by the cloud service provider.

IaaS, as defined by the National Institute of Standards and Technology (NIST), represents a cloud computing model that grants consumers the capability to "provision processing, storage, networks, and other fundamental computing resources" [64]. In this model, end users have greater control over the foundational infrastructure compared to SaaS and PaaS. With IaaS, consumers are responsible for managing and configuring virtual machines, operating systems, storage, and networking components. Unlike SaaS and PaaS, where the focus is on specific applications or development environments, IaaS provides a more versatile solution, allowing organizations to customize and control various aspects of their computing environment. Users have the flexibility to install and configure software, implement security measures, and maintain overall control of their virtualized infrastructure. IaaS is particularly suitable for businesses with diverse and dynamic computing needs, offering a scalable and adaptable solution for managing computing resources without the burden of maintaining physical hardware.

Cloud deployment models encompass various approaches to the provisioning and accessibility of cloud computing resources and services for users. The four main deployment models include public cloud, private cloud, hybrid cloud, and community cloud. The hybrid cloud, a prevalent model, integrates aspects of both public and private clouds. Enterprises strategically leverage on-premises, private, and public cloud resources to create a cohesive hybrid environment. An effective implementation of a hybrid cloud facilitates the smooth transition of data and applications across different environments. This ensures flexibility and scalability while retaining control over sensitive data.

As we delve into the systematic review of literature on cloud computing, these models will serve as a foundational framework for understanding the evolving landscape of this technology.

3 Classification Framework for Systematic Literature Review

At the onset of this analysis, we adapted the classification scheme used by Yang and Tate (2012). We made a few modifications to the scheme to capture advancements in the literature made during the thirteen years following their study period; particularly, this refers to the addition of post-adoption studies. Accordingly, we grouped research areas into 4 themes and 21 sub-themes, adopting the classification model As-Is, except for the addition of a post-adoption sub-theme (see Table 1).

Table 1. Cloud Computing Literature Classification Framework

Themes	Subthemes
Business Issues	Adoption, Post Adoption, Cost, Pricing, Legal and Ethical Issues, Trust, Privacy
Technology Issues	Cloud Performance, Data Management, Data Centre Management, Software Development, Service Management, Security
Conceptualization	Foundational/Introductions, Predictions
Domains & Applications	e-Science, e-Government, Education, Open Source, Mobile Computing, Other Domains

4 Methodology for the Review

A literature review can be conducted in different ways: narrative review, descriptive review, vote counting, and meta-analysis [46]. In this study, the meta-analysis technique was employed to conduct the literature review. The decision to use the meta-analysis approach was driven by its capacity to offer statistical validation for the ongoing research. To study the current state of cloud research, which concerns IS researchers, we adopted a review from the same set of journals as used in the systematic literature review by Wang et al., 2016 [101].

We first searched in the senior scholar's list of premier 11 journals, these being: the European Journal of Information Systems (EJIS), Information Systems Journal (ISJ), Information Systems Research (ISR), Journal of Association for Information Systems (JAIS), Journal of Information Technology (JIT), Journal of Management Information Systems (JMIS), Journal of Strategic Information Systems (JSIS), and MIS Quarterly (MISQ), Decision Support Systems (DSS), Information and Management, Information, and Organization. To this list, additional journals and conference proceedings were added. Additional journals added were the Communications of the Association for Information Systems, Communications of the ACM, and ACM Transactions on Management Information Systems journals, and four top management journals (Management Science, Decision Sciences, Harvard Business Review, and Sloan Management Review). AISeL-based conference proceedings (International Conference on Information Systems (ICIS), Americas Conference on Information Systems (AMCIS)) were also included as the published sources.[1]

The search was conducted by using the phrases "cloud computing", "Infrastructure as a Service", "Platform as a Service", and "Software as a Service". When the search was conducted, these strings were concatenated with the "OR" operator. We searched for these strings in the abstracts, titles, and keywords of the papers. The period chosen was from January 2010 to June 2023. This timespan has been chosen given that systematic literature review papers researching cloud computing exist for the period spanning 2006 to 2018. Cloud computing as a field is maturing, and implementations have only gone up. It was critical to look at the more recently published papers as well. Since the period from 2006 to 2010 has been adequately represented in systematic literature reviews of cloud computing research, we chose to start our search in January 2010.

The search provided 393 articles which were then subjected to manual filtering to eliminate editorials, review articles, and reports. Duplicates and articles related to other disciplines like computer engineering were also removed from consideration. The filtering procedure yielded a total of 245 fully reviewed research articles. These journal articles were further examined to identify content relevant to cloud computing, resulting in a selection of 152 articles for further analysis. Furthermore, we obtained 235 fully reviewed research articles from conference proceedings at ICIS and AMCIS. We have focused our detailed analysis primarily on journal articles, reserving the conference papers for the purpose of assessing the numerical distribution of publications over the years.

The set of 152 journal articles was classified on themes, sub-themes, research methodology employed, theoretical framework utilized, year of publication, publishing outlet (journal), geographical focus, and specific domain if the article was domain specific. The thematic classification was aligned with the framework proposed by Yang and Tate, consisting of 4 overarching themes and 22 sub-themes. The methodology researched was based on qualitative, quantitative, mixed methods, analytical models, and experiments. If the method was unclear, it was assigned a "no method" categorization. If an article used analytical modeling following the queuing or game theoretic framework, the article's methodology was kept as analytical modeling. The geographical focus pertained to the continent where the study concentrated its data collection efforts. In instances where an article's content did not exhibit a specific geographic target and was location agnostic, then we designated the geographical focus as "Global".

---

[1] The conference proceedings were primarily used to assess the year-on-year numerical trends in publications, and they have not been used for detailed analysis.

5   Results and Analysis

5.1   Distribution of Articles by year

Figure 1 illustrates the annual publication trends of journal and conference articles, along with their cumulative sum. It is important to note that data for the year 2023 is available only from January to June. Across all years, conference article submissions consistently outnumber journal article submissions. The submission count witnessed a steady increase from 2010 to 2014. Wang et al. (2016) [101] highlighted the period from 2012 to 2014 as the flourishing stage of cloud computing, evident in the high submission count during this timeframe (114 papers). Subsequently, there was a declining trend in paper counts from 2015 to 2017. However, with the widespread adoption of cloud computing and calls for papers in 2017–2019, there was a resurgence in the number of published papers, reaching a peak of 126 papers. Post-2019, there has been a noticeable decline in publications related to cloud computing.

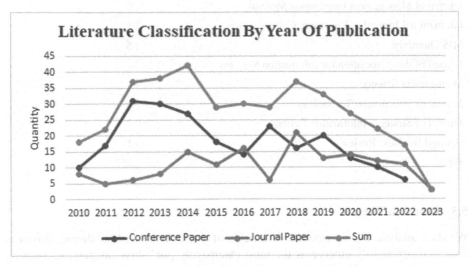

Fig. 1. Literature classification by year of publication

5.2   Publication Outlet

We then analyzed the publication outlets of the articles. Table 2 indicates the distribution of articles by journals they were published. In the senior scholar's list of premier journals, Information and Management, Decision Support Systems, and Information Systems Research, have had the most publications. Communication of the ACM recorded the highest number of studies (22%).

Table 2. Distribution of articles by journal

Journal	No. of Publications
Communications of the ACM	33
Information and Management	17
Decision Support Systems	13
Information Systems Research	11
MIS Quarterly Executive	11
Electronic Commerce Research and Applications	10
European Journal of Information Systems	7
Information Systems Journal	7
ACM Transactions on Management Information Systems	6
Communications of the Association for Information Systems	6
Journal of Management Information Systems	6
International Journal of Electronic Commerce	5
MIS Quarterly	5
Journal of the Association for Information Systems	4
Management Science	4
Journal of Information Technology	3
Journal of Strategic Information Systems	3
Harvard Business Review	1
Total	152

5.3 Research Themes

We then analyze the distribution of articles of each theme and subtheme. Business issues conspicuously emerge as the most extensively published category, accounting for seventy-one articles (47%). It is followed by Technological Issues with forty-three articles (28%), Conceptualization with twenty-seven articles (18%), and the category with the lowest representation is the Domain comprising eleven articles (7%). Five articles covered the literature review of cloud computing and have been taken in the conceptualization theme.

The widespread adoption of cloud computing has spotlighted the business issues related to cloud computing, indicating a growing emphasis on business perspective and that is reflected in the business issues category dominating the publications. Technological issues continue to remain significant, with various technical factors still hindering the expansion of cloud computing. These include issues related to data security, privacy, legal regulations, and energy efficiency [6].

The business issues theme (see Table 3) considers research related to the socio-technical aspects of cloud computing such as adoption, cost, privacy, pricing, legal, trust, and ethics. We have introduced a special sub-theme named post-adoption to call out papers that delve into post-adoption scenarios of cloud computing. These articles explore topics such as the continuance of cloud services, outcomes of cloud computing, value appropriation from cloud investments, and factors contributing to success in cloud implementation scenarios.

Table 3. Distribution of "Business Issues" Articles

Theme	Number of Articles	Percentage
Adoption	21	30%
Post-Adoption	20	28%
Pricing	21	30%
Costing	4	6%
Privacy	1	1%
Legal	2	3%
Trust	1	1%
Ethical Issues	1	1%
Total	71	100%

As evident from Table 3, a significant 58% of the articles in this category focus on the adoption and post-adoption dimensions of cloud computing. Research efforts have concentrated on factors that enable or impede cloud computing adoption and assimilation, and investigation of costs within the cloud environment and compute and storage instance expenses. Likewise, factors that drive pricing by cloud providers were a highly researched area. Notably, pricing was a relatively emerging area of research in earlier literature reviews, but post-2015, it garnered increased attention as cloud service offerings and pricing models matured.

Table 4. Distribution of "Technological Issues" Articles

Themes	Number of Articles	Percentage
Cloud Performance	5	12%
Security	13	32%
Data Management	5	12%
Software Development	4	10%
Data Center Management	4	10%
Service Management	10	24%
Total	41	100%

The focus of the technological issue theme (Table 4) is on the core infrastructure that supports cloud computing. Sub-themes examined under this theme include security, cloud computing performance, data management, data center management, and service management. Our analysis of the literature suggests that security and service management stand out as significant concerns, among technological issues. The previous literature reviews did not have security as the foremost concern. However, widespread adoption of cloud computing and cloud computing-based security breaches have brought this issue to the fore. As cloud usage increases SLA management and service management in general become a critical research area. We also observe that the data center management sub-theme has become critical, primarily on the sustainability concerns surrounding data centers.

Table 5. Distribution of "Conceptualizing Cloud Computing" Articles

Themes	Number of Articles	Percentage
Foundational/Introductions	20	91%
Predictive	2	9%
Total	22	100%

Conceptualizing cloud computing theme (Table 5) contains articles that provide a general view of cloud computing practice and research. The theme is categorized into two sub-themes, Foundational/Introduction and Predictions. A significant majority of articles are foundational works.

The final theme comprises domains (Table 6) in which cloud computing has been applied. The articles in this theme investigate the application of computing in areas such as education, e-science, e-government, mobile computing, open source, and other domains of application. The table below shows a breakdown of articles that researched "Domain issues". This theme had the lowest article count:

Table 6. Distribution of "Domain" Articles

Themes	Number of Articles	Percentage
Education	1	9%
Not For Profit	1	9%
New IT Venture	2	18%
Smart Toys/ Smart Manufacturing	2	18%
Others	5	45%
Total	11	100%

5.4 Distribution of Research Methodology

In our comprehensive literature review, we observed a diverse spectrum of research methodologies. The predominant share, at 59.3%, was attributed to studies employing analytical modeling and simulation. Subsequently, 14.7% of the studies lacked a specified methodology, while 13% utilized quantitative methods. A noteworthy albeit smaller portion of the research landscape included qualitative studies (11.6%) and mixed methods studies (2.5%).

5.5 Distribution of Research Frameworks

The extant literature has examined cloud computing using several pertinent research frameworks including the Technology Adoption Model (TAM), Diffusion of Innovation (DOI), Theory of Reasoned Action (TRA), Resource Based View (RBV), Grounded Theory, Migration Theory, Technology, Organization and Environment (TOE), Knowledge-based view framework. Several papers use more than one theoretical framework to explain the organizational context. On the other hand, many articles did not use a particular theoretical framework to conduct their analysis (e.g. [20, 23, 63]). Table 7 indicates the distribution of articles and their respective research frameworks.

Table 7. Research Framework Classification

Research Framework	Number of Articles	Percentage
No Theory	122	80%
RBV	7	5%
TOE	5	3%
TAM	2	1%
Grounded Theory	2	1%
Migration Theory	2	1%
DOI	2	1%
TAM and TOE	1	1%
TOE and DOI	1	1%
Theory of Reasoned Action	1	1%
TRA and TAM	1	1%
Socio-Technical Theory	1	1%
Economic Theory of Substitution	1	1%
Agency Theory	1	1%
Cognitive-affective-conative-action (CACA)	1	1%
TOE and RBV	1	1%
TOE, Agency Theory, and Knowledge-Based View	1	1%
Total	152	100%

5.6   The Geographic Focus of the Articles

In this category, we investigate the articles based on the geographic focus of the extant literature. We examine the geographical region based on whether it is the source of data or the focus of the articles reviewed. The available literature on cloud computing was categorized according to continents, including cross-continental and global studies. Our analysis (Fig. 2) reveals that 8% of articles have an Asia focus followed by 7% of articles having a European focus, 6% from North America, and 1% with an Australian focus. A significant 78% had no geographical focus and were categorized as having a global focus.

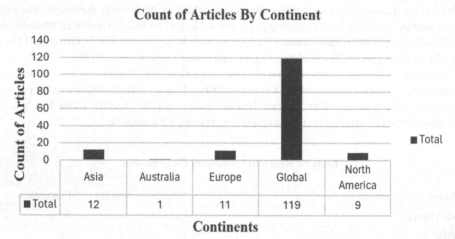

Fig. 2. Geographic Focus of the Articles

The results indicate that most studies did not utilize a specific geographical location as their data source or focus and were therefore classified under the global context. Furthermore, when considering the distribution of articles by continent, it was evident that a substantial number of cloud computing studies originated from Asia, Europe, and North America. We found none in the cross-continent classification. Studies conducted in the Asian region were conducted in countries such as Taiwan, China, Korea, and India (e.g., [12, 14, 41, 97, 111]). On the other hand, research classified under Europe originated from the United Kingdom, Norway, Germany, Finland, and the European Union as a whole (e.g., [9, 72]. Since the existing cloud computing literature has predominantly concentrated on developed nations, it is crucial to conduct additional studies in developing countries and GREAT (Growing, Rural, Emerging, Aspirational, Transitional) domains [18, 37, 38] to address the specific contextual and socio–technical factors within these regions. There is increasing interest and research in examinations of IT phenomena in countries such as India (e.g., [39, 40, 45, 61, 98, 99]), including studies of cloud computing (e.g., [33, 41, 62]). Given the relevance of cloud computing to this context wherein firms are high growth and value-seeking, it is pertinent that more such studies be conducted in the future.

6 Discussion

Our review of the literature sheds light on several themes and issues prevalent in the body of work on cloud computing. We find that business themes have been the focus of most studies, with considerable stress on post-adoption and adoption sub-themes.

6.1 Findings from the Business Issues Category of Studies

The Business Issues category within the realm of cloud computing research is a multifaceted landscape encompassing diverse sub-themes that delve into crucial facets of cloud adoption, post-adoption challenges, cost considerations, legal implications, ethical concerns, trust dynamics, and privacy issues. This section provides a comprehensive overview of findings beginning with a focus on adoption, unraveling the enablers and constraints that shape the decision-making processes for enterprises and individuals. Post-adoption concerns shed light on the continuous utilization of cloud computing and the challenges hindering its seamless integration within organizational frameworks. The cost sub-theme critically evaluates the economic benefits of cloud adoption, urging a nuanced examination of both short-term advantages and long-term cost considerations. Pricing strategies, particularly the dynamics of spot instances, are meticulously analyzed, employing frameworks such as Game Theory to unravel the complexities of cloud pricing. Legal considerations encompass the need for universal laws, certifications, and continuous service certification, while ethical and trust dynamics form critical components in the evaluation of cloud technologies. Privacy issues, including identity and access management, feature prominently in the ethical and legal discourse surrounding cloud adoption.

Adoption. The most extensively studied research area (sub-theme) amongst business issues is cloud adoption and factors that enable adoption in enterprises and individuals or constrain the same [9, 32, 49]. The adoption of IT has been an enduring theme in the overall information systems literature [49, 54, 94, 97, 106, 109]. Studies on cloud computing also examine this notion extensively.

Studies indicate that cloud computing enablers include top management support, relative advantage, technology readiness and competitive pressure, vendor trustworthiness, perceived solution clarity, and cost savings. Factors that have been observed as constraining cloud adoption include security, privacy, a lack of adequate legislation, a shortage of cloud talent, or a lack of availability of technical infrastructure. At both the individual and societal levels, concerns about information privacy, information security, and compliance with regulations are preventing adoption [52]. At the organizational level integration and compliance factors act as impediments to widespread adoption [50, 93].

Additionally, research examining the connection between the significance of physical and knowledge resources for individual firms and the consequent choice of cloud computing deployment models [112] has been studied, indicating that firms with a greater emphasis on physical capital intensity tended to opt for cloud computing outsourcing, while those with a stronger focus on knowledge capital intensity leaned toward utilizing private clouds. Among the service models researched SaaS is the most researched service model. Academic research on SaaS has discussed the adoption of SaaS in enterprises [72]. Research has focused on factors that drive the adoption of the SaaS model from the client's perspective, and theoretical frameworks, such as economic, strategic management, and information systems theories, have been leveraged to study SaaS adoption.

To draw attention to the articles that stress the ongoing utilization of cloud computing and operational, cloud sourcing concerns, and outcomes achieved with cloud computing, we added the post-adoption sub-theme. We have seen a high number of research articles that focus on the post-adoption research sub-theme. This sub-theme aligns with the larger stream of IT business value literature that continues to remain relevant and vibrant, with several recent exemplars of research that examine value-related questions in the context of IT [3, 4, 13, 60, 66, 67, 77, 78, 81, 82, 91].

There are indications that companies face challenges in fully harnessing the advantages of cloud sourcing during its continuous usage. The continuance of cloud computing in enterprises is fraught with barriers [68] including management process barriers, lack of objectives and strategies for cloud sourcing, as well as the inadequate organization of cloud vendor communications. Overcoming these barriers can pave the way towards continuous cloud use. Cloud service providers' technology support has been observed to impact a buyer's utilization of IT services following adoption [79], and enhanced technology support results in higher usage volumes and improved efficiency. A uniform approach to harnessing cloud advantages is not a viable solution, considering unique business process characteristics, the presence of legacy systems, and variations in regulations among different regions [103]. The organization of IT functions and structure can change with the wider adoption of cloud computing [16, 104]. The service quality and user satisfaction in cloud-based scenarios have been measured using the SaaS-Qual instrument [9], comprising six factors: rapport, flexibility, features, security, reliability, responsiveness, and user satisfaction. Papers have also looked at the impact of SaaS on IS governance, IS authority allocation, and factors that influence these allocations, with suggestions on best practices for IS authority [9]. There is a line of research where cloud adoption has been studied along the lens of enabling platform ecosystems. Companies seek to derive advantage of emergent platform ecosystems, collaborating with a diverse group of third-party developers, through embracing cloud technologies [27]. This was also brought out by the multi-year longitudinal study of the SAP company and its cloud platform project [88].

Studies also reveal the catalyzing role of cloud computing in enhancing firm performance [9, 34, 41]. Studies related to the adoption of cloud technology have also explored the Return on Investment (ROI) resulting from migrating to the cloud, highlighting substantial cost reductions of up to 40% achieved by organizations [29]. Depending on the contextual factors in an enterprise, cloud computing may generate business value and the path to the creation could be through decoupling, platformization, and recombination [10]. Cloud computing can aid inter-enterprise collaboration and SC agility, enabling real-time communication, savings in resource consumption, and waste management [87]. The impact of the SaaS service model on the performance of a business has been examined, with specific attention to the influence of the firm's business strategy and its capability to manage business processes [80].

Post-adoption. Post-adoption issues have been studied by understanding the impact of SaaS adoption [104]. Factors analyzing successful SaaS implementation and assimilation have also been researched [105]. However, a lot more needs to be researched for successful SaaS assimilation in enterprises. The transition from traditional IT outsourcing to the cloud-sourcing era has radically changed client–provider relationships [96]. Furthermore, enterprise cloud clients must rethink the role of the internal IT department [16] as well as the characteristics of the outsourcing relationship that defines how clients and cloud providers interact in the era of cloud sourcing [84].

Cost. Articles in the cost sub-theme category have examined the economic benefits of cloud computing from a cloud user perspective whereas the pricing sub-theme focuses on the pricing strategies of the cloud providers. From a cost perspective, studies supporting the argument that cloud adoption has lowered costs have focused on short-term costs [14]. More work needs to be taken up in areas of long-term costs as well as transparency in cloud billing. In many cases, the "renting" of cloud services can get incrementally expensive, and firms may move out of the cloud to their own data center or move to another cloud [65]. More work examining the repatriation of cloud workloads needs to be taken up. Cloud computing resources may be priced on an On Demand, Reserved, or On Spot basis, and different mechanisms in which the pricing and discounts can be optimized exist [59]. Cloud pricing has been examined as an example of digital and information product pricing [30]. The supply of such products is characterized as discontinuous, and their marginal costs are close to zero.

Pricing. Pricing of spot compute instances is also a popular research area. The spot market is an offering where the cloud service providers make available their unused capacity at significantly lower rates (as much as 80 – 90% cheaper) as compared to On-Demand and other instance types. Approximately 30% of the capacity in the global data centers may go unused [43], on account of a conflict between the "rather static capacity of computing resources and the highly volatile day-to-day demand for these resources". To leverage surplus capacities without violating the written SLAs, cloud providers provide spot instances at extremely low rates. Spot instances are used by organizations with workloads that are flexible about run-time and interruptions and spot computing may not be a good use case for real-time applications and systems as it does not guarantee availability. Spot pricing dynamics have been analyzed both in the context of spot instances within a cloud region or between dispersed cloud regions [15, 21, 90]. Most papers have used analytical modeling as the methodology with Game Theory or the Queueing Theory forming the theoretical framework. Cheng et al., 2016 [15] examined the relationships among the spot prices of identical computing resources and demonstrated that their prices differ based on the region in which these resources are located. Singh et al., 2022 [90], examined the spot price dynamics of computing resources in markets within a region but across different zones (sub-geographies within a region). Further, Mukherjee et al., 2021 [69] proposed a new framework for spot price auctions wherein customers bid for future periods but considering the relationships among the prices of other spot instances. Papers have studied spot price dynamics from both the provider's perspective (e.g., Field [52, 54, 56] as well as the consumers' perspective [90]. Hosseini et al., 2020 [29] studied the problem of optimizing compute resources to minimize rental costs by switching between cheaper and more expensive compute clusters based on price-performance schedules. They assert that in the face of confusing and diverse sets of computing resources with varying configurations, switching between compute configurations can optimize costs. On the cost sub-theme, studies support the argument that cloud computing has lowered startup costs; however, long-term costs, as well as transparency in the costing structure, do remain a concern.

Pricing from a SaaS perspective suggests that SaaS providers gain from economies of scale that they may pass off in pricing in a competitive market [59]. But the SaaS model, on account of multi-tenancy, also faces the lack-of-fit costs that users in enterprises that use SaaS may suffer from. Research has concentrated on pricing models in SaaS using econometric studies (e.g., [56, 59]. Cloud supply chains have been analyzed [19].

Legal. From a legal issue sub-theme perspective, legal matters concerning cloud computing have been researched, also focusing on the risks associated with cloud computing and strategies for risk management. Research has focused on legislation to establish appropriate legal frameworks that facilitate the adoption and development of cloud computing [28, 36]. The absence of universal laws is seen as impeding cloud computing adoption in cross-geography scenarios. Cloud providers must adhere to country and industry-specific regulations for which they seek certifications. Studies have sought to understand and "unblackbox" the cloud provider's certification status [50, 51]. These certifications seek to influence decision-making when it comes to cloud sourcing, serving as assurances for future service quality, security, privacy, availability, contract friendliness, and legal compliance. Continuous Service Certification (CSC) that involves the collection and evaluation of certification-related data regarding cloud service operations to verify ongoing compliance with certification criteria has also been proposed [57].

Ethics and Trust. Ethics and Trust are also important considerations evaluated in the literature. The ethical issues sub-theme analyses the cloud computing phenomena from an ethical standpoint, whereas the trust sub-theme examines approaches cloud providers use to gain trust from prospective users. Trust plays a pivotal role in fostering successful business relationships and acts as a crucial factor in determining the adoption of technology. Qualitative studies have extended conceptual models of trust in IT outsourcing providers and IT artifacts to explore unique characteristics of trust within cloud computing environments [52]. Business enterprises adopt cloud integration services to improve collaboration with their trading partners and to deliver quality data mining services. Data-as-a-Service (DaaS) mashup allows multiple enterprises to integrate their data. Business enterprises face challenges not only to protect private data over the cloud but also to legally adhere to privacy compliance rules when trading person-specific data. Studies have researched privacy-preserving business models that allow the collaboration of multiple organizations for data integration [44]. The equitable distribution of social and economic advantages within the cloud ecosystem hinges on the pricing strategies and resource allocation choices made by cloud providers. These decisions directly affect cloud users in terms of resource allocation fairness and have broader implications for social well-being. To fully leverage the potential of cloud computing and to set regulatory standards, frameworks have been developed to quantify the impact of resource allocation and pricing decisions [35]. These frameworks aim to establish a balance between fairness and revenue maximization. However, additional research to seek insights into regulatory policies for cloud neutrality, privacy, and ethical perspective, needs to be done.

Privacy. The privacy sub-theme explores privacy issues from an ethical or legal viewpoint. Within the realm of privacy, Identity and Access Management (IAM) has been a topic of discussion. The improper management of identities can pose security risks to organizations, especially in the context of multi-cloud hybrid workloads and cloud-based IoT solutions. Researchers have examined iDaaS (Identity-as-a-Service), a cloud-based security service that enables companies to delegate the management of employee access to organizational resources, including IAM functions. Privacy considerations also assist in decision-making regarding the placement of workloads on the cloud or on-premises [1].

6.2 Findings from the Technological Issues Category Studies

In this section, we shift the focus to technological issues in cloud computing, delving into six sub-themes: cloud computing performance, security, data management, software development, data center management, and cloud service management. Cloud computing performance studies aim to create scalable infrastructure, optimize workflows, and enhance interoperability. Despite the benefits, effectively addressing customer needs and constraints poses a challenge. Security is a critical concern in cloud adoption, with papers analyzing safeguards and highlighting the shift from IT-as-a-product to IT-as-a-service. The abstraction in cloud computing creates transparency issues and a diminished sense of control, but studies suggest that cloud workloads can reduce information security risks compared to legacy systems. Data management explores large-scale distributed data processing, servitization of products, and knowledge discovery techniques. Software development sub-theme focuses on cloud-native applications, PaaS platforms, and modular applications like microservices, emphasizing the need for further research in adoption and post-adoption scenarios. Data center management emphasizes energy efficiency, power conservation, and environmental considerations. Cloud providers' adoption of green IT is discussed, and research explores cloud computing's impact on users' energy efficiency. Cloud service management covers administration, SLAs, and service models, with a focus on trade-offs in establishing SLAs and the promises of cloud services.

Cloud Computing Performance. Cloud computing performance studies aim at developing cloud-based infrastructure that can scale with users and the complexity and variety of cloud workloads. They focus on conducting comparative studies to quantify performance variations among different clouds [31], improving workflow scheduling and load balancing, optimizing dynamic resources, and enhancing interoperability across various cloud systems. Cloud computing benefits are highly appealing as they provide flexibility guarantees for addressing customer service constraints like downtime and cost, which are negotiated through Quality of Service (QoS) guarantees by cloud providers. Nevertheless, effectively catering to customer needs and specific constraints when delivering cloud services remains a challenge. Factors such as reliability, capacity-oriented availability, and costs play a significant role in the negotiation of these services [17, 22, 111]. Hybrid cloud infrastructures necessitate integrating on-premises software and cloud-based software services. Integration is enabled through two different types of integration methods using an enterprise service bus (ESB) or using an integration platform as a service (iPaaS) like MuleSoft. Studies have compared the above integration mechanisms and when they should be used [112].

Security. Cloud security is a widely researched theme as security remains a critical concern with adopters. The cloud providers must ensure that the service applications, cloud software, and the physical location of the cloud are secure. The business data is stored locally in the cloud. Papers have analyzed security in the cloud and suggested safeguards [7, 25, 53, 58, 76, 107]. The associated shift from IT-as-a-product to IT-as-a-service places enterprise cloud clients in constant dependency on the cloud service provider. Clients entrust their confidential data, as well as the oversight of critical IT infrastructure and applications, to the Internet [5, 73]. The abstraction introduced by cloud computing has resulted in a perceived lack of transparency [100] and a diminished sense of control. When software vendors offer SaaS versions as well the on-premises versions of the software, there are different risk implications. The on-premises version invites undirected (nontargeted) attacks while the SaaS version invites directed (targeted) attacks. In a directed attack the malicious actor incurs expenditure to compromise a specific target, a fixed version of a SaaS product can be that specific target, and by compromising the SaaS version, the malicious actor can impact many customers. However, studies have also demonstrated that cloud workloads can reduce information security risks as opposed to being on on-premises legacy IT systems that do not address contemporary cybersecurity threats adequately [74]. More studies need to happen in the context of security with cloud computing, specifically in the hybrid multi-cloud deployment context, also themes like cloud outsourcing and commensurate security risks should be further studied. In many contexts, hybrid cloud or cloud-assisted IOT environments [107] may be more secure than on-premises IT ecosystems running legacy systems and more studies should analyze those situations.

Data Management. The data management sub-theme addresses specific issues related to large-scale distributed data processing in the cloud and includes data consistency, data mining and algorithms, integrations of distributed datasets, and parallel database management systems. Cloud becomes an enabler for servitization of products. Decision Support Systems can be provided as services by hosting them on the cloud, and the cloud becomes an enabler of scale, scope, and cost economies [2, 20]. Knowledge discovery techniques can help make better decisions, but they are currently out of reach of most users and need high amounts of expertise. A SaaS-based datamining service can solve problems for cost savings and enable faster access to business intelligence systems [113]. Data placement strategies in Industry 4.0, IOT, and edge cloud computing environments with heterogeneous data distribution, have also been studied [24].

Software Development. The software development sub-theme represents a stream of software-developer-oriented literature and includes articles related to developing cloud native applications, analysis of cloud-based programming frameworks, developing software with the PaaS platforms as also development of modular, component-based applications such as microservices-based distributed applications in the cloud. PaaS platforms enable organizations to build innovative custom applications or data, AI, and ML pipelines without managing the platform itself. PaaS varies from IaaS and SaaS because it splits the infrastructure layers in a different manner providing the complete stack all the way to the runtime, to the users. The client organization using the PaaS platform typically provides the application layer as well as the database schemas and objects that run on the database chosen in the PaaS configuration. PaaS capabilities have been shown to have empowered self-organizing development teams and ongoing feedback loops, during development, thereby accelerating. Software development and agility [47]. The evolution of requirements and mechanisms for requirement management have been studied, including in the context of cloud-based enterprise systems, in medium-sized organizations [86]. There are very few studies detailing the adoption of PaaS platforms, other cloud-based development platforms, architectural tenets of cloud-native applications, and post-adoption scenarios for PaaS. This area is a key issue that needs further research.

Data Center Management. The Data Center management sub-theme focuses on the essential component that underpins cloud computing and the data center and emphasizes aspects like energy efficiency, power conservation, and environmental considerations in the design of data centers. Growth in internet and cloud use is causing the growth of data centers. As cloud computing reshapes the energy consumption landscape between service providers and users, comprehending the environmental effects of cloud computing necessitates investigations on both the user and vendor aspects. Green computing aims to minimize the environmental impact of firms and enhance their sustainability through the utilization of IT and IS. Green computing comprises two distinct aspects: Green IS, which pertains to the creation and application of information systems that facilitate sustainable business practices, and Green IT, which is focused on optimizing energy consumption and equipment efficiency. Cloud providers are largely adopting green IT. Google is carbon-neutral in its operations and has a goal to have all its data centers carbon-free by 2030. Microsoft plans to be carbon-negative, water-positive, and zero waste by 2030. Cloud computing can be utilized to enhance both components of green. Factors that encourage cloud-based green IT use also benefits from cloud-based green IS use have been studied [48, 87]. Research has explored cloud computing's influence on users' energy efficiency and has revealed that cloud-based IT services enhance users' energy efficiency, with the impact growing more pronounced after 2010 [75]. The energy efficiency outcomes were found to be heterogenous, with the software-as-a-service (SaaS) model showing the most significant association with improvements in both electric and non-electric energy efficiency, while infrastructure-as-a-service (IaaS) was positively linked primarily to electric energy efficiency, particularly in industries with high IT hardware usage.

Cloud Service Management. Cloud service management discusses the administration of cloud services, including service lifecycle management, publishing, discovering, and selecting cloud-based services. Cloud vendors provide cloud computing services and consequently, papers have analyzed service quality [11], Service Level Agreements (SLAs), contract design, and consequent impacts on adoption. Service management has been researched in the context of service models with the SaaS service model receiving the bulk of research attention. Cloud service providers face intricate trade-offs when establishing SLAs for their services [110]. These trade-offs involve variables such as price, penalty, and the guarantee of service availability (uptime), with resource management strategies playing a crucial role in meeting the SLA requirements. Approaches for specific aspects of cloud provider management have been analyzed [6, 26, 63]. Digging deeper into the promises of cloud computing, Winkler et al., 2014 [103], analyzed the mantras of cloud services (i.e., financial benefits, technological implications, and organizational implications) and described the trade-off for cloud clients. From an in-depth analysis of a single case, they derived nine lessons learned to achieve cloud payoffs. Including multi-sourcing strategies, and involvement of internal IT staff. They also advocate an in-depth analysis of providers as well as contract negotiation.

6.3 Findings from the Conceptualization Category Studies

Cloud computing conceptualization articles have been categorized as foundational or predictive. Foundational articles explore the foundations of cloud computing and its building blocks. The most cited conceptual cloud papers belong to the foundational category (e.g. [6, 63, 100, 108]). Understanding the foundations of cloud computing is critical for its continued adoption and assimilation. There are very few papers in the predictive sub-theme that help us understand the future breakthroughs in cloud computing [32, 63] while some have sought to predict a firm's performance and market reactions from signals of investments in cloud computing [92].

6.4 Findings from the Domain Category Studies

The domain theme concerns itself with the domains in which cloud computing has been applied. The application of cloud computing has been researched across areas such as education [89], edge computing and IoT applications [42, 102], smart toy manufacturer [55]. Through a longitudinal study, a business model for a cloud-based game provider was researched [71]. This research acknowledges the positive transformation cloud computing has brought in these domains and advocates for more cloud-based applications in these areas.

7 Conclusion

This study examines cloud computing literature through a meta-analysis of 152 research articles from 18 information systems-related journals, to take stock of the most recent trends of cloud computing research from the period 2010 to 2023. The findings point out that as cloud computing use in enterprises becomes well established, business issues themes have become the most researched themes. From an earlier stress on cloud adoption studies, the research increasingly focuses on post-adoption concerns around the continuance of services, outcomes, and path to value creation with cloud computing. We call for more research in the areas of security, ethics, legal, and privacy, particularly cross-geography, and cross-industry regulation compliance. We also reiterate our call for more cloud computing related research in GREAT domains such as India.

Research in the realm of cloud computing predominantly focuses on the SaaS service model, while IaaS and PaaS have received comparatively less attention. While pricing strategies for cloud services, particularly in the areas of compute and storage, have garnered significant interest, there is a need for further investigation into the long-term cost implications of adopting cloud computing for enterprise use. Early adopters of cloud computing may not have realized large cost savings in the cloud, and the repatriation of IT workloads from cloud to on-premises is a growing trend. This area needs additional research. On the pricing front, articles have used analytical modeling. These studies need to be validated with quantitative, empirical studies. Few papers have stressed software management and the use of the cloud by the developer community. More research needs to be adopted for studying cloud-native development, microservices-based distributed hybrid applications, and their managerial implications. Patterns of cloud services used by industries have led to the growth of industry cloud, as cloud-based building blocks that help with industry-specific digital solutions. There is a need for research on industry clouds.

This study offers several contributions. To begin with, it presents a comprehensive overview of cloud computing research conducted from January 2010 to June 2023. While this review is not exhaustive, it offers valuable insights into the current landscape of research in this field. Furthermore, only a limited number of literature reviews have scrutinized cloud computing articles published between 2016 and 2023. Our study specifically concentrates on this timeframe. Through this literature review, we identify areas that still lack substantial research attention and highlight themes, methodologies, and theoretical frameworks that warrant further exploration in the domain of cloud computing research. Our meta-analysis can serve as a valuable and high-quality reference source for both academics and practitioners interested in the field of cloud computing.

References

1. Abdalla Mikhaeil, C., James, T.L.: Examining the case of French hesitancy toward IDaaS solutions: technical and social contextual factors of the organizational IDaaS privacy calculus. Inform. Manage. **60**(4), 103779 (2023)
2. Allen, B., et al.: Software as a service for data scientists. Commun. ACM **55**(2), 81–88 (2012)
3. Andrade-Rojas, M.G., Kathuria, A., Lee, H.-H.: Multilevel synergy of IT operational integration: competition networks and operating performance. Prod. Oper. Manage. (forthcoming) (2024)
4. Andrade-Rojas, M.G., Saldanha, T., Kathuria, A., Khuntia, J., Boh, W.F.: How IT overcomes deficiencies for innovation in SMEs: closed innovation versus open innovation. Inform. Syst. Res. (forthcoming) (2024)
5. Anthes, G.: Security in the cloud. Commun. ACM **53**, 16–18 (2010)
6. Armbrust, M., et al.: A view of cloud computing. Commun. ACM **53**, 50–58 (2010)
7. August, T., Niculescu, M.F., Shin, H.: Cloud implications on software network structure and security risks. Inform. Syst. Res. **25**, 489–510 (2014)
8. Bandara, W., Furtmueller, E., Gorbacheva, E., Miskon, S., Beekhuyzen, J.: Achieving rigor in literature reviews: insights from qualitative data analysis and tool-support. Commun. Assoc. Inform. Syst. **37**(8), 154–204 (2015). http://aisel.aisnet.org/cais/vol37/iss1/8
9. Benlian, A.: Is traditional, open-source, or on-demand first choice? Developing an AHP-based framework for the comparison of different software models in office suites selection. Eur. J. Inform. Syst. **20**, 542–559 (2011)

10. Benlian, A., Kettinger, W.J., Sunyaev, A., Winkler, T.J.: Special section: the transformative value of cloud computing: a decoupling, platformization, and recombination theoretical framework. J. Manage. Inform. Syst. **35**, 719–739 (2018)
11. Benlian, A., Koufaris, M., Hess, T.: The role of SaaS service quality for continued SaaS use: Empirical insights from SaaS using firms (2010)
12. Bhattacherjee, A., Park, S.C.: Why end-users move to the cloud: a migration-theoretic analysis. Eur. J. Inform. Syst. 23, 357–372 (2014)
13. Chaturvedi, D., Kathuria, A., Andrade, M., Saldanha, T.: Navigating the Paradox of IT Novelty and Strategic Conformity: The Moderating Role of Industry Dynamism (2023)
14. Chen, F., Lu, A., Wu, H., Li, M.: Compensation and pricing strategies in cloud service SLAs: considering participants' risk attitudes and consumer quality perception. Electron. Commerce Res. Appl. **56**, 101215 (2022)
15. Cheng, H.K., Li, Z., Naranjo, A.: Research note—cloud computing spot pricing dynamics: latency and limits to arbitrage. Inform. Syst. Res. **27**, 145–165 (2016)
16. Choudhary, V., Vithayathil, J.: The impact of cloud computing: should the IT department be organized as a cost center or a profit center? J. Manage. Inform. Syst. **30**, 67–100 (2013)
17. Choudhary, V., Zhang, Z.: Research note—patching the cloud: the impact of SaaS on patching strategy and the timing of software release. Inform. Syst. Res. **26**, 845–858 (2015)
18. Dasgupta, A., Karhade, P., Kathuria, A., Konsynski, B.: Holding space for voices that do not speak: design reform of rating systems for platforms in GREAT economies (2021)
19. Demirkan, H., Cheng, H.K., Bandyopadhyay, S.: Coordination strategies in an SaaS supply chain. J. Manage. Inform. Syst. **26**, 119–143 (2010)
20. Demirkan, H., Delen, D.: Leveraging the capabilities of service-oriented decision support systems: putting analytics and big data in cloud. Decis. Support Syst. **55**, 412–421 (2013)
21. Dierks, L., Seuken, S.: Cloud pricing: the spot market strikes back. Manage. Sci. **68**(1), 105–122 (2022)
22. Ding, S., Xia, C., Wang, C., Desheng, Wu., Zhang, Y.: Multi-objective optimization based ranking prediction for cloud service recommendation. Decis. Support. Syst. **101**, 106–114 (2017)
23. Dong, L., Shu, W., Sun, D., Li, X., Zhang, L.: Pre-alarm system based on real-time monitoring and numerical simulation using internet of things and cloud computing for tailings dam in mines. IEEE Access **5**, 21080–21089 (2017)
24. Xin, Du., Tang, S., Zhihui, Lu., Gai, K., Jie, Wu., Hung, P.C.K.: Scientific workflows in IoT environments: a data placement strategy based on heterogeneous edge-cloud computing. ACM Trans. Manage. Inform. Syst. **13**(4), 1–26 (2022)
25. Ermakova, T., Fabian, B., Kornacka, M., Thiebes, S., Sunyaev, A.: Security and privacy requirements for cloud computing in healthcare: elicitation and prioritization from a patient perspective. ACM Trans. Manage. Inform. Syst. **11**(2), 1–29 (2020)
26. Garrison, G., Kim, S., Wakefield, R.L.: Success factors for deploying cloud computing. Commun. ACM **55**(9), 62–68 (2012)
27. Giessmann, A., Legner, C.: Designing business models for cloud platforms. Inf. Syst. J. **26**(5), 551–579 (2016). https://doi.org/10.1111/isj.12107
28. Gray, A.: Conflict of laws and the cloud. Comput. Law Secur. Rev. **29**(1), 58–65 (2013)
29. Hosseini, L., Tang, S., Mookerjee, V., Sriskandarajah, C.: A switch in time saves the dime: a model to reduce rental cost in cloud computing. Inform. Syst. Res. **31**(3), 753–775 (2020)
30. Huang, K.-W., Sundararajan, A.: Pricing digital goods: discontinuous costs and shared infrastructure. Inf. Syst. Res. **22**(4), 721–738 (2011)
31. Iosup, A., Ostermann, S., Yigitbasi, M.N., Prodan, R., Fahringer, T., Epema, D.H.J.: Performance analysis of cloud computing services for many-tasks scientific computing. IEEE Trans. Parallel Distrib. Syst. **22**, 931–945 (2011)

32. Iyer, B., Henderson, J.C.: Preparing for the future: understanding the seven capabilities cloud computing. MIS Q. Exec. **9**, 2 (2010)
33. Jha, S. and Kathuria, A. Size Matters for Cloud Capability and Performance (2022)
34. Jha, S., Kathuria, A.: How firm age and size influence value creation from cloud computing (2023)
35. Joe-Wong, C., Sen, S.: Harnessing the power of the cloud: revenue, fairness, and cloud neutrality. J. Manage. Inf. Syst. **35**, 813–836 (2018)
36. Joint, A., Baker, E.: Knowing the past to understand the present–issues in the contracting for cloud based services. Comput. Law Secur. Rev. **27**(4), 407–415 (2011)
37. Karhade, P., Kathuria, A.: Missing impact of ratings on platform participation in India: a call for research in GREAT domains. Commun. Assoc. Inf. Syst. **47**(1), 19 (2020)
38. Karhade, P., Kathuria, A., Dasgupta, A., Malik, O., Konsynski, B.R.: Decolonization of digital platforms: a research agenda for GREAT domains. In: Garimella, A., Karhade, P., Kathuria, A., Liu, X., Xu, J., Zhao, K. (eds.) The Role of e-Business during the Time of Grand Challenges. LNBIP, vol. 418, pp. 51–58. Springer, Cham (2021). https://doi.org/10.1007/978-3-030-79454-5_5
39. Karhade, P., Kathuria, A., Konsynski, B.: When choice matters: assortment and participation for performance on digital platforms (2021)
40. Kathuria, A., Karhade, P.P., Konsynski, B.R.: In the realm of hungry ghosts: multi-level theory for supplier participation on digital platforms. J. Manag. Inf. Syst. **37**(2), 396–430 (2020)
41. Kathuria, A., Mann, A., Khuntia, J., Saldanha, T.J.V., Kauffman, R.J.: A strategic value appropriation path for cloud computing. J. Manage. Inf. Syst. **35**(3), 740–775 (2018). https://doi.org/10.1080/07421222.2018.1481635
42. Kaur, J., Kaur, P.D.: CE-GMS: A cloud IoT-enabled grocery management system. Electron. Commer. Res. Appl. **28**, 63–72 (2018)
43. Kepes, B.: 30% of servers are sitting "Comatose" according to research. Forbes https://forbes.com/sites/benkepes/2015/06/03/30-of-servers-are-sitting-comatose-according-to-research (2015)
44. Khokhar, R.H., Fung, B.C.M., Iqbal, F., Alhadidi, D., Bentahar, J.: Privacy-preserving data mashup model for trading person-specific information. Electron. Commer. Res. Appl. **17**, 19–37 (2016)
45. Khuntia, J., Kathuria, A., Andrade-Rojas, M.G., Saldanha, T., Celly, N.: How foreign and domestic firms differ in leveraging IT-enabled supply chain information integration in BOP markets: the role of supplier and client business collaboration. J. Assoc. Inf. Syst. **22**(3), 6 (2021)
46. King, W.R., He, J.: Understanding the role and methods of meta-analysis in IS Research. Commun. Assoc. Inf. Syst. 16, 665–686 (2005)
47. Krancher, O., Luther, P., Jost, M.: Key affordances of Platform-as-a-Service: self-organization and continuous feedback. J. Manage. Inf. Syst. **35**, 776–812 (2018)
48. Kumar, C., Marston, S., Sen, R., Narisetty, A.: Greening the cloud: a load balancing mechanism to optimize cloud computing networks. J. Manage. Inf. Syst. **39**,, 513–541 (2022)
49. Kung, L., Cegielski, C.G., Kung, H.-J.: An integrated environmental perspective on software as a service adoption in manufacturing and retail firms. J. Inf. Technol. **30**, 352–363 (2015)
50. Lansing, J., Benlian, A., Sunyaev, A.: Unblackboxing" decision makers' interpretations of IS certifications in the context of cloud service certifications. J. Assoc. Inf. Syst. **19**(11), 1064–1096 (2018)
51. Lansing, J., Siegfried, N., Sunyaev, A., Benlian, A.: Strategic signaling through cloud service certifications: Comparing the relative importance of certifications' assurances to companies and consumers. J. Strateg. Inf. Syst. **28**, 101579 (2019)

52. Lansing, J., Sunyaev, A.: Trust in cloud computing. ACM SIGMIS Database DATABASE Adv. Inform. Syst. **47**, 58–96 (2016)
53. Lee, J., Cho, D., Lim, G.: Design and validation of the bright internet. J. Assoc. Inform. Syst. **19**, 63–85 (2018)
54. Lee, M.H., Han, S.P., Park, S., Oh, W.: Positive demand spillover of popular app adoption: implications for platform owners' management of complements. Inf. Syst. Res. **34**(3), 961–995 (2023)
55. Li, S., Chen, W., Chen, Y., Chen, C. and Zheng, Z.: Makespan-minimized computation offloading for smart toys in edge-cloud computing. Electron. Commerce Res. Appl. **37**, 100884 (2019)
56. Li, S., Cheng, H.K., Duan, Y., Yang, Y.-C.: A study of enterprise software licensing models. J. Manag. Inf. Syst. **34**(1), 177–205 (2017)
57. Lins, S., Schneider, S., Szefer, J., Ibraheem, S., Ali, A.: Designing monitoring systems for continuous certification of cloud services: deriving meta-requirements and design guidelines. Commun. Assoc. Inf. Syst. **44**(1), 460–510 (2019)
58. Liu, Y., Sheng, X., Marston, S.R.: The impact of client-side security restrictions on the competition of cloud computing services. Int. J. Electron. Comm. **19**(3), 90–117 (2015)
59. Ma, D., Seidmann, A.: Analyzing software as a service with per-transaction charges. Inf. Syst. Res. **26**, 360–378 (2015)
60. Malik, O., Jaiswal, A., Kathuria, A., Karhade, P.: Leveraging BI systems to overcome infobesity: a comparative analysis of incumbent and new entrant firms (2022)
61. Mani, D., Srikanth, K., Bharadwaj, A.: Efficacy of R&D work in offshore captive centers: an empirical study of task characteristics, coordination mechanisms, and performance. Inf. Syst. Res. **25**(4), 846–864 (2014)
62. Mann, A., Kathuria, A., Khuntia, J., Saldanha, T.: Cloud-integration and business flexibility: the mediating role of cloud functional capabilities (2016)
63. Marston, S., Li, Z., Bandyopadhyay, S., Zhang, J., Ghalsasi, A.: Cloud computing — the business perspective. Decis. Support. Syst. **51**(1), 176–189 (2011)
64. Mell, P.M., Grance, T.: The NIST definition of cloud computing. National Institute of Standards and Technology (2011)
65. Metz, C.: The epic story of dropboxs exodus from the amazon cloud empire (2016)
66. Mithas, R., Sambamurthy,: How information management capability influences firm performance. MIS Q. **35**(1), 237 (2011)
67. Mithas, T., Bardhan, G.: Information technology and firm profitability: mechanisms and empirical evidence. MIS Q. **36**(1), 205 (2012)
68. Muhic, M., Bengtsson, L., Holmström, J.: Barriers to continuance use of cloud computing: evidence from two case studies. Inf. Manage. **60**, 103792 (2023)
69. Mukherjee, A., Sundarraj, R.P., Dutta, K.: Time-preference-based on-spot bundled cloud-service provisioning. Decis. Support. Syst. **151**, 113607 (2021)
70. Müller, S.D., Holm, S.R., Søndergaard, J.: Benefits of cloud computing: literature review in a maturity model perspective. Commun. Assoc. Inform. Syst. **37**, 851–878 (2015)
71. Ojala, A.: Business models and opportunity creation: how IT entrepreneurs create and develop business models under uncertainty. Inf. Syst. J. **26**, 451–476 (2015)
72. Oliveira, T., Thomas, M., Espadanal, M.: Assessing the determinants of cloud computing adoption: An analysis of the manufacturing and services sectors. Inf. Manage. **51**, 497–510 (2014)
73. Owens, D. Securing elasticity in the cloud. *Communications of the ACM*, 53, 6 (2010/06 2010), 46–51 (2010)
74. Pang, M.-S., Tanriverdi, H.: Strategic roles of IT modernization and cloud migration in reducing cybersecurity risks of organizations: the case of U.S. federal government. J. Strat. Inf. Syst. **31**, 101707 (2022)

75. Park, J., Han, K., Lee, B.: Green cloud? An empirical analysis of cloud computing and energy efficiency. Manage. Sci. **69**, 1639–1664 (2023)

76. Parno, B., Howell, J., Gentry, C., Raykova, M.: Pinocchio. Commun. ACM **59**, 103–112 (2016)

77. Pye, J., Rai, A., Dong, J.Q.: Business value of information technology capabilities: an institutional governance perspective. Inf. Syst. Res. **35**, 28–44 (2023)

78. Ramakrishnan, T., Kathuria, A., Khuntia, J., Konsynski, B.: IoT value creation through supply chain analytics capability (2022)

79. Retana, G., Forman, C., Narasimhan, S., Niculescu, M.F., Wu, D.J.: Technical support, knowledge transfer, and service demand: evidence from the cloud. SSRN Electron. J. (2012)

80. Rodrigues, J., Ruivo, P., Oliveira, T.: Mediation role of business value and strategy in firm performance of organizations using software-as-a-service enterprise applications. Inf. Manag. **58**(1), 103289 (2021)

81. Saldanha, T.J., Andrade-Rojas, M.G., Kathuria, A., Khuntia, J., Krishnan, M.: How the locus of uncertainty shapes the influence of CEO long-term compensation on IT capital investments. MIS Q. (2023)

82. Sambhara, C., Rai, A., Xu, S.X.: Configuring the enterprise systems portfolio: the role of information risk. Inf. Syst. Res. **33**(2), 446–463 (2022)

83. Sarker, S., Chatterjee, S., Xiao, X., Elbanna, A.: The sociotechnical axis of cohesion for the IS discipline: its historical legacy and its continued relevance. MIS Q. **43**(3), 695–720 (2019)

84. Schlagwein, D., Thorogood, A., Willcocks, L.P.: How commonwealth bank of Australia gained benefits using a standards-based, multi-provider cloud model. MIS Q. Exec. **13**(4), 209–222 (2014)

85. Schneider, S., Sunyaev, A.: Determinant factors of cloud-sourcing decisions: reflecting on the IT outsourcing literature in the era of cloud computing. J. Inf. Technol. **31**(1), 1–31 (2016). https://doi.org/10.1057/jit.2014.25

86. Schneider, S., Wollersheim, J., Krcmar, H., Sunyaev, A.: How do Requirements evolve over Time? A case study investigating the role of context and experiences in the evolution of enterprise software requirements. J. Inf. Technol. **33**(2), 151–170 (2018)

87. Schniederjans, D.G., Hales, D.N.: Cloud computing and its impact on economic and environmental performance: a transaction cost economics perspective. Decis. Support. Syst. **86**, 73–82 (2016)

88. Schreieck, M., Wiesche, M., Krcmar, H.: Capabilities for value co-creation and value capture in emergent platform ecosystems: a longitudinal case study of SAP's cloud platform. J. Inf. Technol. **36**(4), 365–390 (2021)

89. Shiau, W.-L., Chau, P.Y.K.: Understanding behavioral intention to use a cloud computing classroom: a multiple model comparison approach. Inf. Manag. **53**(3), 355–365 (2016)

90. Singh, V.K., Shivendu, S., Dutta, K.: Spot instance similarity and substitution effect in cloud spot market. Decis. Support. Syst. **159**, 113815 (2022)

91. Soh, F., Setia, P.: The impact of dominant IT infrastructure in multi-establishment firms: the moderating role of environmental dynamism. J. Assoc. Inf. Syst. **23**(6), 1603–1633 (2022)

92. Son, I., Lee, D., Lee, J.-N., Chang, Y.B.: Market perception on cloud computing initiatives in organizations: an extended resource-based view. Inf. Manag. **51**(6), 653–669 (2014)

93. Srinivasan, S.: Is security realistic in cloud computing? J. Int. Technol. Inf. Manag. **22**(4), 3 (2013). https://doi.org/10.58729/1941-6679.1020

94. Sun, T., Shi, L., Viswanathan, S., Zheleva, E.: Motivating effective mobile app adoptions: evidence from a large-scale randomized field experiment. Inf. Syst. Res. **30**(2), 523–539 (2019)

95. Templier, M., Paré, G.: Transparency in literature reviews: an assessment of reporting prac-
    tices across review types and genres in top IS journals. Eur. J. Inf. Syst. **27**(5), 503–550
    (2017). https://doi.org/10.1080/0960085X.2017.1398880
96. Trenz, M., Huntgeburth, J., Veit, D.: Uncertainty in cloud service relationships: uncovering
    the differential effect of three social influence processes on potential and current users. Inf.
    Manage. 55, 971–983 (2018)
97. van de Weerd, I., Mangula, I.S., Brinkkemper, S.: Adoption of software as a service in
    Indonesia: examining the influence of organizational factors. Inf. Manage. **53**(7), 915–928
    (2016)
98. Venkatesh, V., Bala, H., Sambamurthy, V.: Implementation of an information and commu-
    nication technology in a developing country: a multimethod longitudinal study in a Bank in
    India. Inf. Syst. Res. **27**(3), 558–579 (2016)
99. Venkatesh, V., Sykes, T.A.: Digital divide initiative success in developing countries: a
    longitudinal field study in a Village in India. Inf. Syst. Res. **24**(2), 239–260 (2013)
100. Venters, W., Whitley, E.A.: A critical review of cloud computing: researching desires and
    realities. J. Inf. Technol. **27**(3), 179–197 (2012)
101. Wang, N., Huigang Liang, Yu., Jia, S.G., Xue, Y., Wang, Z.: Cloud computing research in
    the IS discipline: a citation/co-citation analysis. Decis. Support. Syst. 86, 35–47 (2016)
102. Wang, X., Wang, X.: Multimedia data delivery based on IoT clouds. Commun. ACM **64**(8),
    80–86 (2021)
103. Winkler, T.J., Benlian, A., Piper, M., Hirsch, H.: Bayer healthcare delivers a dose of reality
    for cloud payoff mantras in multinationals. MIS Q. Exec. 13, 4 (2014)
104. Winkler, T.J., Brown, C.V.: Horizontal allocation of decision rights for on-premise
    applications and Software-as-a-Service. J. Manage. Inf. Syst. **30**(3), 13–48 (2013)
105. Wright, R.T., Roberts, N., Wilson, D.: The role of context in IT assimilation: a multi-method
    study of a SaaS platform in the US nonprofit sector. Eur. J. Inf. Syst. **26**(5), 509–539 (2017).
    https://doi.org/10.1057/s41303-017-0053-2
106. Wulf, F., Lindner, T., Strahringer, S., Westner, M.: IaaS, PaaS, or SaaS? The why of cloud
    computing delivery model selection: vignettes on the post-adoption of cloud computing. In:
    The Proceedings of Proceedings of the 54th Hawaii International Conference on System
    Sciences, pp. 6285–6294 (2021)
107. Xiong, Hu., Wang, Yi., Li, W., Chen, C.-M.: Flexible, efficient, and secure access delegation
    in cloud computing. ACM Trans. Manage. Inf. Syst. **10**(1), 1–20 (2019)
108. Yang, H., Tate, M.: A descriptive literature review and classification of cloud computing
    research. Commun. Assoc. Inf. Syst. **31**(1), 2 (2012)
109. Yaraghi, N., Du, A.Y., Sharman, R., Gopal, R.D., Ramesh, R.: Health Information exchange
    as a multisided platform: adoption, usage, and practice involvement in service co-production.
    Inf. Syst. Res. **26**(1), 1–18 (2015)
110. Yuan, S., Sanjukta Das, R., Ramesh, C.Q.: Service agreement trifecta: backup resources,
    price and penalty in the availability-aware cloud. Inf. Syst. Res. **29**(4), 947–964 (2018)
111. Zhang, G., Ravishankar, M.N.: Exploring vendor capabilities in the cloud environment: a
    case study of Alibaba cloud computing. Inf. Manage. 56, 343–355 (2019)
112. Zhang, X., Yue, W.: Integration of on-premises and cloud-based software: the product
    bundling perspective. J. Assoc. Inform. Syst. 21, 1507–1551 (2020)
113. Zorrilla, M., García-Saiz, D.: A service oriented architecture to provide data mining services
    for non-expert data miners. Decis. Support. Syst.. Support. Syst. **55**(1), 399–411 (2013).
    https://doi.org/10.1016/j.dss.2012.05.045

Digital Assets and Decentralized Finance – Emerging Research Opportunities for Information Systems

Himanshu Warudkar(✉)

Indian School of Business, Hyderabad, India
himanshu_warudkar2024@efpm.isb.edu

Abstract. This article explores the transformative impact of Decentralized Finance (DeFI) on the financial ecosystem and its implications for Information Systems. As global financial regulators adapt to the rise of DeFI, a decentralized blockchain network facilitates financial transactions through smart contracts, disrupting traditional intermediaries such as banks and exchanges. The decentralized nature of DeFI offers competitive, contestable, composable, and non-custodial financial ecosystems, presenting opportunities for efficiency and cost reduction. To architect DeFI solutions effectively, understanding the technology's layers and factors influencing adoption is crucial. The article introduces the Three-Layered DeFI Stack Reference (DSR) Model, emphasizing the Settlement Layer, DLT Application Layer, and DeFI Compositions. Architectural decisions involving permissioned or permissionless blockchains, database choices, trust considerations, and transaction interactions are explored. Considering the infancy of research on DeFI in Information Systems, the article proposes a research agenda. It categorizes potential research into the design and deployment of DeFI systems and the adoption and implications of these systems. The study also highlights the need for investigating the relationship between the extensiveness, evolvability, and enabling attributes of DeFI technology (3Es) and its real-world value, vision, and viability (3Vs). The research agenda aims to contribute to the understanding of DeFI's impact on information systems, offering exciting prospects for exploration in emerging and global markets.

Keywords: Decentralized Finance (DeFI) · Blockchain Technology · Information Systems · Digital Transformation · Financial Ecosystem

1 Introduction to Decentralized Finance (DeFI)

Financial regulators in leading economies of the world are creating frameworks for managing and using Decentralized Finance (DeFI)[1]. Decentralized finance (DeFI) is a system in which users conduct financial transactions through a decentralized blockchain

---

[1] For an overview of DeFI, see https://finreg.sg/answers/nature-of-decentralised-finance-DeFI-242/how-is-decentralised-finance-DeFI-regulated-in-singapore-610.

© The Author(s), under exclusive license to Springer Nature Switzerland AG 2024
A. Kathuria et al. (Eds.): WeB 2022, LNBIP 508, pp. 89–98, 2024.
https://doi.org/10.1007/978-3-031-60003-6_6

network directly using smart contracts, without using financial intermediaries, such as banks, brokerages, or centralized exchanges (e.g., stock exchanges[2], central depositories[3]). These smart contracts replicate and replace the roles played by intermediary financial institutions to offer services such as trading, borrowing, lending, or insuring. The decentralized nature of the transactions and the lack of regulated intermediaries can revolutionize, disrupt, and disintermediate traditional financial markets [2, 21, 25].

The financial system performs many crucial economic growth and stability functions, such as allocating resources to their most productive use, moving capital from agents (economies, corporations, individuals) with surpluses to those with DeFIcits, and providing efficient means for moving wealth across time and countries. These functions are usually carried out by intermediaries such as banks, brokers, and exchanges (e.g., stock exchanges, central depositories) connected by payment systems (e.g., Society for Worldwide Interbank Financial Telecommunication – SWIFT)[4]. These intermediaries serve as centralized nodes or connections that govern aspects such as who gets access to the financial system and provide customers with essential services such as record keeping, verification of transactions, settlement, liquidity, and security. This approach implies that intermediaries perform many of the core functions in the system and help implement regulatory goals such as tax reporting, anti-money-laundering laws or consumer financial protection. As a result, these intermediaries can hold significant power based on their preferential access to customers and data – often resulting in a monopoly or duopoly structure. If not properly harnessed and regulated, this centralized position can be a source of outsized economic rents and can lead to considerable inefficiencies. It can also lead to inherent fragility and systematic risk if core intermediaries become corrupted or investors lose trust in the system [21].

The invention of blockchain technology, also called distributed ledger, public database, Internet of value, digital infrastructure, network, and platform, led to early applications such as bitcoins. Blockchain-based smart contracts are expected to automate exchanges of information and ownership regardless of geographical location or institutional environment, thereby overcoming the centralized nature of financial services described earlier [7]. Smart contracts are programs stored on a blockchain that run when predetermined conditions are met. They are typically used to automate the execution of an agreement (contract) such that all participants can be immediately sure of the outcome without any intermediary's involvement or loss of time. Smart contracts can also automate a workflow, triggering the next action when conditions are met[5].

DeFI is emerging in the form of Blockchain-based applications, which will eliminate various transaction costs associated with paper-based administrative work, intermediating and monitoring, and dispute resolution. Other such applications include DAO (decentralized autonomous organization), dApp (decentralized application), NFT (non-fungible token), Web 3.0, and the Metaverse.

---

[2] See https://www.nseindia.com.
[3] See https://www.dtcc.com/.
[4] For more information, see https://www.swift.com/homepage.
[5] For more details, see https://ethereum.org/en/developers/docs/smart-contracts/.

2 Getting the Architecture Right for DLT-Based Digital Transformation

The vision of the TOGAF architecture framework from The Open Group[6] is *"Boundaryless Information Flow achieved through global interoperability in a secure, reliable, and timely manner describes seven levers of digital transformation"*. TOGAF describes seven levers of digital transformation based on the premise that digital transformation is fundamentally a strategy and an operating model change [18, 34]. Technological advancements such as Distributed Ledger Technology (DLT) are leveraged to improve human experiences and operational efficiencies and to evolve the products and services to which customers will remain loyal. It is the consequence of:

- The ability to handle information in the digital form.
- Using digital technologies to manage the process of creating, capturing, and analyzing information to deliver perceptive human-machine interaction experience (Fig. 1).

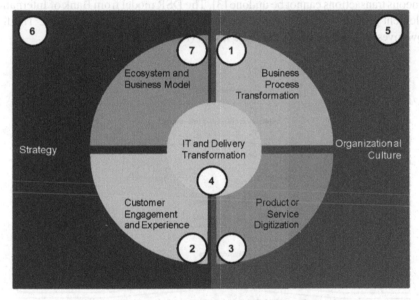

Fig. 1. Seven Layers of TOGAF Digital Transformation

The seven levers of TOGAF digital transformation are about framing a complete problem statement and comprehensively realizing outcomes. Strategy, Ecosystem and Business Model, and Customer Engagement and Experience frame the problem statement. Business Process Transformation, Product or Service Digitization, and Organizational Culture are operational steps to realize the strategy. IT and delivery transformation span both sides and help realize agility, efficiency, and decision-support goals. DeFI

---

[6] More information is available at https://www.opengroup.org/togaf.

enables the Business Model transformation and Product or Service Digitization through the disintermediation of intermediaries in financial services transactions.

To get the architecture of DeFI right, a deep understanding of DeFI needs to be built in both the practitioner and academic community, and various factors affecting the adoption and implementation of DeFI are required. To aid that, a Decentralized Stack Reference (DSR) model has been proposed by the Bank for International Settlement (BIS) [2].

Some of the advantages of DeFI are that it is a competitive, contestable, composable, and non-custodial financial ecosystem built on technology that does not require a central organization to operate. These same advantages mean that it has no safety net, and regulators are only now starting to understand the usage of this technology and associated issues [33]. The underlying ecosystem is competitive as novel intermediaries—miners or validators—compete to process and settle transactions. This also means that users can choose from different financial protocols; these are contestable as anyone can become an intermediary, deploy a protocol, or even start a new ledger. DeFI does not come with any safety net as it lacks protection from criminal conduct or investor fraud and erroneous transactions cannot be undone [3]. The DSR model from Bank of International Settlement provides a three-layered approach towards understanding DeFI. The figure below gives us a brief view of the three layers (Fig. 2):

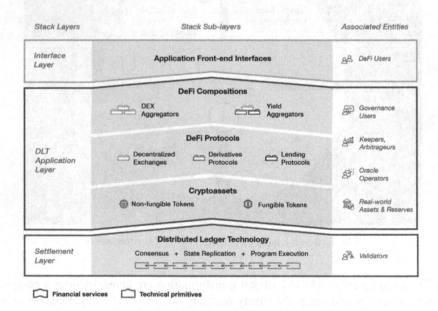

Fig. 2. Three Layered DeFI Stack Reference (DSR) Model (Adapted from [21]

Layer 1 - Settlement Layer: This layer is responsible for completing financial transactions and discharging the obligations of all involved parties. This involves the resolution of potential conflicts and finding consensus on the current state of a system [23]. In

DeFI, this functionality is typically provided by DLTs such as Ethereum[7] or Solana[8] that provide a globally distributed computing infrastructure, consensus protocols and an execution environment for smart contracts, which are the core components of all DeFI protocols.

Layer 2 – DLT Application Layer: This layer comprises applications implemented through smart contracts:

Cryptoassets are DLT applications that facilitate the transfer of value across the DeFI ecosystem.

A *DeFI Protocol* is a DLT application implemented by smart contracts, utilizing crypto assets and providing certain financial service functionality, e.g., lending protocols, derivatives protocols, and decentralized exchanges (DEXs) based on the offered functionalities. Functionality is realized through financial functions such as the pooling of liquidity provided by multiple users, the supply of collateral, or the swap of crypto assets. Certain parts are specific to a particular protocol type, while others are used in several protocols and across different categories.

DeFI Compositions enable a specific type of DeFI protocol, also implemented by a set of smart contracts, that provide novel financial services by using services of other DeFI protocols.

Layer 3 – Application Front-end Interfaces - Provides the user interfaces for users to transact on the DLT and buy products.

Architecting DLT solutions involves making critical decisions around the requirements, baselines, features, functions, and scalability of the blockchain being evaluated or proposed. Deciding whether to use a permissioned or permissionless blockchain is crucial and determining which features are essential to an enterprise when considering blockchain services [8]. This depends on the requirements of the use case, i.e., whether an organization needs privacy or not for its transactions. If privacy is required, organizations should choose a permissioned blockchain. The decision between two blockchains, e.g., Hyperledger Fabric or R3 Corda, could be based solely on having or not having channels. Decisions will need to be made based on the following:

- Databases
- Trust
- Third parties
- Transaction interaction

For example, a typical decision tree for using a permissioned vs. permissionless blockchain is based on the following factors. If the answer to any of these is "No," then organizations do not need to use a blockchain and instead should go for a Master / Slave database.

- Need for a shared common database?
- Multiple parties involved?

---

[7] For more information, see https://ethereum.org/.
[8] For more information, see https://solana.com/.

- Parties involved have conflicting incentives and/or are not trusted?
- Rules governing participants are not uniform.
- Need for an objective, immutable log?
- Rules of transactions stay the same frequently.
- Are transactions public?

Several other issues need to be addressed in architecting and designing DeFI solutions. These include but are not limited to the nature of business i.e., globally distributed or locally concentrated, efficiencies expected out of the implementation, security of the underlying DLT framework used, agility of the organization and its ability to adapt to changes in business processes, business continuity requirements [8].

3   Factors Affecting the Success of DeFI

To identify the factors that affect the success of DeFI, one can think of the DLT as a General-Purpose Technology (GPT). To that extent, GPT is usually characterized by its pervasive "input in many downstream sectors" (extensiveness), "inherent potential for technical improvements" (evolvability), and "innovational complementarities" (enabling). These are commonly referred to as the 3Es. [7].

"*Extensiveness*" of DeFI would depend on the enhanced trust in data that it would need to bring along with greater efficiency in exchanging information and value. Given the inherent lack of a safety net as explained earlier, trust becomes a crucial factor.

"*Evolvability*" is about the evolution of DLT as a technology itself. Starting with early use cases of Blockchain 1.0 with focus on cryptocurrencies, Blockchain 2.0 evolved to uses around "privacy, smart contract, non-native asset blockchain tokens and capabilities." Blockchain 3.0 extended capabilities further to decentralized applications (dApps) and DeFI. Blockchain 4.0 incorporates AI and blockchain to inform and automate decision-making. Interoperability between permissioned and permissionless blockchains is improving owing to technical improvements such as enhanced cross-chain data processing capabilities. Thus, as a potential GPT, blockchain (DLT) would need to co-evolve with complementary technologies and new use cases would emerge from there.

"*Enabling*" new business processes and models due to the efficient circulation of assets using DLT. The use of DLT in securing and spurring the exchange of digital assets, such as NFTs is becoming an attractive use cases. NFTs are non-fungible tokens representing ownership of items with certain intrinsic value to the owners e.g., bonds[9]. NFTs are created through a minting process on the blockchain and a creator or owner outlines the fundamental details of an item, broadcasts the information on a blockchain, triggering a smart contract function, and creating a token with a unique identifier minted to it. The identifier makes the token non-fungible and indelibly attaches it to its owner.

Considering the growing interest in DLT applications for real business, hype is often associated with it. Although hailed as the "trust machine," blockchain has been mistrusted

---

[9] https://www.euromoney.com/article/2b97clbq6u418q664cb9c/capital-markets/hsbc-orion-tok enizes-commercial-bank-money-and-sterling-bonds.

by potential adopters due to a lack of understanding of its seemingly contradictory features (e.g., transparency vs. anonymity) and the negative headlines associated with cryptocurrency theft and speculative moves in NFT markets. Use cases and business models have served as proofs of concept to improve the understanding of blockchain, but technology adoption at scale is required; as such, the "diffusion of innovation" for DLT is yet to happen [7, 8, 25].

Practitioners adopt blockchain by finding value in solutions, setting a long-term vision, and building viability. To measure the real-world value of DLT adoption, 3Vs are an important [7]. Only then the full technological capabilities of DLT can be translated into real-world use cases despite the uncertainties surrounding its potential.

Extensive Use Cases and Value Creation. Although DLT can be applied extensively in multiple sectors, applying a universal approach to the value proposition for diverse use cases is incorrect. For example, the use of DeFI is appropriate only when there is inter-organizational data sharing, and contracts across multiple parties involved. It must be remembered that although DLT can serve as a valuable solution in many sectors, a successful use case starts from a pain point: a business problem, not a technology or a solution. DeFI is not a silver bullet for all use cases in finance.

Evolving Technology and Vision for Adoption. All major blockchain frameworks are open source, giving DLT three main advantages: adaptation, supporting ecosystems, and interoperability. Therefore, organizations stand to benefit from cooperation within broader open-source communities. As such, having a vision for adopting DeFI is critical, and most DeFI implementations so far have been executed through a consortium of financial institutions[10].

Enabling Technology and Viable Solutions. Blockchain or DLT, being an enabling technology, needs to be integrated with other solutions to function in the real world, and in doing so, it provides the potential for innovations. In the context of DeFI, integration with traditional IT systems within the organization is vital. DeFI also needs to be integrated with user applications within an organization and between organizations to function as an enabling infrastructure that allows secure and tamper-proof data transactions.

4   An Information Systems Research Agenda for DeFI

Research on DeFI within the field of Information Systems is in its infancy. A recent systematic literature review of DeFI identifies three levels of abstraction (micro, meso, and macro) and seven subcategories [22]. Extant research at the micro-level examines aspects of individual components of the DeFI landscape. Research on the micro-level of the DeFI landscape has been categorized into three subcategories based on their topic of interest. These subcategories include financial smart contract research, which aims to analyze the design of financial smart contract languages, financial tokens in DeFI, which studies the various forms of store-of-value created using smart contracts, and DeFI DApps, which involves building and researching prototypes of DeFI services [22].

---

[10] For details, see https://www.ecb.europa.eu/paym/groups/pdf/omg/2022/220317/item-2_Toke nisation-cash-securities.pdf.

At the meso-level, researchers delve into the study of individual DeFI blockchain systems and explore the challenges associated with scaling beyond these systems. This level is thus further divided into two research objectives. In the first objective, DeFI single-chain ecosystem insights, authors analyze empirical DeFI patterns and largely focus on Ethereum, which has the highest amount of transaction data. The second objective, Scaling beyond stand-alone DeFI ecosystems, involves investigating how to connect different blockchain systems for DeFI, such as Ethereum and Cardano, and incorporate off-chain data like non-crypto-asset prices [22].

At the macro-level, scholars take a holistic approach to analyzing the DeFI ecosystem and explore its impact beyond the ecosystem, including on financially excluded populations, the legacy financial system, the need for regulation, and the potential long-term evolution [22].

In line with other calls for research in information systems that have appeared in this volume in the past [11–13], I call for research on DeFI by information systems researchers. There are exciting research opportunities in Information Systems within the realm of DeFI. These opportunities can be broadly categorized into two genres: 1) the design and deployment of DeFI systems and 2) the adoption and implications of DeFI systems. The first genre can utilize various methodologies like design science and computational simulation to advance the technical aspects of DeFI by exploring new designs, implementations, and instantiations of DeFI and associated technologies. The second genre can investigate the factors that may increase or reduce the adoption of DeFI at the country, organizational, or individual levels, or the impacts and implications of such adoption at any of these levels. Both research streams can run parallel to existing literature that has a long mature history in the field. For example, there are many studies that examine the adoption of various information technologies [10, 19, 29, 35, 37]. Other studies seek to understand the motivations for the adoption of specific technologies or antecedents to organizational or managerial attention toward information technologies in general [4, 14, 20, 27, 29, 32, 36]. Similarly, there is a vibrant stream of research that examines the business value of information technology [4, 9, 16, 17, 24, 26, 28–31].

The relationship between 3Es and 3Vs of DLT needs to be explored further in the context of Information Systems research. For example, the linkage between blockchain technology's extensiveness, evolvability, and enabling (3Es) attributes does not always end up with value, vision, and viability (3Vs) in blockchain use cases [7]. As such, identifying the factors associated with architectural and integration patterns, organizational receptiveness to DLT, and extensiveness of use cases for which DLT is being used vs. the value attribution could be an interesting area of research in the field of information systems.

Finally, a point to note is that DeFI has the potential to both dissolve as well as fortify national boundaries. Thus, research in this area should not be confined to WEIRD domains – emerging markets and GREAT domains [6, 11, 12] offer intriguing and the most promising possibilities for future research. Implications for topics like digital innovation [1, 5], digital globalization [17, 28], and the business value of digital technologies in emerging economies are immense [15, 16].

References

1. Andrade Rojas, M.G., Kathuria, A., Lee, H.-h.: Improving innovation efficiency through competition networks and digitized operational integration. In: Academy of Management Proceedings, p. 21570. Academy of Management Briarcliff Manor, NY 10510 (2020)
2. Auer, R., Haslhofer, B., Kitzler, S., Saggese, P., Victor, F.: The technology of decentralized finance (DeFi). Digit. Financ. 1–41 (2023)
3. Belshe, M.: A 5-Pronged Approach to Sensible Crypto Regulation After FTX. CoinDesk, City (2023)
4. Chaturvedi, D., Kathuria, A., Andrade, M., Saldanha, T.: Navigating the paradox of IT novelty and strategic conformity: the moderating role of industry dynamism. In: ICIS 2023 Proceedings, p. 14 (2023)
5. Cho, W., Malik, O., Karhade, P., Kathuria, A.: Need for speed in the sharing economy: how IT capability drives innovation speed? In: Hawaii International Conference on System Sciences (2022)
6. Dasgupta, A., Karhade, P., Kathuria, A., Konsynski, B.: Holding space for voices that do not speak: design reform of rating systems for platforms in GREAT economies. In: Proceedings of the 54th Hawaii International Conference on System Sciences (2021)
7. Du, J., Nielsen, B.B., Welch, C.: From buzzword to biz world: realizing blockchain's potential in the international business context. California Manag. Rev. **66**, 00081256231202266 (2023)
8. Holbrook, J.: Architecting Enterprise Blockchain Solutions. Wiley (2020). https://doi.org/10.1002/9781119557722
9. Hsieh, J.J.P.-A., Rai, A., Xu, S.X.: Extracting business value from IT: a sensemaking perspective of post-adoptive use. Manage. Sci. **57**(11), 2018–2039 (2011)
10. Karahanna, E., Chen, A., Liu, Q.B., Serrano, C.: Capitalizing on health information technology to enable digital advantage in US hospitals. MIS Q. **43**(1), 113–140 (2019)
11. Karhade, P., Kathuria, A.: Missing impact of ratings on platform participation in India: a call for research in GREAT domains. Commun. Assoc. Inf. Syst. **47**(1), 19 (2020)
12. Karhade, P., Kathuria, A., Dasgupta, A., Malik, O., Konsynski, B.R.: Decolonization of digital platforms: a research agenda for GREAT domains. In: Garimella, A., Karhade, P., Kathuria, A., Liu, X., Xu, J., Zhao, K. (eds.) The Role of e-Business during the Time of Grand Challenges. LNBIP, vol. 418, pp. 51–58. Springer, Cham (2021). https://doi.org/10.1007/978-3-030-79454-5_5
13. Karhade, P., Kathuria, A., Malik, O., Konsynski, B.: Digital platforms and infobesity: a research agenda. In: Garimella, A., Karhade, P., Kathuria, A., Liu, X., Xu, J., Zhao, K. (eds.) WeB 2020. LNBIP, vol. 418, pp. 67–74. Springer, Cham (2021). https://doi.org/10.1007/978-3-030-79454-5_7
14. Kathuria, A., Fontaine, A., Prietula, M.: Acquiring IT competencies through focused technology acquisitions (2011)
15. Kathuria, A., Karhade, P.P., Konsynski, B.R.: In the realm of hungry ghosts: multi-level theory for supplier participation on digital platforms. J. Manage. Inform. Syst. **37**(2), 396–430 (2020)
16. Kathuria, A., Karhade, P.P., Ning, X., Konsynski, B.R.: Blood and water: information technology investment and control in family-owned businesses. J. Manag. Inf. Syst. **40**(1), 208–238 (2023)
17. Khuntia, J., Kathuria, A., Saldanha, T.J., Konsynski, B.R.: Benefits of IT-enabled flexibilities for foreign versus local firms in emerging economies. J. Manag. Inf. Syst. **36**(3), 855–892 (2019)
18. Khuntia, J., Saldanha, T., Kathuria, A., Tanniru, M.R.: Digital service flexibility: a conceptual framework and roadmap for digital business transformation. Eur. J. Inform. Syst. **33**(1), 61–79 (2024)

19. Lee, M.H., Han, S.P., Park, S., Oh, W.: Positive demand spillover of popular app adoption: implications for platform owners' management of complements. Inf. Syst. Res. **34**(3), 961–995 (2023)
20. Li, X., Hsieh, J.J.P.-A., Rai, A.: Motivational differences across post-acceptance information system usage behaviors: an investigation in the business intelligence systems context. Inf. Syst. Res. **24**(3), 659–682 (2013)
21. Makarov, I., Schoar, A.: Cryptocurrencies and decentralized finance (DeFi). National Bureau of Economic Research (2022)
22. Meyer, E., Welpe, I.M., Sandner, P.G.: Decentralized finance—a systematic literature review and research directions. In: The Proceedings of ECIS (2022)
23. Mills, D., et al.: Distributed Ledger Technology in Payments, Clearing, and Settlement (2016)
24. Mithas, S., Whitaker, J., Tafti, A.: Information technology, revenues, and profits: exploring the role of foreign and domestic operations. Inf. Syst. Res. **28**(2), 430–444 (2017)
25. Murray, A., Kuban, S., Josefy, M., Anderson, J.: Contracting in the smart era: The implications of blockchain and decentralized autonomous organizations for contracting and corporate governance. Acad. Manag. Perspect. **35**(4), 622–641 (2021)
26. Pye, J., Rai, A., Dong, J.Q.: Business value of information technology capabilities: an institutional governance perspective. Inform. Syst. Res. 35, 3-8 (2023)
27. Saldanha, T. J., Andrade-Rojas, M. G., Kathuria, A., Khuntia, J. and Krishnan, M. How the Locus of Uncertainty Shapes the Influence of CEO Long-term Compensation on IT Capital Investments (2021)
28. Saldanha, T.J., Sahaym, A., Mithas, S., Andrade-Rojas, M.G., Kathuria, A., Lee, H.-H.: Turning liabilities of global operations into assets: IT-enabled social integration capacity and exploratory innovation. Inf. Syst. Res. **31**(2), 361–382 (2020)
29. Saldanha, T.J.V., Kathuria, A., Khuntia, J., Konsynski, B.R.: Ghosts in the machine: how marketing and human capital investments enhance customer growth when innovative services leverage self-service technologies. Inf. Syst. Res. **33**(1), 76–109 (2022)
30. Saldanha, T.J.V., Lee, D., Mithas, S.: Aligning information technology and business: the differential effects of alignment during investment planning, delivery, and change. Inf. Syst. Res. **31**(4), 1260–1281 (2020)
31. Sambhara, C., Rai, A., Xu, S.X.: Configuring the enterprise systems portfolio: the role of information risk. Inf. Syst. Res. **33**(2), 446–463 (2022)
32. Sun, T., Shi, L., Viswanathan, S., Zheleva, E.: Motivating effective mobile app adoptions: evidence from a large-scale randomized field experiment. Inf. Syst. Res. **30**(2), 523–539 (2019)
33. Tierno, P. What Happened at FTX and What Does It Mean for Crypto? Congressional Research Service, City (2022)
34. Weritz, P., Braojos, J., Matute, J., Benitez, J.: Impact of strategic capabilities on digital transformation success and firm performance: theory and empirical evidence. Eur. J. Inform. Syst. 1–21 (2024)
35. Xu, Y., Ghose, A., Xiao, B.: Mobile payment adoption: an empirical investigation of alipay. Inform. Syst. Res. **0**, 0 (2023)
36. Xue, L., Ray, G., Zhao, X.: Managerial incentives and IT strategic posture. Inf. Syst. Res. **28**(1), 180–198 (2017)
37. Yaraghi, N., Du, A.Y., Sharman, R., Gopal, R.D., Ramesh, R.: Health information exchange as a multisided platform: adoption, usage, and practice involvement in service co-production. Inf. Syst. Res. **26**(1), 1–18 (2015)

How Do Family Businesses Embark on Digital Transformation? A Call for Future IS Research

Abhishek Sachdeva[1]([✉]), Abhishek Kathuria[1] [iD], Prasanna Karhade[2] [iD], and Sougata Ray[1]

[1] Indian School of Business (ISB), Hyderabad, India
abhishek_sachdeva@isb.edu
[2] CUHK Business School, Sha Tin, Hong Kong SAR, China

Abstract. This paper presents novel pathways for Information Systems (IS) research within the context of family business. As these enterprises navigate the impacts of digital transformation, understanding the intersection of IS and familial commerce has become imperative. Specifically, we address the following questions: (1) What are the key intersections between IS research questions and the nuanced context of family businesses? (2) How can IS researchers contribute to the understanding and advancement of family businesses within the context of India, and in GREAT (Growing, Rural, Eastern, Aspirational, and Transitional) economies more broadly? Our extensive literature review showcases emerging trends in family business research and lessons from history and practice that are valuable for family firms in GREAT nations such as India. We also review existing IS research on issues centered around the family business context. Underscoring unexplored research inquiries that resonate with insights from Indian business history, we advocate for further research at the crossroads of IS and family business, acknowledging the existing scarcity of scholarly contributions within this domain.

Keywords: Information Systems (IS) research · Family businesses · Digital transformation · GREAT nations · Indian business history

1 Introduction: A Primer on Family Business

"Family-owned businesses are firms in which family members, related by blood or marriage, own equity as individuals or groups." [70].

Family-owned enterprises are the driving force behind global socio-economic progress and the generation of wealth. These companies, which range from small-scale operations to large corporations, have consistently demonstrated their widespread geographical presence. According to a 2018 study by the Family Firm Institute, family-run companies represent about two-thirds of all businesses worldwide. Their contribution to the annual global gross domestic product (GDP) ranges from 70 to 90 percent. Family-owned enterprises also support job creation globally, accounting for 50 to 80 percent of new jobs in several countries[1]. Developing economies, in particular, have benefited

---

[1] See https://economictimes.indiatimes.com/familybusinessforum/insights/why-family-busine sses-are-better-equipped-to-go-global/articleshow/66860347.cms.

© The Author(s), under exclusive license to Springer Nature Switzerland AG 2024
A. Kathuria et al. (Eds.): WeB 2022, LNBIP 508, pp. 99–118, 2024.
https://doi.org/10.1007/978-3-031-60003-6_7

from the economic externalities of these firms. Hence, we focus our call on Information Systems (IS, from now on) and family businesses in GREAT (Growing, Rural, Eastern, Aspirational, and Transitional) nations [66].

In this article, we bring together the vast literatures on Family Business and on Information Systems (IS) and review previous scholarly contributions to propose a future line of work. This chapter will benefit researchers in IS who are (i) optimistic about outcomes at the forefront of digital capabilities and familial relations in business (ii) preparing to teach digital adoption and transformation to stakeholders of a family business who seek professional intervention in managerial and governance capacities (iii) advising practitioners on technological innovation in the family enterprise ecosystem. We intend to be holistic in our review of existing academic inputs and present perspectives that are both informational and stimulating.

2   Current Perspectives in Family Business Literature

Early contributions in management literature establish various definitions and features of family business. The definition of family business has varied based on the number of family members involved, the split of ownership, and the degree of their influence in governance [41, 119]. The following accounts, such as [35, 77], and [61], amongst others, proposed that definitions of family business incorporate the impact of family aspirations and involvement on firm performance. A concurrent theme of econometric analysis in family business prioritized the granular nature of day-to-day and generational involvement, the role of a CEO, and the composition of the governing board to establish identification strategies, further narrowing the definition of family business [19, 53, 94, 116, 118].

Subsequent scholarship in family business determined rules (or conventions) to interpret mechanisms on investment policy, shareholding structure, potential costs and benefits of family ownership and cost of debt financing [3, 5, 12, 38]. Scholars used agency theory to explain intra-firm mechanisms in family businesses with high ownership concentration. This research uncovered that majority shareholders employ their control to engage in profit-driven actions that negatively impact the wealth of minority shareholders [51, 84, 94, 121]. A greater concentration of voting rights can provide stronger incentives for controlling shareholders to obtain private benefits. Family-owned businesses are perceived as possessing these intangible advantages and tend to be less inclined to decrease their ownership stakes to maintain control. To be more precise, family firms represent a unique category of enterprises in which primary shareholders are deeply dedicated to the business and exhibit a higher degree of reluctance to dilute control due to their aversion to control-related risks [96, 133].

A body of research also enhanced the foundational study of control dynamics in family businesses by highlighting roles of the family in consolidating majority ownership within their own familial circles. Controlling family shareholders easily advocate for self-interests by restricting recruitment of professional executives or by considerably raising firm dividends or their own remuneration [45, 49, 121]. This form of entrenchment results in certain expropriation practices of the controlling family shareholders wielding power over minority shareholders and ultimately reducing firm profitability [43, 50, 52,

58, 99]. Nonetheless, a comparative line of scholarly output showed that the distinctive features of family firms have a positive effect on their corporate behavior. The family's interest in the long-term survival of the business as well as its concern for maintaining the reputation of the firm and the family, lead the family to avoid acting opportunistically regarding the obtained earnings [3, 24, 134]. 'Fairness' of their values, stability, and capital preservation are often evaluated in line with reputation building and income needs [35, 46].

In summary, the evidence regarding ownership dynamics in family firms does not present a consensus regarding the outcomes of family ownership, plausibly due to the lack of rigorous methodologies. [43, 49] and [58] offer early explanations for founding family firms with concentrated ownership structures reporting lower profits. [3, 24], and [134] conclude differently on firm performance. Family businesses that do not have a professional CEO tend to observe favorable outcomes in their firm performance.

A branch of literature that delves into how families enhance their unique familial qualities through technology is in alignment with research in the field of information systems. This research sheds light on the behavior of family businesses in the age of digitalization. Digital transformation involves transitioning from a conventional organization that carries out digital initiatives to a digital-centric organization with an all-encompassing strategy that positions digital technology as the core of its business [57, 80, 132]. Family businesses view digital transformation as an opportunity to improve processes and gradually discover applications in redesigning business models, raising firm innovativeness, and hiring relevant talent [19, 26, 27, 39, 74]. The relationship between family control, firm performance, and digital innovation becomes more intricate as family members of different generations adapt to these multi-dimensional transitions [16]. In transitionary phases of a succession, these relations affect business innovation driven by successors' knowledge quotient and their ability to assimilate new technologies in agreement with the present generation of proprietors [13, 113, 139]. The coexistence of different generations carries with it the gravitas of experiences [11, 56, 87] and presents new opportunities for information systems research in transaction atmospheres of knowledge transfer and support of knowledge work.

3 An In-Practice Outlook

3.1 International Presence of Families in Trade

Geography, socio-economic climate, and offspring upbringing shape the progression and scope of family businesses. These factors have influenced mediation (a conflict resolution approach in which an impartial third party, known as the mediator, helps the conflicting parties to engage in negotiations aimed at addressing the issues that separate them, see [107]) and succession practices in some of the world's oldest businesses such as *Cartier* (France), *Great Eagle Holdings* (Hong Kong SAR China), *Hoshi Ryokan* (Japan), and *Rushworth's Music House* (the UK). The interrelationship between family leader habitus and accumulation of capital has also created positive spillovers in the cultural economy of countries, better identified as contemporary cultural hotspots [20, 88]. Family businesses have also contributed to many other sectors. These include agro-industry and food, electricity, e-commerce and digital services, hotels, information technology, petrochemicals, pharmaceuticals, renewable energy, textiles, and water infrastructure.[2]

3.2 A Brief Family Business History of GREAT Nations

Compared to families in developed markets, families in GREAT markets tend to be larger, more cohesive, and more respectful of hierarchy. Such families are also typically less open to conversations about mortality. In the past, these features of familial commerce have presented several barriers to innovation, an outcome common during the Second Industrial Revolution. During this period, several family firms in various parts of the world failed to capitalize on economies of scale and scope [37]. However, Chinese family firms were an exception to this trend. They maintained their cost-control approach while building their presence in the silk-reeling industry during the First Opium War of 1840.

Family business group affiliation hinges on three vital components: authority, exchange, and network [90, 98]. While Chinese firms tend to place a higher emphasis on the network aspect, Korean familial commerce places even greater importance on authority [55, 63, 128]. Korean chaebols, which represent conglomerates or financial cliques, emphasize patrilineal lineage, consanguine continuity, and ancestor worship. They are categorized based on their founding periods. In the late 1950s, self-made entrepreneurs capitalized on preferential grant allocations, government property disposals, and favorable tax and finance arrangements to establish companies like Hyundai, Samsung, and Lucky-Goldstar. The chaebols of the 1960s emerged due to foreign loans obtained for a series of five-year plans, including groups such as Hanjin, Korea Explosive, and Sangyong. Much later, in the 1970s, family-affiliated enterprises such as Daewoo, Sunkyong, and Lotte were established, driven by rapid growth in exports and domestic demand.

On the governance front, regional macroeconomic shocks have played a role in initiating the repair [8, 112]. The Asian Financial Crisis of 1997 exposed many family enterprises that had direct affiliations with domestic banks in various operational capacities. The episode also led to the financial collapse of major family groups such as the Tejapaibul Family (Bangkok Metropolitan Bank) and the Wanglee Family (Nakornthon Bank Group) due to their failure to secure recapitalization. However, the Ratanarak Family (Bank of Ayudhya), the Sophonpanich Family (Bangkok Bank), and the Lamsam Family (Thai Farmers Bank) continued to prosper. Typical strategies for course correction included aligning individual interests in governance, resolving intra-family conflicts related to ownership concentration, ensuring long-term succession, and prioritizing survival.

3.3 Family Business Dynamics in India: A Comprehensive Overview

While the architecture of family business appears stable and well-established in developing countries of the east, its texture is dynamic and more vibrant in India. The country is

---

[2] *USA*: Cargill, Bechtel Group and Kohler; *Australia*: BGC, Hancock Prospecting and Peregrine Corporation; *Thailand*: Charoen Pokphand Group and Central Group; *Philippines*: Ayala Corporation, JG Summit Holdings and SM Investments.

one of the world's most populous, the third-largest economy by purchasing power parity (PPP), and the fastest-growing major economy in the post-COVID-19 era [125]. It has a rich civilizational history dating back several millennia. Family-owned businesses have been the dominant form of commerce in this country for centuries. Although India contributed nearly a quarter to the global GDP in the 16th century, four centuries of colonial misrule left the country's economy and status in tatters. After gaining independence, India has experienced substantial growth, especially after abandoning the socialist economic model in the early 1990s. The country is home to over 1.48 million companies, of which nearly 75% are family-owned[3].

For many years, the Indian economy has been a prime example of the positive spillovers created by the burgeoning entrepreneurial spirit of domestic family businesses. Historical developments in independent (liberalized) India brought about a change in the entrepreneurial attitude (ease of doing business) in many such firms. *Jehangir Ratanji Dadabhoy (JRD) Tata and Sumant Moolgaokar's setup of TELCO (Tata Locomotive and Engineering Company), Rahul Bajaj's tenure as MD of Bajaj Auto,* and *the 1993 post-split group diversification of T.V. Sundaram Iyengar's Business Empire (TVS Group)* are all trailblazing cues of navigating through competitive pressures with exemplary vision and firm leadership (see Table 1).

Table 1. A timeline of events representative of evolution in Indian Family Businesses (1990-Present).

Time Period	Business Strategies and Examples
Early 1990s	1. Family businesses in India compete with MNCs 2. Economic liberalization in 1991 opens access to global technology and capital markets 3. Pharmaceutical firms serve low-cost markets and innovate 4. Emergence of new business houses such as *Dr. Reddy's, Bharti Enterprises,* and *Sun Pharma*
Early 2000s	1. Some Indian business groups expand globally for economies of scale. (E.g., *Bharat Forge* acquires German firm *Carl Dan Peddinghaus*) 2. National challenges and reforms shape Indian family business' strategies 3. Strategies include resource-seeking, asset-seeking and market-seeking behaviours
Mid-2010s	1. Indian businesses introduce higher-margin products and explore overseas markets. Example: Aurobindo Pharma expands product portfolio and acquires *Actavis's* Western European operations 2. Indian businesses buy small firms in developed countries for technology and marketing competencies. Example: *Asian Paints* acquires *Berger International* and invests in manufacturing facilities in emerging markets
Ongoing	1. Strategic alliances, technical tie-ups, and joint ventures with global partners are common Example: Motherson Sumi Systems Limited (MSS) partners with international tier-one auto component companies. MSS expands manufacturing and technological capabilities with 24 international manufacturing facilities
Overall	Indian family businesses adapted to changing business landscape through innovation and customer-focused commerce. Evolution from local competition to global expansion and strategic acquisitions

---

[3] See (1) https://www.newindianexpress.com/opinions/2023/mar/07/family-in-indian-family-businesses-is-key-to-growth-2553735.html.and (2) https://www.statista.com/statistics/100 8330/india-number-of-registered-active-companies-by-type/#:~:text=As%20of%20June%202 022%2C%20there,south%20Asian%20country%20of%20India.

In recent times, India has strengthened its position by resisting pressure to join trade blocs, fostering bold electrification efforts[4], and reinforcing military bonds within the APAC region (see [65, 108]). These strategic developments not only bolster India's emergence as a fast-growing economy but also contribute to creating a safer environment for business growth. They enhance national security, improve infrastructure, and ensure fair competition, resulting in a stable and conducive business landscape. This environment has also allowed many families to deeply entrench themselves in India's business landscape and play entrepreneurial roles in various forms, ranging from traditional businesses to startups. Furthermore, common practices such as transgenerational family participation, a strong sense of tradition, and long-term commitment have significantly contributed to job creation and economic growth, making such enterprises integral to India's economic development. As the country continues to integrate into the global economy, family firms will maintain a cornerstone relationship with its economic development while seeking opportunities to blend tradition with innovation.

3.4 Motivation for Advancing Research in Family Business

Given the significance of family businesses, academic research on family business has a long-standing tradition in the management sciences. This tradition has led to the creation of several journals dedicated to the study of family businesses, as well as research centres and programs focused on addressing issues relevant to family businesses. Surprisingly, the literature in Information Systems (IS) appears bereft of engagement with the family business literature, with only a few notable exceptions [54, 64, 70, 102, 109, 110, 115]. In this manuscript, we propose an agenda and call for IS research in the context of Family Businesses in GREAT economies in general, and in India, in particular.

We advance a research agenda on possible avenues for research through which IS researchers can conduct research inquiries related to family business issues. Besides providing a holistic review of family business literature in a previous section (see Sect. 2), we discuss the following in the remainder of this manuscript: First, we elaborate on our call for IS research in family business in the context of India. Second, we review of literature where IS research questions intersect with the family business context. Finally, we present future directions for IS research in the context of family businesses.

4 Call for IS Research: Flare for Digital in the Home Ground

Given the rich history of family businesses in India and the country's growing role in the global economy, it is pertinent and imperative for IS researchers to examine issues related to information systems and family businesses in the Indian context. Further, since 2015, India has introduced new policy campaigns to transform the country on several fronts. Digital India is one such program that strives to create a digitally empowered society and knowledge economy by improving technological infrastructure in the country (see [111] for further motivation on the Digital India program). This initiative promises to

---

[4] See https://www.ceew.in/publications/access-to-electricity-availability-and-electrification-per centage-in-india.

provide new business opportunities in areas such as online education, cloud computing, and financial technologies [69]. However, it is also changing how customers interact with existing businesses as digital infrastructure seeps through as a core utility for both parties. The face of 'emergence' has pivoted from national shocks to a digital epoch that demands existing businesses to factor in digital capabilities. In the context of family firms, evidence of this remains sparse. Therefore, a call for IS research will establish current interactions among people, data, and technology associated with family businesses. Before researchers begin such an examination, it is important to understand the existing work within the IS literature related to family business. In the following section, we present a summary of this literature.

In recent years, more emphasis has been placed on digital transformation in family businesses. One of the early contributions [30] investigated how the involvement of family in management affects a firm's development of Internet of Things (IoT) innovations, specifically focusing on exploratory IoT innovations. Their longitudinal analysis of listed German firms between 2002 and 2013 shows that a negative relationship exists. Furthermore, the degree of technological diversification, especially in unrelated areas, moderates this relationship. The study also presented implications for practice that generalize the risk-averse behavior of family-managed firms, prioritizing family goals over exploratory IoT innovations. Therefore, for firms aiming to lead in digital transformation, it is advisable to lower the proportion of family members in the top management team.

Other research [122] emphasizes the need for a managerial perspective on digital transformation in family businesses. The authors generalize their focus on technology and analyze how small and medium-sized family firms manage digital transformation considering firm-specific resource constraints. They conducted 127 semi-structured interviews across 15 firms in Germany, Austria, and Switzerland. All firms in their sample operate in the manufacturing sector and are at different stages of digital transformation. Their case analyses help identify a three-stage process of digital transformation, encompassing process digitalization, product and service digitalization, and business model digitalization. It also uncovers triggers for each stage and the dynamic capabilities required for successful transformation. This allows the authors to highlight combinations of factors that either enable or hinder the development of dynamic capabilities, influencing the speed and effectiveness of the digital transformation journey.

Several studies in the past have highlighted the lack of empirical evidence to explain the factors driving barriers to digital transformation (see [48, 91] amongst others). Many other studies vouch for analyzing the strategic value of digital transformation in small and medium-sized firms (see [105, 117, 132] amongst others). [14] exploit these themes in tandem to identify causal linkages that drive barriers to digital transformation among small family firms in Brazil. Using techniques of structural equation modeling, they analyze the effect of digitalization strategies and barriers to digital transformation on the use of technologies.

In addition to a review of literature at the intersection of family business and digital transformation, we create a thematic map to capture all related contributions (see Fig. 1). This allows us to build on our literature search without filters on region and further highlight research trends in an important branch of IS (see [132]). Four primary thematic categories emerge in this map (Basic, Motor, Emerging/Declining, and Niche Themes). Studies under the Basic theme form the foundation of the literature (see [120]). Motor themes highlight the driving forces in this research, including technological change, investment, and the integration of digital tools into family business operations. Niche themes reveal specialized areas of focus within the family business and digital transformation literature (for family-related studies in the Manufacturing & Services Industry theme, see [10, 25, 89, 137]).

In the Emerging or Declining category, we observe a greater focus on dynamic themes in this field. These themes encompass studies related to urban design and regional economics, which investigate how economic actors within a geographic-social structure contribute to the growth of family firms (see [13]) and promote organizational resilience practices differently in family firms in rural and urban areas (see [22]). Emerging works that come closest to family business and IS identify factors that motivate the adoption of artificial intelligence (see [129]) and evaluate the impact of generational involvement in business digitalization (see [23, 97]). In contrast, declining themes may pertain to areas that were once prominent but have received less attention over time (Under Company Information theme studies that utilize the case-study approach, see [7, 78, 106]).

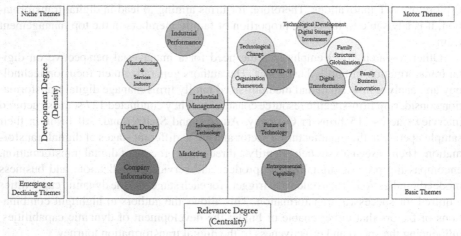

Fig. 1. Development-Relevance Plot of Emerging Themes on Digital Transformation and Family Business in Academic Literature. Source: *Scopus Database and Authors' Calculation.*

Two other key exemplars that align most closely with the scope of our review are [102] and [70]. The first [102] makes pioneering contributions to IS research by studying the relationship between IT investment and family businesses in India. Family firms typically hold mixed preferences for IT investment due to their inhibitions towards risky, long-term investment. However, such investments do contribute to succession and survival over multiple generations. These dynamics gain further intricacy due to the employment of family-affiliated managers versus the enlistment of professional managers. By establishing a theoretical framework on socioemotional wealth, Ning et al. explain the distinct moderating influences exerted by family and professional management controls on the correlation between family ownership and IT investment. They find that family ownership exerts a negative influence on IT investment, family management amplifies this association, while professional management weakens this relationship.

The second [70], expand upon the research direction introduced by [102] by emphasizing the importance of family ownership in the context of future IS scholarship. Family-owned enterprises exhibit variations in their strategic objectives and actions, functioning as a source of both wealth and social standing for their familial proprietors. In relation to this, the authors advance the nature of ownership and executive management as sources of heterogeneity in IT investment and its business value. They find that family ownership negatively influences IT investment as owners are likely to avoid investments in IT that are frivolous, reduce information asymmetry, or leave auditable digital trails. Furthermore, the negative influence of family ownership on IT investment is weakened when a career professional is appointed in the senior-most executive position of a family-owned business. This is because professional executives strive to utilize IT for control and performance benefits, and family owners desire to use IT to monitor and control the non-family professional executive. Family ownership also weakens the negative influence of environmental hostility on the relationship between IT investment and firm performance, as family-owned businesses incur less dynamic adjustment costs and maintain better alignment between IT and business strategy.

5   Future Directions of Research in IS and Family Business

In this section, we delve into IS within the realm of family businesses, highlighting six avenues of future research in greater detail. First, firm-level studies contain various kinds of heterogeneity that may interplay with family dynamics. This may have implications for strategic decisions and IT-related outcomes that may also adjust depending on the regulatory environment in some geographies [21, 101]. The Resource-based View (RBV) of family business theory can address some implications considering the organizational behavior of family firms [60]. According to this view, the family becomes a distinctive resource and brings its values, traditions, and intergenerational knowledge into the strategic IT decision-making process. In line with [21, 93, 123, 124], and [101], understanding how family-specific resources, such as the family's collective experience and commitment to preserving the legacy, shape IT adoption and impact is paramount.

Second, prior research has explored the impact of IT implementation in the context of competitive measures [15, 32]. Organizations actively seek IT innovations to support their strategies [86]. However, understanding the role of IT as a supporter or driver of business value is essential [18, 100, 138]. Socioemotional wealth (SEW) theory (see [17]) can explain the underlying mechanisms of this dynamic, suggesting that family businesses may prioritize IT investments that align with family values, legacy preservation, and socioemotional endowments. Nevertheless, limited evidence exists on whether IT, as a supporter or enabler, can enhance the agility and long-term sustainability of family firms [47, 85, 127].

Third, while existing research has explored the economic implications of IT investments [36, 82, 104], a critical area for future research lies in understanding the strategic underpinnings of IT-related decisions within family businesses. These decisions are often intertwined with the aspiration to maintain control within the family, aligning with the RBV theory's emphasis on resources that are representative of sustained competitive advantages. RBV suggests that family firms should leverage their unique internal resources to create and maintain advantages in the market. Therefore, future research can delve into how the family's resource pool, including its values, traditions, and shared knowledge, influences strategic IT decisions and their impact on business outcomes. By exploring the role of these family-specific resources, researchers can gain deeper insights into how family businesses create and sustain competitive advantages through IT adoption and utilization, in alignment with the RBV framework.

Fourth, a current strand of literature examines the role of family business group (FBG) affiliation in promoting innovation. According to findings reported by [33], the affiliation of an enterprise with an FBG expedites the transfer of technological knowledge and financial resources. However, in cases where FBGs choose to diversify, this strategy backtracks on the progress made in innovativeness. The trends in innovation and knowledge transfer are similar in small and medium enterprises. [59] report that R&D intensity and FBG affiliation share a positive relationship and that this effect is more prominent in relatively larger firms and in firms with greater FBG ownership. While these innovation effects are significant across a range of firms in terms of their size, IS researchers have a role to play in teasing out the impact of IT innovation and its implications for FBG ownership in a developing country context in general and India in particular.

Fifth, a related branch of literature in FBG affiliation studies the impact of market-oriented institutional change on foreign subsidiary performance (see [28, 73, 95] amongst others). [76] offer a formative study that divides market-oriented institutional change as a discrete event into phases of friction and convergence at the institutional level. This temporal construct shows that FBG-affiliated firms benefit from internationalization in periods of convergence over friction. Research in the Economics of IS can employ novel identification strategies to recontextualize resource curse and capture paradoxical situations in which firms underperform due to institutional shocks, despite leveraging IT and digital capabilities at the firm and business-group level.

Sixth, India and other GREAT nations provide IS researchers with an opportunity to study family businesses given its rich culture, history, and civilization norms (for recent top conference exemplars, see [68, 102, 109], amongst others. For recent journal exemplars, see [69] and [70]). It also provides ground to the lives of the mind to examine the nature, structure, and function of IT in family enterprises. The century-long legacy of the Murugappa family (Murugappa Group in 1900), mass media innings of Ramnath Goenka (The Indian Express in 1932), and Dhirubhai Ambani's (Reliance Industries in 1966) zeal to train investors in remote parts of the country offer bankable wisdom for IS researchers. In the past, these groups have accommodated differences in linguistic preferences and invited more diversity in their customer base. Today, this strategy can raise trendsetting questions about multilingual information systems, machine translation, and the impact of language on technology adoption in family businesses. Cultural variability has also laid out varying degrees of repayment flexibility across the Group's customers. This flexibility can be recontextualized to study how family enterprises adapt technology to suit the diverse cultural expectations of their customers. A convincing case can also be made on the impact of cultural factors on technology acceptance and usage across family enterprises in India, thereby extending the limited prior literature on cultural aspects of IT value in global and GREAT contexts [62, 66, 75, 114, 130, 131]. Last, these groups have navigated through economic turmoil and gained cognizance of product portfolios that cater to the country's large urban-rural divide (see Figs. 2, 3, 4, 5 Panels A-D). IS research can draw attention to questions on the response of family firms to technology accessibility, affordability, and the digital divide.

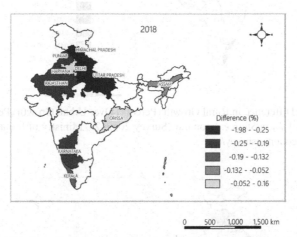

Fig. 2. Panel A. Difference in Rural Growth (Percent) Over Urban Growth (Percent) in Internet Subscribers - 2018. *Data Source*: Economic Survey 2022–23, Ministry of India. https://www.ind iabudget.gov.in/economicsurvey/

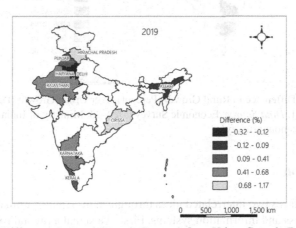

Fig. 3. Panel B. Difference in Rural Growth (Percent) Over Urban Growth (Percent) in Internet Subscribers - 2019. *Data Source*: Economic Survey 2022–23, Ministry of India. https://www.ind iabudget.gov.in/economicsurvey/

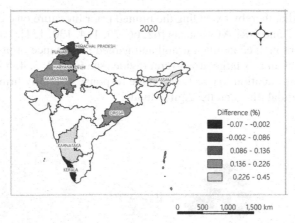

Fig. 4. Panel C. Difference in Rural Growth (Percent) Over Urban Growth (Percent) in Internet Subscribers - 2020. *Data Source*: Economic Survey 2022–23, Ministry of India. https://www.ind iabudget.gov.in/economicsurvey/

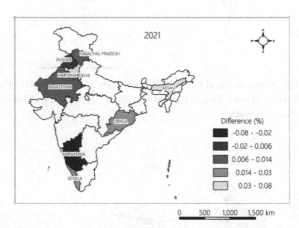

Fig. 5. Panel D. Difference in Rural Growth (Percent) Over Urban Growth (Percent) in Internet Subscribers - 2021. *Data Source*: Economic Survey 2022–23, Ministry of India. https://www.ind iabudget.gov.in/economicsurvey/

6 Conclusion

Our chapter surfaces two interrelated ideas through an in-depth examination of research in family business and information systems. First, we signal a pivotal role of the family in absorbing innovative contributions from industry practice into their entrepreneurial ventures. Second, we explore previous contributions on the impact of information systems initiatives in family enterprises. We also propose novel pathways for future research in GREAT nations that capture sustainable change over short-term effects of technology, linguistic features, and digital capabilities. This book chapter outlines a research agenda that combines these impressions, addressing intersections that are expected to remain central over the next decade. There is an increasing emphasis on India as both a context and a source of data and theories in the IS literature. Building on previous calls for research in IS [66, 71], our work contributes to a rich tradition of advancing the field through research agendas. Notably, these prior calls have recently gained significant traction within the IS literature, particularly in the context of India. This research agenda offers a roadmap for future investigations in IS, emphasizing the enduring significance of these confluence points and their potential to shape the impact of the discipline.

References

1. Alexander, L., Van Knippenberg, D.: Teams in pursuit of radical innovation: a goal orientation perspective. Acad. Manag. Rev. **39**(4), 423–438 (2014)
2. Alter, S., Sherer, S.A.: A general but readily adaptable model of information system risk. Commun. Assoc. Inf. Syst. **14**(1), 1–28 (2004)
3. Anderson, R.C., Reeb, D.M.: Founding-family ownership and firm performance: evidence from the S&P 500. J. Financ. **58**(3), 1301–1328 (2003)
4. Anderson, R.C., Duru, A., Reeb, D.M.: Investment policy in family-controlled firms. J. Bank. Finance **36**(6), 1744–1758 (2012)
5. Anderson, R.C., Mansi, S.A., Reeb, D.M.: Founding family ownership and the agency cost of debt. J. Financ. Econ. **68**(2), 263–285 (2003)
6. Anderson, R.C., Reeb, D.M., Zhao, W.: Family-controlled firms and informed trading: evidence from short sales. J. Financ. **67**(1), 351–385 (2012)
7. Ano, B., Bent, R.: Human determinants influencing the digital transformation strategy of multigenerational family businesses: a multiple-case study of five French growth-oriented family firms. J. Family Bus. Manage. **12**(4), 876–891 (2022)
8. Arrondo-García, R., Fernández-Méndez, C., Menéndez-Requejo, S.: The growth and performance of family businesses during the global financial crisis: the role of the generation in control. J. Fam. Bus. Strat. **7**(4), 227–237 (2016)
9. Astrachan, C.B., Botero, I., Astrachan, J.H., Prügl, R.: Branding the family firm: a review, integrative framework proposal, and research agenda. J. Fam. Bus. Strat. **9**(1), 3–15 (2018)
10. Ates, A., Acur, N.: Making obsolescence obsolete: execution of digital transformation in a high-tech manufacturing SME. J. Bus. Res. **152**, 336–348 (2022)
11. Bąkiewicz, A.: Cultural embeddedness of family business succession: the perspective of next generation. Int. J. Contemp. Manage. **19**(1), 7–27 (2020)
12. Banalieva, E.R., Eddleston, K.A.: Home-region focus and performance of family firms: the role of family vs non-family leaders. J. Int. Bus. Stud. **42**, 1060–1072 (2011)
13. Baù, M., Chirico, F., Pittino, D., Backman, M., Klaesson, J.: Roots to grow: family firms and local embeddedness in rural and urban contexts. Entrep. Theory Pract. **43**(2), 360–385 (2019)
14. Begnini, S., Oro, I.M., Tonial, G., Dalbosco, I.B.: The relationship between the use of technologies and digitalization strategies for digital transformation in family businesses. J. Family Bus. Manage. (2023). https://doi.org/10.1108/JFBM-06-2023-0087
15. Benitez-Amado, J., Walczuch, R.M.: Information technology, the organizational capability of proactive corporate environmental strategy and firm performance: a resource-based analysis. Eur. J. Inf. Syst. **21**, 664–679 (2012)
16. Bergfeld, M.M.H., Weber, F.M.: Dynasties of innovation: highly performing German family firms and the owners' role for innovation. Int. J. Entrep. Innov. Manag. **13**(1), 80–94 (2011)

17. Berrone, P., Cruz, C., Gomez-Mejia, L.R.: Socioemotional wealth in family firms: theoretical dimensions, assessment approaches, and agenda for future research. Fam. Bus. Rev. **25**(3), 258–279 (2012)
18. Bharadwaj, A., El Sawy, O.A., Pavlou, P.A., Venkatraman, N.: Digital business strategy: toward a next generation of insights. MIS Q. **37**(2), 471–482 (2013). https://doi.org/10.25300/MISQ/2013/37:2.3
19. Botero, I.C.: Effects of communicating family ownership and organisational size on an applicant's attraction to a firm: an empirical examination in the USA and China. J. Fam. Bus. Strat. **5**(2), 184–196 (2014)
20. Bourdieu, P.: Social space and symbolic power. Sociol Theory **7**(1), 14–25 (1989). https://doi.org/10.2307/202060
21. Brennan, N.M., Subramaniam, N., Van Staden, C.J.: Corporate governance implications of disruptive technology: an overview. Br. Account. Rev. **51**(6), 100860 (2019)
22. Brewton, K.E., Danes, S.M., Stafford, K., Haynes, G.W.: Determinants of rural and urban family firm resilience. J. Fam. Bus. Strat. **1**(3), 155–166 (2010)
23. Bürgel, T.R., Hiebl, M.R.: Conflict management strategies and the digitalization of family firms: the moderating role of generational ownership dispersion. IEEE Trans. Eng. Manage. (2023)
24. Burkart, M., Panunzi, F., Shleifer, A.: Family firms. J. Finance **58**(5), 2167–2201 (2003)
25. Camino-Mogro, S.: TFP determinants in the manufacturing sector: the case of Ecuadorian firms. Appl. Econom. Anal. **30**(89), 92–113 (2022)
26. Cassia, L., De Massis, A. V., Pizzurno, E.: An exploratory investigation on NPD in small family businesses from Northern Italy. Int. J. Bus. Manage. Social Sci. **2**(2), 1–14 (2011)
27. Cassia, L., De Massis, A.V., Pizzurno, E.: Strategic innovation and new product development in family firms: an empirically grounded theoretical framework. Int. J. Entrep. Behav. Res. **18**(2), 198–232 (2012)
28. Castaldi, S., Gubbi, S.R., Kunst, V.E., Beugelsdijk, S.: Business group affiliation and foreign subsidiary performance. Glob. Strateg. J. **9**(4), 595–617 (2019)
29. Castillo, J., Wakefield, M.W.: An exploration of firm performance factors in family businesses: do families value only the "bottom line"? J. Small Bus. Strateg. **17**(2), 37–52 (2006)
30. Ceipek, R., Hautz, J., De Massis, A., Matzler, K., Ardito, L.: Digital transformation through exploratory and exploitative internet of things innovations: the impact of family management and technological diversification. J. Prod. Innov. Manag. **38**(1), 142–165 (2021)
31. Celly, N., Kathuria, A., Subramanian, V.: Overview of Indian MNCs. In: Thite, M., Wilkinson, A., Budhwar, P., (Eds.), Emerging Indian Multinationals: Strategic Players in a Multipolar World. Oxford University Press (2016).
32. Chakravarty, A., Grewal, R., Sambamurthy, V.: Information technology competencies, organizational agility, and firm performance: enabling and facilitating roles. Inf. Syst. Res. **24**(4), 976–997 (2013)
33. Chang, S.J., Chung, C.N., Mahmood, I.P.: When and how does business group affiliation promote firm innovation? a tale of two emerging economies. Organ. Sci. **17**, 637–656 (2006)
34. Chen, C.L., Lin, Y.C., Chen, W.H., Chao, C.F., Pandia, H.: Role of government to enhance digital transformation in small service business. Sustainability **13**(3), 1028 (2021)
35. Chua, J.H., Chrisman, J.J., Sharma, P.: Defining the family business by behavior. Entrep. Theory Pract. **23**(4), 19–39 (1999)
36. Clemons, E.K., Row, M.C.: Information technology and industrial cooperation: the changing economics of coordination and ownership. J. Manag. Inf. Syst. **9**(2), 9–28 (1992)
37. Colli, A., Howorth, C., Rose, M.: Long-term perspectives on family business. Bus. Hist. **55**(6), 841–854 (2013)

38. Covin, J.G., Slevin, D.P.: Strategic management of small firms in hostile and benign environments. Strateg. Manag. J. **10**(1), 75–87 (1989)
39. Craig, J.B., Dibrell, C., Garrett, R.: Examining relationships among family influence, family culture, flexible planning systems, innovativeness, and firm performance. J. Fam. Bus. Strat. **5**(3), 229–238 (2014)
40. Davenport, T.H., Short, J.E.: The new industrial engineering: information technology and business process redesign. MIT Sloan Manag. Rev. **31**(4), 11–27 (1990)
41. Davis, J.A., Tagiuri, R.: Bivalent attributes of the family firm. Santa Barbara, CA.: Owner Managed Business Institute (1982)
42. De Toni, A.F., De Zan, G., Battistella, C.: Organisational capabilities for internal complexity: an exploration in the Coop stores. Bus. Process. Manag. J. **22**(1), 196–230 (2016)
43. DeAngelo, H., DeAngelo, L.: Controlling stockholders and the disciplinary role of corporate payout policy: a study of the times mirror company. J. Financ. Econ. **56**(2), 153–207 (2000)
44. Del Giudice, M.: Discovering the Internet of Things (IoT) within the business process management: a literature review on technological revitalization. Bus. Process Manage. J. **22**(2), 263–270 (2016)
45. Demsetz, H.: The structure of ownership and the theory of the firm. J. Law Econom. **26**(2), 375–390 (1983)
46. Du, X., Jian, W., Du, Y., Feng, W., Zeng, Q.: Religion, the nature of ultimate owner, and corporate philanthropic giving: Evidence from China. J. Bus. Ethics **123**(2), 235–256 (2014). https://doi.org/10.1007/s10551-013-1804-1
47. Duncan, N.B.: Capturing flexibility of information technology infrastructure: a study of resource characteristics and their measure. J. Manag. Inf. Syst. **12**(2), 37–57 (1995)
48. Eller, R., Alford, P., Kallmünzer, A., Peters, M.: Antecedents, consequences, and challenges ofsmall and medium-sized enterprise digitalization. J. Bus. Res. **112**, 119–127 (2020)
49. Fama, E.F., Jensen, M.C.: Separation of ownership and control. J. Law Econom. **26**(2), 301–325 (1983)
50. Fan, J.P., Wong, T.J.: Corporate ownership structure and the informativeness of accounting earnings in East Asia. J. Account. Econ. **33**(3), 401–425 (2002)
51. Francis, J., LaFond, R., Olsson, P., Schipper, K.: The market pricing of accruals quality. J. Account. Econ. **39**(2), 295–327 (2005)
52. Francis, J., Schipper, K., Vincent, L.: Earnings and dividend informativeness when cash flow rights are separated from voting rights. J. Account. Econ. **39**(2), 329–360 (2005)
53. Gallucci, C., Santulli, R., Calabrò, A.: Does family involvement foster or hinder firmperformance? the missing role of family-based branding strategies. J. Fam. Bus. Strat. **6**(3), 155–165 (2015)
54. Garimella, A., Karhade, P., Kathuria, A., Liu, X., Jennifer, X., Zhao, K. (eds.): The Role of e-Business during the Time of Grand Challenges: 19th Workshop on e-Business, WeB 2020, Virtual Event, December 12, 2020, Revised Selected Papers. Springer International Publishing, Cham (2021)
55. Gatfield, T., Youseff, M.: A critical examination of and reflection on the Chinese family business unit and the Chinese business clan. Fam. Bus. Rev. **14**(2), 153–158 (2001)
56. Ge, B., Campopiano, G.: Knowledge management in family business succession: current trends and future directions. J. Knowl. Manag. **26**(2), 326–349 (2022)
57. Ghosh, S., Hughes, M., Hodgkinson, I., Hughes, P.: Digital transformation of industrial businesses: a dynamic capability approach. Technovation **113**, 102414 (2022)
58. Gomez-Mejia, L.R., Nunez-Nickel, M., Gutierrez, I.: The role of family ties in agency contracts. Acad. Manag. J. **44**(1), 81–95 (2001)
59. Guzzini, E., Iacobucci, D.: Ownership as R&D incentive in business groups. Small Bus. Econ. **43**, 119–135 (2014)

60. Habbershon, T.G., Williams, M.L.: A resource-based framework for assessing the strategic advantages of family firms. Fam. Bus. Rev. **12**(1), 1–25 (1999)
61. Holt, D.T., Rutherford, M.W., Kuratko, D.F.: Advancing the field of family business research: further testing the measurement properties of the F-PEC. Fam. Bus. Rev. **23**(1), 76–88 (2010)
62. Hsieh, R., Keil,: Understanding digital inequality: comparing continued use behavioral models of the socio-economically advantaged and disadvantaged. MIS Q. **32**(1), 97 (2008). https://doi.org/10.2307/25148830
63. Jeong, S.H., Kim, H., Kim, H.: Strategic nepotism in family director appointments: evidence from family business groups in South Korea. Acad. Manag. J. **65**(2), 656–682 (2022)
64. Jha, S., Kathuria, A.: Size matters for cloud capability and performance. In: Proceedings of the Americas Conference on Information Systems (AMCIS), Minneapolis (2022)
65. Joshi, Y., Mukherjee, A.: From denial to punishment: the security dilemma and changes in India's military strategy towards China. Asian Security **15**(1), 25–43 (2019)
66. Karhade, P., Kathuria, A.: Missing impact of ratings on platform participation in India: a call for research in GREAT domains. Commun. Assoc. Inf. Syst. **47**(1), 19 (2020)
67. Karhade, P., Kathuria, A., Dasgupta, A., Malik, O., Konsynski, B.R.: Decolonization of Digital Platforms: A Research Agenda for GREAT Domains. In: Garimella, A., Karhade, P., Kathuria, A., Liu, X., Jennifer, Xu., Zhao, K. (eds.) The Role of e-Business during the Time of Grand Challenges: 19th Workshop on e-Business, WeB 2020, Virtual Event, December 12, 2020, Revised Selected Papers, pp. 51–58. Springer International Publishing, Cham (2021). https://doi.org/10.1007/978-3-030-79454-5_5
68. Kathuria, A., Karhade, P.P.: You Are Not You When You Are Hungry: Machine Learning Investigation of Impact of Ratings on Ratee Decision Making. In: Xu, J.J., Zhu, B., Liu, X., Shaw, M.J., Zhang, H., Fan, M. (eds.) WEB 2018. LNBIP, vol. 357, pp. 151–161. Springer, Cham (2019). https://doi.org/10.1007/978-3-030-22784-5_15
69. Kathuria, A., Karhade, P.P., Konsynski, B.R.: In the realm of hungry ghosts: multi-level theory for supplier participation on digital platforms. J. Manag. Inf. Syst. **37**(2), 396–430 (2020)
70. Kathuria, A., Karhade, P.P., Ning, X., Konsynski, B.R.: Blood and water: information technology investment and control in family-owned businesses. J. Manag. Inf. Syst. **40**(1), 208–238 (2023)
71. Kathuria, A., Khuntia, J., Karhade, P., Ning, X.: Don't ever take sides with anyone against the family: family ownership and information management. In: Proceedings of the Americas Conference on Information Systems, Cancun (2019)
72. Kathuria, R., Kathuria, N., Kathuria, A.: Competitive priorities as trade-offs or mutually supportive: a glimpse from an emerging economy. In: Thakur, R., Srivastava, V., Bhatia, S., Sharma, J., (Eds.), Management Practices for the New Economy. Bloomsbury, India (2017)
73. Khanna, T., Palepu, K.: The future of business groups in emerging markets: long-run evidence from Chile. Acad. Manag. J. **43**(3), 268–285 (2000)
74. Khuntia, J., Kathuria, A., Andrade-Rojas, M.G., Saldanha, T., Celly, N.: How foreign and domestic firms differ in leveraging IT-enabled supply chain information integration in BOP markets: the role of supplier and client business collaboration. J. Assoc. Inf. Syst. **22**(3), 6 (2021)
75. Khuntia, J., Kathuria, A., Saldanha, T.J., Konsynski, B.R.: Benefits of IT-enabled flexibilities forforeign versus local firms in emerging economies. J. Manag. Inf. Syst. **36**(3), 855–892 (2019)
76. Kim, H., Kim, H., Hoskisson, R.E.: Does market-oriented institutional change in an emergingeconomy make business-group-affiliated multinationals perform better? an institution-based view. J. Int. Bus. Stud. **41**, 1141–1160 (2010)

77. Klein, S.B., Astrachan, J.H., Smyrnios, K.X.: The F-PEC scale of family influence: construction, validation, and further implication for theory. Entrep. Theory Pract. **29**(3), 321–339 (2005)
78. Koh, A., Kong, E., Timperio, G.: An analysis of open innovation determinants: the case study of Singapore based family-owned enterprises. Europ. J. Family Bus. **9**(2), 85–101 (2019)
79. Kotwal, A., Ramaswami, B., Wadhwa, W.: Economic liberalization and Indian economic growth: what's the evidence? J. Econom. Lit. **49**(4), 1152–1199 (2011)
80. Kraus, S., Durst, S., Ferreira, J.J., Veiga, P., Kailer, N., Weinmann, A.: Digital transformation in business and management research: an overview of the current status quo. Int. J. Inf. Manage. **63**, 102466 (2022)
81. Kumar, N., Aggarwal, A.: Liberalization, outward orientation and in-house R&D activity of multinational and local firms: a quantitative exploration for Indian manufacturing. Res. Policy **34**(4), 441–460 (2005)
82. Kumar, R.L.: A note on project risk and option values of investments in information technologies. J. Manag. Inf. Syst. **13**(1), 187–193 (1996)
83. Kumaraswamy, A., Mudambi, R., Saranga, H., Tripathy, A.: Catch-up strategies in the Indian auto components industry: domestic firms' responses to market liberalization. J. Int. Bus. Stud. **43**, 368–395 (2012)
84. La Porta, R., Lopez-de-Silanes, F., Shleifer, A., Vishny, R.: Investor protection and corporategovernance. J. Financ. Econ. **58**(1–2), 3–27 (2000)
85. Lee, O.K., Sambamurthy, V., Lim, K.H., Wei, K.K.: How does IT ambidexterity impact organizational agility? Inf. Syst. Res. **26**(2), 398–417 (2015)
86. Lu, K., (Ram) Ramamurthy,: Understanding the link between information technology capability and organizational agility: an empirical examination. MIS Q. **35**(4), 931 (2011). https://doi.org/10.2307/41409967.
87. Lyons, R., Ahmed, F.U., Clinton, E., O'Gorman, C., Gillanders, R.: The impact of parental emotional support on the succession intentions of next-generation family business members. Entrepreneurship & Regional Development, pp. 1–19 (2023)
88. Maclean, C., Harvey, J., Press: Business elites and corporate governance in France and the UK. FPSC, Palgrave Macmillan UK, London (2006). https://doi.org/10.1057/9780230511736
89. Manzaneque, M., Diéguez-Soto, J., Garrido-Moreno, A.: Technological innovation inputs, outputs and family management: evidence from Spanish manufacturing firms. Innovation **20**(4), 299–325 (2018)
90. Masulis, R.W., Pham, P.K., Zein, J.: Family business groups around the world: financing advantages, control motivations, and organizational choices. Rev. Finan. Stud. **24**(11), 3556–3600 (2011)
91. Silva, C., de Mattos, G., Pellegrini, G.H., Dolfsma, W.: Systematic literature review on technological transformation in SMEs: a transformation encompassing technology assimilation and business model innovation. Manage. Rev. Quart. (2023). https://doi.org/10.1007/s11301-023-00327-7
92. McWatters, C.S., Chen, Q., Ding, S., Hou, W., Wu, Z.: Family business development in mainland China from 1872 to 1949. Bus. Hist. **58**(3), 408–432 (2016)
93. Mikalef, P., Pateli, A., van de Wetering, R.: IT architecture flexibility and IT governance decentralisation as drivers of IT-enabled dynamic capabilities and competitive performance: the moderating effect of the external environment. Eur. J. Inf. Syst. **30**(5), 512–540 (2021)
94. Miller, D., Le Breton-Miller, I., Lester, R.H., Cannella, A.A., Jr.: Are family firms really superior performers? J. Corp. Finan. **13**(5), 829–858 (2007)
95. Minetti, R., Yun, S.G.: Institutions, bailout policies, and bank loan contracting: evidence from Korean chaebols. Rev. Finan. **19**(6), 2223–2275 (2015)

96. Mishra, C.S., McConaughy, D.L.: Founding family control and capital structure: the risk of loss of control and the aversion to debt. Entrep. Theory Pract. **23**(4), 53–64 (1999)

97. Mondal, A., Chakrabarti, A.B.: Knowledge management through information and communication technology investments: the story of Indian family firms. South Asian J. Bus. Stud. (2023). https://doi.org/10.1108/SAJBS-12-2021-0456

98. Morck, R., Yeung, B.: Agency problems in large family business groups. Entrep. Theory Pract. **27**(4), 367–382 (2003)

99. Morck, R., Yeung, B., Yu, W.: The information content of stock markets: why do emerging markets have synchronous stock price movements? J. Financ. Econ. **58**(1–2), 215–260 (2000)

100. Nambisan, S.: Information technology and product/service innovation: a brief assessment and some suggestions for future research. J. Assoc. Inf. Syst. **14**(4), 1 (2013)

101. Napitupulu, I.H.: Internal control, manager's competency, management accounting information systems and good corporate governance: evidence from rural banks in Indonesia. Glob. Bus. Rev. **24**(3), 563–585 (2023)

102. Ning, X., Karhade, P., Kathuria, A., Khuntia, J.: Influence of Ownership and Management on IT Investment in Indian Family Firms. In: Lang, K.R., Xu, J., Zhu, B., Liu, X., Shaw, M.J., Zhang, H., Fan, M. (eds.) WeB 2019. LNBIP, vol. 403, pp. 185–193. Springer, Cham (2020). https://doi.org/10.1007/978-3-030-67781-7_17

103. Pereira, C.S., Durão, N., Moreira, F., Veloso, B.: The importance of digital transformation in international business. Sustainability **14**(2), 834 (2022). https://doi.org/10.3390/su14020834

104. Pererva, P., Kuchynskyi, V., Kobielieva, T., Kosenko, A., Maslak, O.: Economic substantiationof outsourcing the information technologies and logistic services in the intellectual and innovative activities of an enterprise. Eastern-Europ. J. Enterprise Technol. **4**(13), 112 (2021)

105. Persaud, A., Zare, J.: Beyond technological capabilities: the mediating effects of analytics culture and absorptive capacity on big data analytics value creation in small-and medium-sized enterprises. IEEE Trans. Eng. Manage. (2023)

106. Pirraglia, E., Giuliani, F., De Cicco, R., Di Berardino, C., Palumbo, R.: The role of emotions in B2B product advertising on social media: a family business case study. J. Family Bus. Manage. **13**(1), 146–165 (2022)

107. Prince, R.A.: Family business mediation: a conflict resolution model. Fam. Bus. Rev. **3**(3), 209–223 (1990)

108. Raju, M.H., Ahmed, Z.: Effect of military expenditure on economic growth: evidence from India Pakistan and China using co integration and causality analysis. Asian J. German Europ. Stud. **4**, 1–8 (2019)

109. Ramakrishnan, T., Kathuria, A., Khuntia, J.: An Empirical Investigation of Analytics Capabilities in the Supply Chain. In: Lang, K.R., Jennifer, Xu., Zhu, B., Liu, X., Shaw, M.J., Zhang, H., Fan, M. (eds.) WeB 2019. LNBIP, vol. 403, pp. 56–63. Springer, Cham (2020). https://doi.org/10.1007/978-3-030-67781-7_6

110. Ramakrishnan, T., Kathuria, A., Khuntia, J., Konsynski, B.: IoT value creation through supply chain analytics capability. In: Proceedings of the International Conference on Information Systems (ICIS), Copenhagen (2022)

111. Ray, S., Bhadra, S.: "Indian family firms in emerging digital economy: an analysis of digitaltechnology adoption" In: Tony Fu-Lai Yu & Ho-Don Yan (Eds.) Handbook of Asian Family Business-Governance, Succession, and Challenges in the Age of Digital Disruption, Routledge, London (2021)

112. Reynolds, S., Fowles, R., Gander, J., Kunaporntham, W., Ratanakomut, S.: Forecasting the probability of failure of Thailand's financial companies in the Asian financial crisis. Econ. Dev. Cult. Change **51**(1), 237–246 (2002)

113. Rondi, E., De Massis, A., Kotlar, J.: Unlocking innovation potential: a typology of family business innovation postures and the critical role of the family system. J. Fam. Bus. Strat. **10**(4), 100236 (2019)
114. Saldanha, T.J., Sahaym, A., Mithas, S., Andrade-Rojas, M.G., Kathuria, A., Lee, H.H.: Turning liabilities of global operations into assets: IT-enabled social integration capacity and exploratory innovation. Inf. Syst. Res. **31**(2), 361–382 (2020)
115. Saldanha, T., Kathuria, A., Khuntia, J., Konsynski, B.: It's a dangerous business, going out your door: overcoming institutional distances through IS. In: Proceedings of the International Conference on Information Systems (ICIS), Austin (2021)
116. Santiago, A., Pandey, S., Manalac, M.T.: Family presence, family firm reputation andperceived financial performance: empirical evidence from the Philippines. J. Fam. Bus. Strat. **10**(1), 49–56 (2019)
117. Saura, J.R., Palacios-Marqués, D., Barbosa, B.: A review of digital family businesses: settingmarketing strategies, business models and technology applications. Int. J. Entrep. Behav. Res. **29**(1), 144–165 (2023)
118. Sciascia, S., Mazzola, P.: Family involvement in ownership and management: exploring nonlinear effects on performance. Fam. Bus. Rev. **21**(4), 331–345 (2008)
119. Shanker, M.C., Astrachan, J.H.: Myths and realities: family businesses' contribution to the US economy—A framework for assessing family business statistics. Fam. Bus. Rev. **9**(2), 107–123 (1996)
120. Sharma, P., Chrisman, J.J., Gersick, K.E.: 25 years of family business review: reflections on the past and perspectives for the future. Fam. Bus. Rev. **25**(1), 5–15 (2012)
121. Shleifer, A., Vishny, R.W.: A survey of corporate governance. J. Financ. **52**(2), 737–783 (1997)
122. Soluk, J., Kammerlander, N.: Digital transformation in family-owned Mittelstand firms: a dynamic capabilities perspective. Eur. J. Inf. Syst. **30**(6), 676–711 (2021)
123. Steininger, D.M.: Linking information systems and entrepreneurship: a review and agenda for IT associated and digital entrepreneurship research. Inf. Syst. J. **29**(2), 363–407 (2019)
124. Tafti, A., Rahmati, P., Mithas, S., Krishnan, M.S.: How human resource and information systems practices amplify the returns on information technology investments. J. Assoc. Inf. Syst. **23**(5), 1150–1183 (2022)
125. The World Bank.: India - The World Bank Data. The World Bank in India (2023). https://data.worldbank.org/country/india
126. Thite, M., Wilkinson, A., Budhwar, P. (eds.): Emerging Indian Multinationals: Strategic Players in a Multipolar World. Oxford University Press (2016). https://doi.org/10.1093/acprof:oso/9780199466467.001.0001
127. Tiwana, A., Konsynski, B.: Complementarities between organizational IT architecture and governance structure. Inf. Syst. Res. **21**(2), 288–304 (2010)
128. Tsui-Auch, L.S., Lee, Y.J.: The state matters: management models of Singaporean Chinese and Korean business groups. Organ. Stud. **24**(4), 507–534 (2003)
129. Upadhyay, N., Upadhyay, S., Al-Debei, M.M., Baabdullah, A.M., Dwivedi, Y.K.: The influence of digital entrepreneurship and entrepreneurial orientation on intention of family businesses to adopt artificial intelligence: examining the mediating role of business innovativeness. Int. J. Entrep. Behav. Res. **29**(1), 80–115 (2023)
130. Venkatesh, V., Rai, A., Sykes, T.A., Aljafari, R.: Combating infant mortality in rural India: Evidence from a field study of eHealth Kiosk Implementations. MIS Q. **40**(2), 353–380 (2016). https://doi.org/10.25300/MISQ/2016/40.2.04
131. Venkatesh, V., Sykes, T., Zhang, X.: ICT for development in rural India: a longitudinal study of women's health outcomes. MIS Q. **44**(2), 605–629 (2020)
132. Verhoef, P.C., et al.: Digital transformation: a multidisciplinary reflection and research agenda. J. Bus. Res. **122**, 889–901 (2021)

133. Villalonga, B., Amit, R.: How do family ownership, control and management affect firm value? J. Financ. Econ. **80**(2), 385–417 (2006)
134. Wang, D.: Founding family ownership and earnings quality: founding family ownership. J. Account. Res. **44**(3), 619–656 (2006). https://doi.org/10.1111/j.1475-679X.2006.00213.x
135. Weill, P.: The relationship between investment in information technology and firm performance: a study of the valve manufacturing sector. Inf. Syst. Res. **3**(4), 307–333 (1992)
136. Yang, B., Nahm, A., Song, Z.: Succession, political resources, and innovation investments of family businesses: evidence from China. Manag. Decis. Econ. **43**(2), 321–338 (2022)
137. Yew, J.L.K., Gomez, E.T.: Advancing tacit knowledge: Malaysian family SMEs in manufacturing. Asian Econom. Papers **13**(2), 1–24 (2014)
138. Yoo, Y., Boland, R.J., Jr., Lyytinen, K., Majchrzak, A.: Organizing for innovation in the digitized world. Organ. Sci. **23**(5), 1398–1408 (2012)
139. Zybura, J., Zybura, N., Ahrens, J.P., Woywode, M.: Innovation in the post-succession phase of family firms: Family CEO successors and leadership constellations as resources. J. Fam. Bus. Strat. **12**(2), 100336 (2021)

Towards AI-Driven Transport and Logistics

Amandeep Dhaliwal(✉)

SLM-PG, School of Learning and Management, Manav Rachna International Institute of
Research and Studies, Faridabad, India
Amandeep.slm@mriu.edu.in

Abstract. Artificial intelligence (AI) has witnessed widespread adoption across
various organizational domains, including transport & logistics, wherein its applications range from driver assistance to parcel sorting and inventory planning to
many more. The paper systematically elucidates the landscape of the usage of AI
in these domains and seeks to investigate and analyze its opportunities and challenges. It focuses on assessing the importance and significance of the utilization of
intelligent and autonomous transport as well as cleaner transport modalities. The
methodology employed in this report is grounded in exploratory and descriptive
analysis, focusing predominantly on a thorough examination of existing literature,
empirical scientific research publications, and prior and ongoing AI initiatives. The
results thus meticulously present the various facets of the existing challenges and
opportunities faced by organizations, activities, and individuals in the adoption of
AI technology and systems in the Transport and logistics sectors.

Keywords: Artificial Intelligence (AI) · Transport · Logistics · Autonomous
Vehicles · Intelligent Transport Systems (ITS)

1 Introduction

In the context of India, a nation propelled by its transport and logistics sectors, this
study delineates their pivotal role in driving economic growth. Positioned as a major
economic hub globally, The Netherlands boasts high-quality physical infrastructure and
exceptionally efficient transport and logistics sectors. However, akin to numerous European counterparts, these sectors confront challenges such as congestion, delays, and
accidents, resulting in time loss, escalated costs, and heightened environmental impacts.
Such challenges imperil economic sectors, thereby influencing overall economic growth,
public health, and well-being. The application of AI innovation emerges as a promising solution to address these challenges. AI, a rapidly evolving technology, holds the
potential to enhance decision-making processes, rendering transport and logistics more
efficient, secure, and sustainable [1].

The rapid evolution of AI in the transport and logistics sectors presents an opportunity
to optimize operations, enhance efficiency, and curtail costs through improved planning,
precise forecasting, and outcome prediction. However, the seamless integration of AI
technology into daily operational activities hinges on how organizations navigate the

© The Author(s), under exclusive license to Springer Nature Switzerland AG 2024
A. Kathuria et al. (Eds.): WeB 2022, LNBIP 508, pp. 119–131, 2024.
https://doi.org/10.1007/978-3-031-60003-6_8

synergy between AI and human cognition and interactions in problem-solving contexts [2]. While AI can contribute significantly to solving transport-related issues, especially in optimizing traffic management, predicting network-wide traffic conditions, addressing safety concerns, and enhancing interconnectivity between transport modes, it is imperative to acknowledge the complementary role of human judgment, culture, norms, and beliefs in decision-making processes.

Three overarching aspects that characterize the application of AI in the transport and logistics sectors include, firstly, sensing, which pertains to constructing a world model based on data fusion, and the challenges associated with communication and data sharing between entities in the transportation system. Pre-processing and validating shared data are critical for AI system development [3]. The second aspect, thinking, underscores the capabilities of AI systems in analyzing observed world models and predicting future scenarios, contingent upon the accuracy and reliability of the data utilized. Lastly, acting involves the system's capacity to identify potential actions, predict outcomes, and offer advice for decision-making, either autonomously or under human supervision. However, autonomous action by AI systems currently faces challenges related to ethical considerations, values, standards, and legal frameworks governing decision-making processes [4].

2 Literature Review

Globally, the surge in Artificial Intelligence (AI) publications has been remarkable, escalating from 162,444 in 2010 to 334,500 in 2021, driven by heightened collaborations between researchers from the USA and China, as well as China and the UK [5]. Notably, this academic research has translated into practical industrial applications, manifesting in a substantial annual growth rate of 76.9% in AI-related patents since 2010. The predominant form of published work comprises peer-reviewed research papers (51.5%), followed by conference papers (21.5%), with the remainder distributed across depositories (17%), books, book chapters, and theses (10.1%).

Early studies explored the application of neural network systems in urban traffic flows, demonstrating the feasibility of predicting traffic flow for short durations with high accuracy [6, 7]. Recent studies discuss leveraging AI techniques like Light Gradient Boosting Machine for real-time prediction models in automated driving scenarios [8]. Additionally, a new study proposed a convolutional neural network model within a semi-supervised federated learning framework to accurately identify travel modes from GPS data [9].

In routing optimization, the incorporation of AI-based models, such as Neural Networks and intelligent routing heuristics, has demonstrated substantial improvements. The superiority of Neural Network applications in logistics facility routing decisions, outperforming existing heuristics by a significant margin, was examined [10] while a machine-learning model based on Dijkstra's algorithm for predicting vehicle driving conditions and speed, achieving an impressive accuracy of 95% was also proposed [11]. Another was the employment of Ant Colony Optimization with real-time big data in Hadoop for routing optimization, showcasing a significant reduction in processing time [12].

In addressing traffic management challenges, a traffic-light scheduling framework was proposed using deep reinforcement learning, aiming to balance traffic flow and prevent congestion in dense urban areas [13]. Another notable study constructed a collective, cumulative effect prediction model for train delays, showcasing the application of AI in predicting delays in multi-scenario real-time train operations [5].

The aviation sector has witnessed AI applications predicting flight delays, turnaround time delays, and fuel consumption, which utilized a cascading neural network to predict flight delays [14], while another applied Particle Swarm Optimization to predict fuel consumption in maritime logistics [15]. Another study utilized a self-organized constructive neural network for estimating trip fuel consumption in the aviation sector, demonstrating significant improvements [16].

Despite these advancements, certain limitations, such as the "black box" nature of neural network methods and machine learning, pose challenges due to uncertainties in the relationship between input and output. The complexity of creating artificial and mechanical intelligence, coupled with the understanding of human-based information and behavior, underscores the current limitations of AI applications in transportation, primarily confined to specific Intelligent Transportation Systems (ITS) applications.

In logistics and supply chains, the integration of AI applications has demonstrated substantial benefits, with estimated significant reductions in logistics costs, inventory levels, and service levels [17]. Noteworthy areas of AI application include real-time tracking and monitoring, smart warehousing, loading/unloading optimization, carrying solutions, packaging innovation, processing and distribution optimization, and intelligent information processing systems.

Empirical studies have conducted comprehensive reviews of AI applications in logistics, identifying prevalent AI techniques such as artificial neural networks, metaheuristics, and simulation frameworks [18]. Firm-level studies have explored the determinants of AI adoption in transport and logistics, emphasizing factors like firm size and Absorptive Capacity (AC) [19].

In conclusion, while AI technologies currently accelerate evolutionary changes, their potential for revolutionary transformations in the transport and logistics sectors remains evident [20]. The ongoing research landscape continues to unravel new avenues, fostering a deeper understanding of AI applications and their impact on efficiency.

3 Applications of AI in Transportation

Artificial Intelligence (AI) technology holds significant potential for addressing various challenges within the transportation sector, encompassing operational processes, traffic management, safety, cybersecurity and privacy, policy and planning, travel behavior and demand, and employment ethics [21]. While common perceptions associate AI applications primarily with connected and autonomous vehicles (CAVs), such as driverless cars and drones, its utilization extends beyond these domains to encompass multi-modal transportation systems, including road, air, rail, and sea transport.

Prominent real-world applications of AI in transportation include Car Autonomous Vehicles (CAVs), Unmanned Aerial Vehicles (UAVs), and Personal Aerial Vehicles (PAVs), such as eVTOL (electric vertical takeoff and landing) air taxis and drones [22].

UAVs, in particular, serve diverse functions ranging from intelligence, surveillance, and reconnaissance to environmental monitoring, surveying, weather monitoring, and disaster control. Notably, UAVs contribute significantly to tasks like traffic control, cargo transport, and emergency search and rescue operations.

The current AI market in transport and traffic management predominantly focuses on hardware and systems facilitating the gathering and processing of real-time data. Devices and sensors, outdoor cameras, automatic identifiers, digital assistance, and GPS-based vehicle locators constitute key components [23]. The copious data generated from these devices and vehicles underpin the development of Intelligent Transportation Systems (ITS) and traffic management systems (TMS). AI and Machine Learning augment these systems, enabling accurate predictions (e.g., delivery time prediction solutions) and supporting decision-making for traffic management authorities and transportation companies [24].

Successful implementation of these AI-enhanced systems hinges on effective data sharing across various entities within the entire transport and logistics supply chains. These chains comprise subsystems encompassing transport flows and modes, logistics data, routing, vehicles, passengers, mapping and planning traffic information, parking management, safety management, and emergency response, among others.

Several practical instances illustrate AI applications in ITS systems and transportation and traffic management. Key application areas of AI technology and systems include:

Autonomous and Unmanned Systems: Traditional processes in transport and logistics are progressively yielding to AI-based autonomous and unmanned systems. These technologies are witnessing increased adoption and maturity, leading to substantial transformations in the transport and logistics sectors.

The introduction of self-driving autonomous vehicles represents a groundbreaking shift in the transport sector. Three innovative technologies are poised to steer this transition: self-driving autonomous vehicles, unmanned aerial vehicles (UAVs), and personal aerial vehicles (PAVs), such as eVTOL air taxis and drones [23].

The development of autonomous vehicles hinges on AI technologies, particularly in perception (utilizing sensors and computer vision) and path planning, where AI algorithms process incoming data and make decisions in real time. These decisions are informed by the continuous analysis of big data encompassing various parameters, such as other road users, vehicle types, and weather conditions.

AI application technology empowers autonomous vehicles to recognize objects, identify obstacles and interpret road signs and markings [25]. The continuous development of deep learning and knowledge acquisition ensures these vehicles adapt and improve their capabilities over time, responding to new and varied surroundings.

Established automotive industry players, including BMW, Daimler, Ford, Toyota, and VW, integrate AI as a critical component in their autonomous vehicle development strategies. New entrants like Tesla, Google, and Waymo employ proprietary AI and engineering manufacturing techniques. A global network of companies, such as Bosch, Mobileye, Nvidia, Quanergy, and ZF, supports both traditional and advanced components, contributing to the development of autonomous vehicles.

Secondly, with regard to delivery drones, these unmanned aerial vehicles play a pivotal role in scenarios where delivering products proves challenging or impractical due to factors such as road conditions, safety concerns, reliability, or sustainability [26]. Notably, in the healthcare industry, delivery drones offer businesses a means to reduce transport and logistics costs while circumventing the need for substantial investments in expensive storage facilities.

Thirdly, Unmanned Aerial Vehicles (UAVs) and Personal Aerial Vehicles (PAVs), encompassing drones and unmanned aircraft systems, find application in a limited number of sectors. The development of UAVs in the transport and logistics sectors is currently in the developmental phase [27]. Presently, UAVs are predominantly utilized in security and military tasks, including intelligence, surveillance, reconnaissance, border patrol, target identification, counterinsurgency, attack and strike, civil security control, and law enforcement. Moreover, they are increasingly being employed in civil and environmental domains such as environmental monitoring, surveying, geospatial activities, remote sensing, aerial mapping, weather monitoring, meteorology, forest fire detection, emergency search and rescue, disaster control and management, wireless coverage, cloud support, and communication relays.

Anticipated advancements in high-power-density batteries, long-range and low-power micro-radio devices, cost-effective airframes, and potent microprocessors and motors are expected to bring AI technology and wireless technologies to the aviation sector and air transport. UAVs, facilitated by these improvements, have the potential to offer robust solutions for commercial transport of goods and persons [15].

AI-Based Traffic Management Support Systems: AI is instrumental in supporting decision-making to optimize the performance of multimodal transportation systems. Examples include AI-powered Integrated Transportation Management Systems (ITMS) that incorporate predictive and adaptive self-monitoring transportation systems. These AI systems, leveraging deep learning neural networks trained on historical travel time and event data, aid in predicting real-time multimodal delays due to factors such as road congestions, incidents, and repair work [28]. By employing AI algorithms, planners can optimize delivery routes, adjust schedules in response to unexpected disruptions, and mitigate congestion, emissions, and energy consumption. Such applications enhance travel time, planning, timely deliveries, and overall operational efficiency, thereby minimizing logistics costs for companies [29].

Real-time Traffic Management Optimization and Coordination: AI is employed to predict arrivals, queues, and delays for vehicles and pedestrians. Real-time traffic signal optimization systems based on Machine Learning (ML) and automated traffic signal performance measures enhance traffic management and coordination. AI-based decision support systems generate personalized and real-time multimodal travel information, offering alternative door-to-door multimodal options in the event of disruptions [30]. This capability enables highly personalized travel time information, and fosters improved travel times, experiences, dynamic pricing, and safety.

Incident Management: Traffic managers use AI to mitigate congestion by identifying the time, location, and severity of incidents. AI-based algorithms and systems proactively detect and predict incidents using data from various sources, including sensors, video cameras, images, and Connected Vehicle (CV) messages [31]. These systems process and analyze vast amounts of data, identify patterns, and accurately identify objects in the environment. Additionally, they offer opportunities to address issues related to urban network crashes, incident detection, and management in urban areas, enhancing the management of urban traffic flows through safety metrics.

Asset Management and Maintenance: AI is applied to develop machine vision applications that address the operation, maintenance, and enhancement of physical assets over their lifecycle, thereby reducing costs [32].

In summary, AI applications in Intelligent Transportation Systems (ITS) contribute significantly to efficiency, mobility, and safety. These applications involve identifying and applying strategies to optimize systems, allocating resources economically, improving mobility for multimodal transportation modes, reducing congestion, recommending optimal routes using real-time data, enhancing incident response and prediction, and improving the monitoring and management of assets [33]. Key AI functions contributing to the application and adoption of AI in transportation include non-linear prediction application to traffic demand modeling, control functions application to dynamic signal control and route guidance, pattern recognition applied to automatic detection and image processing for traffic data collection, clustering application to the identification of specific drivers based on behavior, planning application to AI-based decision support systems for transport planning, and optimization application to designing optimal traffic/transit networks and developing optimal work plans for maintenance or timing plans for a group of traffic signals [34].

4 AI in Logistics and Supply Chain

In the domain of logistics, artificial intelligence (AI) is recognized as a pivotal facilitator for initiatives aimed at establishing smart logistics and supply chains. These endeavors aspire to achieve end-to-end visibility, enhance logistics transportation, optimize warehousing, streamline distribution processes, and provide efficient information services, thereby contributing to reductions in emissions and environmental pollution and fostering time and cost savings [35]. Prominent companies within the logistics sector are strategically incorporating AI and machine learning as integral components to elevate real-time decision-making concerning competitiveness, performance, costs, inventories, asset management, and personnel. Additionally, this adoption of AI technologies holds the potential to transform resource planning systems into more sophisticated AI systems and analytics, ranging from semi-autonomous to fully automated implementations [36].

In essence, integrating AI technology into the logistics sector stands to enhance the efficacy of Information Technology (IT) systems by establishing connectivity across all stakeholders along the logistics supply chain networks. This improvement manifests in various logistic activities, including but not limited to order processing, consignment tracking, transport planning, asset and fleet management, and inventory management. However, the development of an AI-based smart logistics system, rendering it perceptible through enhanced visibility (sensing), necessitates a substantial volume of diverse data types from various sources. Such data encompasses information related to weather, traffic situations, congestion, water levels, and transport planning [37]. Achieving this objective relies on fostering close collaboration for data sharing among all stakeholders within the logistics supply chains. Furthermore, the availability of clean, reliable, and validated data is imperative for the successful development and implementation of AI-based logistics systems.

Ideally, resolving challenges related to data sharing and ensuring data interoperability empowers organizations to develop sophisticated AI-driven systems grounded in Machine Learning (ML) solutions. These systems exhibit dynamic predictive and forecasting capabilities, providing accurate and real-time visibility into logistics operations and furnishing support for informed decision-making [38].

At the strategic level, the incorporation of AI systems in the logistics sector holds the promise of autonomous management of logistics processes through the deployment of robots and autonomous AI support systems, exemplified by autonomous warehouses. On a tactical level, AI technology aids in the management of planning, fleet, and asset maintenance, among other essential facets.

Numerous logistics activities and domains are witnessing the integration of AI technology, propelling the transition toward AI-based smart logistics systems. These applications span diverse sectors, including operational management, logistics planning, warehouse management, unmanned distribution, sorting, packing, site selection, and customer services. The primary domains and activities where AI is prominently employed in the logistics sector are outlined and discussed below:

Logistics Planning: Logistics planning involves critical elements such as scenario and numerical analysis, which are pivotal for planning and fleet management. Components like position tracking systems for vehicles and goods, travel time and mileage calculations, routing optimization, determination of required vehicles, and associated costs can be significantly enhanced through the adoption of AI solutions, particularly machine learning [39]. Integration with existing IT systems allows automation of logistics tasks such as order status inquiries, consignment tracking, inventory management, and order processing. Machine Learning technologies integrated into Transportation Management Systems (TMS) provide tailored and accurate recommendations for customers, optimizing supply chain flows and reducing drive time, fuel usage, costs, and emissions [40].

Intelligent Route Optimization: Efficient route optimization is paramount for transport and logistics operators, particularly in the last-mile delivery process, which constitutes a substantial portion of total transportation costs. The application of AI in route optimization, employing artificial intelligence modeling in tandem with fleet management optimization, proves beneficial [41]. It enables logistics companies to enhance overall delivery runs by identifying the most efficient routes and considering real-time adjustments based on demand fluctuations. This not only reduces travel costs and accelerates logistics processes but also ensures optimal utilization of vehicle fleets and resources. Improved accuracy in demand prediction further allows significant operational cost reduction by optimizing the number of dispatched vehicles and enhancing manpower planning [42].

Predictive Logistics: The unpredictable nature of demand and planning in the transport and logistics sectors underscores the importance of predictive logistics. AI plays a crucial role in shifting logistics operations toward proactive, dynamic processes through predictive intelligence. Predictive modeling, particularly for last-mile logistics, involves combining artificial intelligence modeling with delivery scheduler and route planning optimization to predict the probability of delivery success [43]. This approach aligns with sustainability goals by reducing environmental impacts from transport and logistics activities. Predictive network management, utilizing AI modeling techniques, enhances the performance of logistics operations by predicting factors such as freight transit time delays. This application can extend to predictive risk management in diverse industries managing components from global suppliers [44].

Automated Warehouses and Warehouse Management: While only a small percentage of businesses currently use AI technology in their warehouses, projections indicate a significant increase in adoption by 2026 [40]. AI-based automated warehouses offer advantages in real-time data utilization for predictive modeling, tracking, managing, and monitoring inventories throughout the transportation and delivery process. This reduces costs related to human errors, enhances order-picking speed and accuracy, and subsequently boosts customer satisfaction and business revenue [45]. The application of AI for automated classification and identification of goods in warehouses, coupled with predictive modeling, allows adjustments of stocking levels to actual demand, thereby preventing overstocking or shortages. Machine learning facilitates the adjustment of stocking levels to actual demand, avoiding overstocking or shortages. The integration of AI solutions with warehouse automation, image recognition, and predictive modeling further enhances safety, identifies suspicious activities, and enables real-time predictions for more accurate demand forecasting [46]. The expected growth in the warehouse robotic market is anticipated to revolutionize the autonomous classification and management of goods in warehouses through AI technology, robots, and intelligent algorithms supported by IoT, big data, and cloud computing. Several multinational companies already operate fully automated warehouses using AI-driven technologies and robotics, exemplified by Amazon's extensive use of robots in their fulfillment centers [47].

The utilization of drones in conjunction with AI-based computer vision technology facilitates visual inspections to detect damages comprehensively, including their depth and type, enabling prompt resolution. Furthermore, AI finds application within warehouses, enhancing predictive maintenance of equipment by leveraging data collected from diverse sensors without direct connectivity. The integration of machine learning-powered analytics tools augments predictive analytics, identifying patterns within sensor data. This empowers technicians to intervene proactively before equipment failures occur, thereby mitigating downtime costs and asset failures.

Data Analytics: In contemporary business IT systems, the standardization of data collection, classification, analysis, and application of predictive intelligence analytical tools, either synchronized with AI platforms or autonomously, is becoming increasingly prevalent. The logistics sector, characterized by a substantial volume of valuable data, utilizes AI-based data analytics applications for predicting demand and enhancing visibility within the logistics supply chain [48]. The vast reservoir of historical and transactional data proves instrumental in conducting advanced analytics, revealing patterns, and facilitating future predictions. Notably, logistics companies deploy AI-based data analytics applications in diverse domains such as planning and route optimization, freight management, predictive maintenance, and dynamic pricing. Machine learning algorithms aid sales and marketing departments in analyzing customer behavior, predicting demand in real time, and adapting to changes in demand, supply, competition prices, and subsidiary product prices [49].

In Route Optimization and Freight Management – The applied AI models determine the most efficient routes for vehicles, leveraging AI web-based traffic platforms to provide real-time information on road conditions, works, weather, and congestion [50]. Fleet management, enhanced by AI, allows fleet managers to increase competitiveness, optimize existing fleet utilization, and reduce maintenance costs through intelligent sensors tracking shipments, driving times, stops, driver habits, and vehicle technical conditions. AI data analytics models contribute to inventory and yield optimization, identifying and predicting areas of inventory performance [11].

Back Office AI: While many current back-office processes in logistics companies still involve manual tasks, there is a noticeable trend towards digitalization and automation. Logistics companies engage in the digital exchange of documents and automated document processing within logistics supply chains. Furthermore, intelligent business process automation, encompassing AI, robotic process automation (RPA), and process mining technologies, is employed to automate back-office tasks comprehensively [51]. Hyper-automation technologies find applications in scheduling and trucking, report generation, and email processing. Notably, there exists a distinction between RPA automation and AI, where RPA focuses on rule-based systems enhancing accuracy and speed, while AI represents intelligent systems capable of sensing, interacting, and learning from human decisions to aid in decision-making.

The successful adoption and subsequent impact of AI technologies within the transport and logistics supply chain sectors hinge on a multitude of factors, necessitating careful consideration by companies intending to integrate AI effectively.

5 Conclusion

Over the past two decades, the transportation sector has witnessed a pronounced acceleration in digitalization and automation, leading to a surge in data collection through IoT devices, sensors, and other technologies. Within this evolving landscape, AI emerges as a transformative force, offering solutions to prevalent challenges in operational processes, traffic management, safety, cybersecurity, privacy, policy and planning, travel behavior and demand, and employment ethics.

The efficacy of AI algorithms relies significantly on the availability of substantial volumes of high-quality data. In the transport industry, diverse data sources, including GPS tracking, sensor data, and customer transaction records, contribute to the dataset. Several AI technologies are poised to significantly impact the transport & Logistics sector. The rapid development of technologies such as autonomous vehicles (e.g., self-driving trucks and cars), delivery drones, Unmanned Aerial Vehicles (UAVs), and Personal Aerial Vehicles (PAVs) holds transformative potential for the transport and logistics industry. The elimination of the need for human drivers in autonomous vehicles presents opportunities to enhance safety, reduce costs, and improve supply chain efficiency. However, challenges may arise for some companies lacking the resources necessary to access and analyze such data effectively. Significantly, the integration of AI systems with prevailing IT infrastructure becomes paramount. The successful adoption of AI necessitates investments in IT infrastructure upgrades and employee training to proficiently engage with new AI systems. Also, given the intricate regulatory landscape of the transport and logistics industry spanning local, national, and international levels, adherence to regulations and legal rules is critical. Certain regulations may impose restrictions on the use of specific AI technologies, such as autonomous vehicles, or mandate compliance with stringent standards related to data privacy and security. Lastly, the adoption of AI technology entails substantial investments, encompassing the development and deployment costs of AI systems, maintenance, and support. Companies must ascertain the generation of adequate revenue to offset these costs. Beyond economic considerations, the broader societal and ethical impacts of AI adoption, encompassing privacy, safety, employment, and bias-related concerns, necessitate careful evaluation. Transport and logistics companies must align their AI initiatives with overarching social and ethical values.

References

1. Tang, C.S., Veelenturf, L.P.: The strategic role of logistics in the industry 4.0 era. Transp. Res. Part E: Logist. Transport. Rev. **129**, 1–11 (2019). https://doi.org/10.1016/j.tre.2019.06.004
2. Wang, J., Chen, S., Liu, Y., Lau, R.: Intelligent Metaverse Scene Content Construction. IEEE Access. (2023)
3. Hawkins, J., Habib, K.N.: Integrated models of land use and transportation for the autonomous vehicle revolution. Transp. Rev. **39**(1), 66–83 (2019). https://doi.org/10.1080/01441647.2018. 1449033
4. Wang, X., Wong, Y.D., Kim, T.Y., Yuen, K.F.: Does consumers' involvement in e-commerce last-mile delivery change after COVID-19? an investigation on behavioral change, maintenance, and habit formation. Electron. Commer. Res. Appl. **60**, 101273 (2023). https://doi.org/ 10.1016/j.elerap.2023.101273
5. Zhang, D., Peng, Y., Zhang, Y., Daohua, W., Wang, H., Zhang, H.: Train time delay prediction for high-speed train dispatching based on spatio-temporal graph convolutional network. IEEE Trans. Intell. Transp. Systems **23**(3), 2434–2444 (2022). https://doi.org/10.1109/TITS.2021. 3097064
6. Ledoux, C.: An urban traffic flow model integrating neural networks. Transp. Res. Part C Emerg. Technol. **5**, 287–300 (1997)
7. Dia, H., Dilmegani, G.: An object-oriented neural network approach to short-term traffic forecasting. Eur. J. Oper. Res. **131**, 253–261 (2001)
8. Feng Zhou, X., Yang, J., de Winter, J.C.F.: Using eye-tracking data to predict situation awareness in real time during takeover transitions in conditionally automated driving. IEEE Trans. Intell. Transport. Syst. **23**(3), 2284–2295 (2022). https://doi.org/10.1109/TITS.2021.3069776
9. Zhu, Y., Liu, Y., Yu, J.J.Q., Yuan, X.: Semi-supervised federated learning for travel mode identification from GPS trajectories. IEEE Trans. Intell. Transport. Syst. **23**(3), 2380–2391 (2022). https://doi.org/10.1109/TITS.2021.3092015
10. Becker, T., Illigen, C., McKelvey, B., Hülsmann, M., Windt, K.: Using an agent-based neural-network computational model to improve product routing in a logistics facility. Int. J. Prod. Econ. **174**, 156–167 (2016)
11. Hu, W., Wu, H., Cho, H., Tseng, F.: Optimal route planning system for logistics vehicles based on artificial intelligence. J. Internet Technol. **21**, 757–764 (2020)

12. Lakshmanaprabu, S.K., et al.: An effect of big data technology with ant colony optimization based routing in vehicular Ad Hoc networks: towards smart cities. J. Cleaner Prod. **217**, 584–593 (2019)
13. Kumar, N., Mittal, S., Garg, V., Kumar, N.: Deep reinforcement learning-based traffic light scheduling framework for SDN-enabled smart transportation system. IEEE Trans. Intell. Transport. Syst. **23**(3), 2411–2421 (2022). https://doi.org/10.1109/TITS.2021.3095161
14. Chung, S.H., Ma, H.L., Chan, H.K.: Cascading delay risk of airline workforce deployments with crew-pairing and schedule optimization. Risk Anal. **37**, 1443–1458 (2017)
15. Lee, H., Aydin, N., Choi, Y., Lekhavat, S., Irani, Z.: A decision support system for vessel speed decision in maritime logistics using weather archive big data. Comput. Oper. Res. **98**, 330–342 (2018)
16. Khan, W., Habib ur Rehman, M., Zangoti, H.M., Afzal, M., Armi, N., Salah, K.: Industrial Internet of Things: Recent Advances, Enabling Technologies, and Open Challenges. Computers & Electrical Engineering. **81**, (2019). https://doi.org/10.1016/j.compeleceng.2019.106522
17. McKinsey, Company: Succeeding in the AI supply-chain revolution. Article (2021)
18. Toorajipour, R., Sohrabpour, V., Nazarpour, A., Oghazi, P., Fischl, F.: Artificial intelligence in supply chain management: a systematic literature review. J. Bus. Res. **122**, 502–517 (2021)
19. Rey, A., Panetti, E., Maglio, R., Ferretti, M.: Determinants in adopting the Internet of Things in the transport and logistics industry. J. Bus. Res. **131**, 584–590 (2021)
20. Avetisyan, B.R., Druzhinina, N.S., Daudov, I.M.: Neural networks and artificial intelligence as trends for the development of the future. J. Phys.: Conf. Series **1582**(1), 012005 (2020). https://doi.org/10.1088/1742-6596/1582/1/012005
21. Nikitas, A., Michalakopulou, K., Tchouamou, E., Karampatzakis, D.: Artificial Intelligence, Transport and the Smart City: Definitions and Dimensions of a New Mobility Era (2020)
22. Abduljabbar, R., Dia, H., Liyanage, S., Bagloee, S.A.: Applications of artificial intelligence in transport: an overview. Sustainability. **11**, 189 (2019). https://doi.org/10.3390/su11010189
23. Ahangar, M.N., Ahmed, Q.Z., Khan, F.A., Hafeez, M.: A survey of autonomous vehicles: enabling communication technologies and challenges. Sensors. **21**, 706 (2021). https://doi.org/10.3390/s21030706
24. Burmeister, B., Haddadi, A., Matylis, G.: Application of multi-agent systems in traffic and transportation. IEE Proceedings - Software. **144**, 51–60 (1997). https://doi.org/10.1049/ip-sen:19971023
25. Yağdereli, E., Cemal Gemci, A., Aktaş, Z.: A study on cyber-security of autonomous and unmanned vehicles. J. Defense Model. Simul.: Appl., Methodol. Technol. **12**(4), 369–381 (2015). https://doi.org/10.1177/1548512915575803
26. Chowdhury, M., Sadek, A., Ma, Y., Kanhere, N., Bhavsar, P.: Applications of artificial intelligence paradigms to decision support in real-time traffic management. Transp. Res. Rec. **1968**, 92–98 (2006). https://doi.org/10.1177/0361198106196800111
27. Das, S.: Artificial Intelligence in Highway Safety. Texas A&M Transportation Institute. Texas A&M University, USA (2022)
28. Ouallane, A.A., Bahnasse, A., Bakali, A., Talea, M.: Overview of road traffic management solutions based on IoT and AI. Procedia Comput. Sci. **198**, 518–523 (2022). https://doi.org/10.1016/j.procs.2021.12.279
29. Sumalee, A., Ho, H.W.: Smarter and more connected: future intelligent transportation system. IATSS Research. **42**, 67–71 (2018). https://doi.org/10.1016/j.iatssr.2018.05.005
30. Alanazi, F.: A systematic literature review of autonomous and connected vehicles in traffic management. Appl. Sci. **13**, 1789 (2023). https://doi.org/10.3390/app13031789
31. Yue, W., Li, C., Wang, S., Xue, N., Wu, J.: Cooperative incident management in mixed traffic of cavs and human-driven vehicles. IEEE Trans. Intell. Transp. Syst. **24**, 12462–12476 (2023). https://doi.org/10.1109/TITS.2023.3289983

32. Transportation, U.S.D.: Artificial Intelligence and Machine Learning; ITS deployment evaluation. In: USDOT, ITS Joint Program Office (JPO. Washington D.C (2021)
33. Vasudevan, M., Townsend, H., Dang, T.N., O'Hara, A., Burnier, C., Ozbay, K.: Identifying Real-World Transportation Applications Using Artificial Intelligence (AI): Summary of Potential Application of AI in Transportation. In: U.S. Department of Transportation, Intelligent Transportation Systems (ITS) Joint Program Office (JPO (2020)
34. Iyer, L.S., et al.: AI enabled applications towards intelligent transportation. Trans. Eng. **5**, 72–96 (2021)
35. Song, Y., Yu, F.R., Zhou, L., Yang, X., He, Z.: Applications of the Internet of Things (IoT) in smart logistics: a comprehensive survey. IEEE Internet Things J. **8**, 4250–4274 (2021)
36. Gesing, B., Peterson, S.J., Michelsen, D.: Artificial Intelligence in Logistics. DHL/IBM joint report. DHL Customer Solutions & Innovation. GOA. (2018)
37. Prudhvi, G.S., Pai, V.S.: A Study on Supply Chain Management-Logistics Solutions with implementation of AI, (2022)
38. Issaoui, Y., Khiat, A., Haricha, K., Bahnasse, A., Ouajji, H.: An advanced system to enhance and optimize delivery operations in a smart logistics environment. IEEE Access. **10**, 6175–6193 (2022). https://doi.org/10.1109/ACCESS.2022.3141311
39. Boute, R.N., Udenio, M.: AI in Logistics and Supply Chain Management. In: Merkert, R., Hoberg, K. (eds.) Global Logistics and Supply Chain Strategies for the 2020s: Vital Skills for the Next Generation, pp. 49–65. Springer International Publishing, Cham (2023). https://doi.org/10.1007/978-3-030-95764-3_3
40. Damaj, I., Al Khatib, S.K., Naous, T., Lawand, W., Abdelrazzak, Z.Z., Mouftah, H.T.: Intelligent transportation systems: a survey on modern hardware devices for the era of machine learning. J. King Saud Univ. – Comput. Inform. Sci. **34**, 5921–5942 (2022). https://doi.org/10.1016/j.jksuci.2021.07.020
41. Osamy, W., Khedr, A.M., Salim, A., Ali, A.I.A., El-Sawy, A.A.: A review on recent studies utilizing artificial intelligence methods for solving routing challenges in wireless sensor networks. PeerJ Comput. Sci. **8**, e1089 (2022). https://doi.org/10.7717/peerj-cs.1089
42. Ding, Y., Hu, Y., Hao, K., Cheng, L.: MPSICA: an intelligent routing recovery scheme for heterogeneous wireless sensor networks. Inf. Sci. **308**, 49–60 (2015). https://doi.org/10.1016/j.ins.2015.03.001
43. Babiceanu, R.F.: Predictive logistics models for autonomous vehicles deployment in adversarial environments. In: 2023 IEEE Conference on Artificial Intelligence (CAI), pp. 92–94 (2023). https://doi.org/10.1109/CAI54212.2023.00047
44. Sathish Kumar, P.J., Petla, R.K., Elangovan, K., Kuppusamy, P.G.: Artificial Intelligence Revolution in Logistics and Supply Chain Management. In: Kanthavel, R., Ananthajothi, K., Balamurugan, S., Karthik Ganesh, R. (eds.) Artificial Intelligent Techniques for Wireless Communication and Networking, pp. 31–45. Wiley (2022). https://doi.org/10.1002/9781119821809.ch3
45. Nguyen, D.C., et al.: 6G Internet of Things: a comprehensive survey. IEEE Internet Things J. **9**, 359–383 (2022). https://doi.org/10.1109/JIOT.2021.3103320
46. Nguyen, V.-A.-T., et al.: Artificial Intelligence Based Solutions to Smart Warehouse Development: A Conceptual Framework. In: Hassanien, A.E., Rizk, R.Y., Snášel, V., Abdel-Kader, R.F. (eds.) The 8th International Conference on Advanced Machine Learning and Technologies and Applications (AMLTA2022), pp. 115–124. Springer International Publishing, Cham (2022). https://doi.org/10.1007/978-3-031-03918-8_11
47. Kamali: Smart warehouse vs. traditional warehouse - Google Scholar, https://scholar.google.com/scholar_lookup?&title=Smart%20warehouse%20vs%20traditional%20warehouse%E2%80%93review&journal=CiiT%20Int.%20J.%20Autom.%20Auton.%20Syst.&volume=11&issue=1&pages=9-16&publication_year=2019&author=Kamali%2CA, last accessed 2023/12/02

48. Ben Ayed, A., Ben Halima, M., Alimi, A.M.: Big data analytics for logistics and transportation. In: 2015 4th International Conference on Advanced Logistics and Transport (ICALT), pp. 311–316 (2015). https://doi.org/10.1109/ICAdLT.2015.7136630

49. Wang, G., Gunasekaran, A., Ngai, E.W.T., Papadopoulos, T.: Big data analytics in logistics and supply chain management: certain investigations for research and applications. Int. J. Prod. Econ. **176**, 98–110 (2016). https://doi.org/10.1016/j.ijpe.2016.03.014

50. Comi, A., Russo, F.: Emerging information and communication technologies: the challenges for the dynamic freight management in city logistics. Front. Future Transp. **3**,(2022). https://doi.org/10.3389/ffutr.2022.887307

51. Adorno, O. do A.: Business process changes on the implementation of artificial intelligence. https://www.teses.usp.br/teses/disponiveis/12/12139/tde-08042021-011316/, (2020). https://doi.org/10.11606/D.12.2020.tde-08042021-011316

Author Index

© The Editor(s) (if applicable) and The Author(s), under exclusive license
to Springer Nature Switzerland AG 2024
A. Kathuria et al. (Eds.): WeB 2022, LNBIP 508, p. 133, 2024.
https://doi.org/10.1007/978-3-031-60003-6

Printed in the United States
by Baker & Taylor Publisher Services

Printed in the United States
by Baker & Taylor Publisher Services